THE
FARINGDON BRANCH
AND
UFFINGTON STATION

THE
FARINGDON BRANCH
AND
UFFINGTON STATION

ADRIAN VAUGHAN

AMBERLEY

To my friend John Morris,
Who visited me at Clink and
Who searched for me at Royal Oak,
This book is affectionately dedicated.

Frontispiece: No. 5016 *Montgomery Castle,* passing Uffington with the 1.15 Paddington–Bristol express on 26 April 1959. Photographed by R. C. Riley from the road bridge as he waited for the Swindon–Faringdon special excursion to arrive. (Transport Treasury)

First published 1979

This revised edition published 2010

Amberley Publishing Plc
Cirencester Road, Chalford,
Stroud, Gloucestershire, GL6 8PE
www.amberley-books.com

Copyright © Adrian Vaughan 2010

The right of Adrian Vaughan to be identified as the Author of this work has been asserted in accordance with the Copyrights, Designs and Patents Act 1988.

ISBN 978-1-4456-0105-2

British Library Cataloguing in Publication Data.
A catalogue record for this book is available from the British Library.

Typeset in 10pt on 12pt Sabon.
Typesetting and Origination by FONTHILLDESIGN.
Printed in the UK.

Contents

Note for the Second Edition

I am very pleased that Amberley Publishing has kindly given me the opportunity to revise this history of the station where I first became a signalman. In the course of re-working the book, I have had the most helpful and generous co-operation in the matter of illustrations from Jim Brown, Roger Carpenter, Richard Casserley, Alyson Roger and Emma Whinton-Brown, the last two named working for English Heritage in Swindon.

Adrian Vaughan,
Barney,
Norfolk,
2010

Sources of Information

The material for this book was gathered largely from the working timetables, reports, minutes, statistics and plans held in the Transport Archive of the Public Record Office, late of 66 Porchester Road, London, and now in the process of removal to Kew, Surrey. During the three years that I was preparing this book, 1973–76, I searched all the Great Western Railway working timetables from 1864 to 1958, the GWR locomotive records, milk traffic returns and hundreds of other documents looking for any mention of Faringdon or Uffington. Information concerning the various layouts at Uffington or Faringdon, fatalities, statistics about the level crossing were gleaned from Board of Trade records then held at Ashridge Park but now at Kew. As a result of the centralisation of records at Kew, previous document reference numbers may well have been rendered obsolete, so there is no point in their inclusion here. County newspapers at Swindon, Oxford and Reading were consulted and also the hoard of early minutes and letters of the Faringdon Railway Company held at the Berkshire Record Office, Reading. Mr E. T. McDermott's *History of the Great Western Railway* vol. 2, Cecil J. Allen's pamphlet, *British Express Trains*, Jim Russell's *GWR Coaches* and *GWR Locomotives* were among some of the books used to clear up small points. The Signalling Record Society supplied the diagram of Uffington station's layout in the 1930s, and Mr Tony Cook of the Signalling Record Society supplied some closure dates.

One cannot know all that happened to a railway through one hundred years of history, and there are bound to be omissions, but I believe that what information has been included is accurate. I would be very pleased to hear from readers who can throw further light upon the history of the Faringdon branch or Uffington station.

Acknowledgements

Many people helped me to write this book, sparing a thought and some time just at the right moment. There were the kind ladies and gentlemen who took the trouble to answer my advertisement in a Swindon paper and sent some illuminating lines concerning their memories of the railway: Mrs V. G. Broome of Highworth, Mrs Hunt of Swindon and Mr and Mrs Wheeler of Faringdon. David Castle, an old friend from Wantage, heard about the book and supplied an unusual view of Faringdon station and a print of the 1878 poster in his possession which threw new light on the change of gauge on the branch. Sean Bolan, a long-standing friend of some six feet, took a break from drawing in Bath to look idly, of course, through the Journal of the Historical Model Railway Society and was riveted – in a manner of speaking – by a photograph of a broad gauge train passing Uffington and informed me straight away. Mr J. H. Slinn of the HMRS was kind enough to send me a copy of the photograph. Ralph Clark sent me the address for John H. Meredith, who produced some interesting prints. Dr Ian Allen and Dr Hollick actually entrusted me with precious negatives. Mr R. C. Riley and Mr R. H. G. Simpson contributed prints without which the book would be the poorer. Jim Russell spent some of his valuable time searching for the most suitable photographs from among his collection of half a million or so and also patiently answered my enquiries about locomotives and carriages. Shortly before the book went to press, when I had despaired of finding any more pictures, Mrs Singleton decided to take a few prints of Faringdon station and of her father, Arthur Taylor, driver of No. 219 in case anyone there would be interested to see them. They were a thrilling windfall. Through Mrs Singleton I traced Ted Glanville, now over ninety and once fireman to Arthur Taylor. Ted was very happy to talk about the old days, identified most of the men in the photographs, put me right about work on Faringdon shed. With his daughter and son-in-law's wonderful hospitality tucked away under my belt, I spent a pleasant afternoon at their house and came away with the necessary information to make Chapter 9 more accurate.

The staff of Swindon Reference Library were not only helpful but interested in the project and made me feel at home whenever I turned up on some obscure quest. The firm of Crowdy & Rose, who own the building that was once the office of George Haines, went to the trouble of making a search of the building for me, found a great deal of material and sent it safely to the Berkshire Record Office where it is now available for all to see. The Public Record Office in Porchester Road, Paddington, otherwise known as 'BTC Archives', always a happy place to visit, was made even happier by my friend, Harry the Porter, who spent days fetching dozens of books for me and I would also like to record my thanks to the proprietors of the Italian café a few yards down the Porchester Road where one was always served promptly with piping hot egg, sausage and chips at lunchtime. The midday visit to this remarkable establishment was a feature of a day's research and will be sorely missed now that the Archive has been moved to Kew. The charming lady behind her little counter has helped many a book to be written by serving good food to hungry researchers.

Many thanks are also due to Walt Thomas, who was signalman at Uffington for nearly fifty years and who wrote a very useful letter to me when he was over ninety. Chief Inspector Alan Peck of Swindon searched fruitlessly for information on broad gauge engines on the branch but he was able to send me a magazine article about a remarkable station master at Faringdon. I would also like to thank Nicola Gale, my editor at Amberley Publishing, for her kind assistance. Finally, I must thank John Morris for preparing the splendid diagrams and for keeping his eyes open for details of information of use in this book when all the time he was busily engaged in his own historical researches.

Index to Figures and
Tables in the Text

Introduction

The railway to Faringdon was built out of equal parts of local patriotism, concern for personal prestige and the desire to make speculative investments. It was nearly destroyed owing to its founders' mismanagement in times of hardship but survived to serve the town in better times by the intervention of a great railway company. In the hands of this company it served the area well through the summer of England's Imperial power, through the miserable winter of an enormous war and into a new age when its monopoly in local transport was first challenged. New forms of haulage slowly reduced the railway's popularity, but the great company continued to operate it. Another war of even greater duration and ferocity than the last gave the line a new lease of life, but when peace was declared, the railway sank swiftly to lower levels of use than had ever been known. It carried on in a dreamy twilight until the death of the great company brought darkest night and a new master. Three years later, the branch went into a coma ending in death twelve years later, 104 years after its conception. During the first fifty years, it encouraged trade and industry in Faringdon when the town's population was declining, and in the age of the petrol engine, it was working quietly away in the background, carrying the heavy traffic that road hauliers could not, or would not, handle. Elderly residents of Faringdon remember the line now for a variety of reasons. Mr Wheeler said, 'As a young man just after the first war I used to go to the football at Swindon and then to see a show. I didn't have much money in those days and used to save the fare to Uffington by walking there and back along the line.' Picnic parties used the line as Mrs Hunt recalls: 'When we were very young and lived in Swindon, Mum and Dad used to take us fishing. I can remember going on the Faringdon line because Dad used to hire a lovely pony and trap at the pub near Faringdon station to take us to the Thames at Radcot bridge.' A child of the East End of London has more serious memories of the line. She wrote,

> ... on September 2nd, 1939, I was one of thousands of children evacuated from London under the threat of war ... and as far as I know our train travelled from Bow Road in the East End of London to Uffington, non-stop. During the wait for the branch train I thought that Uffington station was right out in the wilds. A shower of rain had made everything fresh, I'd never seen such green nor smelt the air so fresh. It was the start of a new era in my life for I never returned to live in London again.

A delightful letter. The most helpful and charming letter of all came from Mrs Wheeler, who worked hard to give as much information as she could.

> The Faringdon Railway used to be on the edge of the town and was used mainly for goods and passengers who wanted to go to Swindon, Reading and London or

on excursions to the sea-side or to the races. We lived not far from the railway and my children, when they were very small, used to love to watch the trains shunting backwards and forwards and we found it very useful to go on excursions to the sea-side so we made good use of the railway, though we cannot do it now. Children used to love putting pennies on the line for the train to flatten and one very stupid boy put his watch on one day. We once went to Bournemouth and it took nearly all day to get there, we just saw the sea and it was time to come back. The sawmills by the station where my husband and his father worked used to have carts called 'timber bobs' pulled by horses, and the trees were sawn into boards for coffins and furniture and were sent away by train. The farmers sent their milk to London by the early train but now it is collected at the farms by road transport and the station dairy is shut. With the coming of the buses 'the powers that be' decided that they didn't need the railway and now I daresay they wish they'd kept it. The station has been taken over by an undertaker who has made the old waiting room into a Chapel of Rest. The men who worked on the line have either moved away or passed on.

I offer this book as a member of that group of railwaymen who have moved away, to be a memorial to the railway and its servants who have passed on, in the hope that their exertions will be recorded and never forgotten.

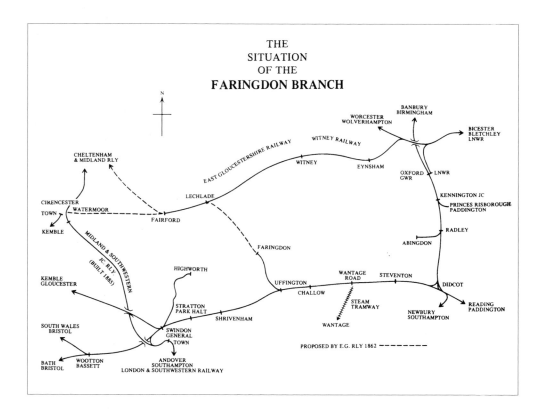

CHAPTER I

Setting the Scene

The town of Faringdon occupies a position roughly halfway along a ridge that extends from Oxford, in the west, to Highworth in the east, a distance of about thirty miles, and separates the Vale of White Horse in the south, from the valley of the Upper Thames to the north. Though the ridge is not high, the abruptness of its wooded rise from the level fields on each side enables the traveller to enjoy views over pastoral landscapes to a southern horizon formed by the chalk downs of Berkshire and to the limestone hills of the Cotswolds in the north. The ridge is at its greatest elevation around its midway point, 450 feet above sea level and 200 feet above the surrounding plains, when it drops steeply before rising gradually towards the east, and in this hollow, the town had its beginnings. The low point was the obvious place by which travellers could cross the ridge, and the town grew round a junction of five ways. The road from Reading struggled up to the 'pass', out of the mire of the Vale, to cross the Oxford–Swindon road and go north-west along a secondary ridge, which kept travellers out of the worst of the Thames floods as they trudged on towards Lechlade and Gloucester. Kings, bishops, abbots and workmen rode or walked on this road between the great Benedictine abbeys of Reading and Gloucester, which is today known simply as the A417. A fifth road left the town heading north, straight down into the marshes of the upper Thames, en route for Burford and the Midland counties.

The strategic importance of Faringdon is obvious, and its position was enhanced by the presence of the Thames, which flows roughly parallel only a few miles to the north; a military force that held the ridge would also command the river and its few bridges thus making a formidable barrier to north/south movements. At the end of the twelfth century, a castle was raised on the heights east of the town, and from the high ramparts, a watch could be kept on the river crossings. The existence of the castle increased the trade of Faringdon, but the former, despite the apparent strength of its position, has left no mark upon the history of the country except in the manner of its departure from the world. During the Civil War, 1640–45, the place was held for the King under Sir Henry Vaughan and was besieged. Only when the cause was quite hopeless did Sir Henry surrender to Cromwell, and this was weeks after the King had given himself up to Parliament.

How glad a traveller must have been, two hundred years ago, to see the lights of Faringdon shining ahead as he forced his horse through the muddy ruts of the Gloucester road in the falling dusk. There were three large inns at the town: the Bell, Crown and the Green Dragon. The first two still provide shelter and refreshment but the third was demolished to make way for the Corn Hall. The three were well situated around the diverging ways and Market Square. (The Salutation at the top of the square is a newer establishment.) For 650 years, large and small fairs were held in the square, the first dating from 1227, organised by the Abbot of Beaulieu, who was granted a charter by the King. In 1486, another charter was granted to the abbey for a three-day fair during the feast of Pentecost. In 1594, all these privileges and monies passed into the hands of a layman, some friends of the tyrannical king. After the Reformation, fairs were held on Candlemas Day, 18 February, Whit Tuesday and St Luke's Day, 13 October. Besides these, there was also the Statute Fair held on the Tuesday before and the Tuesday after Michaelmas – the Hiring fairs when men and women looked for another year's employment. Whether just the weekly fair or one of these great gatherings, the day chosen was always a Tuesday. When the branch railway was built, the timetable had to have special provisions for the first Tuesday of each month.

Another ancient action to have some bearing upon the branch line was the grant of lands at Faringdon to Oriel College in 1326. In 1860, the new railway was planned to cut across these lands, and the Fellows of Oriel were the only landowners to give into the compulsory purchase order gracefully, taking company bonds instead of cash for their compensation, which was a great help to the finances of the little company.

During the first half of the nineteenth century, Faringdon seems to have been a rip-roaring sort of place, particularly at the times of the great fairs when the usual brisk flow of traffic through the town was blocked by huge crowds of farmers, merchants, thieves and beggars, who shoved and elbowed their way across the packed town. Highway robbery, always a problem on the lonely roads approaching the town, increased at these times, as did drunkenness, cattle stealing and pocket picking, all of which went largely unreprimanded in the absence of a police force. To add to the confusion, herds of cattle and flocks of sheep for sale at the marts blocked the narrow lanes of the town as well as the main thoroughfares, thus preventing any bypassing manoeuvres on the part of those not concerned with the sales. If the weather were wet, floods gathered at the foot of the hill from Oxford, just where the market was taking place, and gallons of cow muck were churned with the running mud by thousands of hobnailed boots. So well known – or infamous – did the Faringdon fairs become that they were awarded the doubtful accolade of visits by students from Oxford, who drove over in their 'flys' to see some 'fun' or to manufacture some should it be lacking.

The Highworth to London stagecoach, *Defiance*, gave a thrice-weekly service to London via Wantage and Reading, leaving Faringdon from the Bell at 7 a.m. Royal Mail coaches called daily at the Green Dragon (the site now occupied by the Cornmarket Hall) on their way from Oxford to Bristol and London to Stroud via Lechlade and Cirencester. Freight-carrying stage wagons also called in the town on their lumbering progress between Wales, the West of England and London. The main roads used by these public conveyances were largely in the care of Turnpike Trusts. The route from Faringdon to Gloucester via Lechlade and Cirencester had been 'turnpiked' in 1726, that between Faringdon, Abingdon and Henley in 1733, and the road to Wantage and from there to Wallingford in 1752. Other roads were in the care of the parish authorities and were generally in a ruinous condition. The Wilts & Berks Canal took its serpentine course through the Vale and brought goods to Longcot, about five miles from the town, but in winter, the narrow lanes were so full of mud and water that this may as well have been 500 miles for all the cartage that could take place. For this reason, Faringdon and its satellite villages had to be self-supporting communities, producing locally the bricks, bread and beer, shoes, clothing and furniture that the population required.

The decline of Faringdon dates from 1841, when the Great Western Railway opened its line from London to Bristol, resulting in the town becoming less important as a centre along a line of east–west communication. When the Swindon–Gloucester branch came into being, Faringdon's usefulness to the world beyond the clustering villages came to an end. Trade in the town seems to have improved after the opening of the Faringdon branch railway – but from a low base, and the decline in the town's population was continuous, a 25 per cent reduction being experienced between 1866 and 1911. In the census of 1931, the downward trend still had not been reversed.

A station called Faringdon Road was opened at the 64 mile post of the Great Western Railway in 1841. This was seven and a half miles from the town, and a shuttle service of passenger and freight conveyances quickly developed. A few people gained employment in connection with the shuttle, in particular at the Prince of Wales public house hard by the new station. Coal, coke, bricks and sawn timbers were some of the heavy imports, while wheat, milk, cattle, sheep and round timber were exported. In the space between the main road, the pub and the station, a market place was established with, centrally, a kiosk or pulpit for the accommodation of the auctioneer. The station was very important to the area, and in 1862, 35,000 people passed over its platforms. A passenger at Paddington could have a telegram sent to the landlord of the Prince of Wales for a fee of one shilling, instructing him to have a riding horse ready to meet the train or carriage horses ready to pull the private conveyance which the GWR would load onto a flat truck, surely the Victorian equivalent of Godfrey Davis's 'Rail-Drive' and the Motorail service all rolled into one.

But the railway line had bypassed Faringdon, and by 1860, the town was a backwater. The noise and throng of the Regency period seemed highly desirable when seen through the mists of thirty years, and as the strength of England grew, at home and abroad, the rising tide of nationalism floated feelings of local valour and these feelings were affronted – a town without a railway was hardly a town at all.

What sort of place was Faringdon when these feelings of local patriotism began to blossom? It had a mill, maltings and a brewery so that local grain could be processed for bread and beer. Coal being now cheaply available because of the Great Western Railway and easily conveyed over a well-maintained road to the station, the town had a gasworks. The cobbled streets were lit by gas, as were the better-off homes in the town. Every country trade was practised in the town, from blacksmith and wheelwright to nurseryman and greengrocer. The postal service between Faringdon and the rest of England was remarkably good with next-day deliveries to all main cities. The town's population of nearly 4,000 was the thin soil in which two newspapers managed to grow. One was the *Faringdon Advertiser*, the other *The Faringdon Free Press* owned by Jeremiah Smith, inventor of the gummed envelope and agent for two insurance companies. Few businessmen in Faringdon plied a single trade, the small population forcing them to diversify their interests. Undoubtedly, the man to do this most successfully was George Haines, solicitor. He was also 'Clerk to the Guardians of the Workhouse', 'Clerk to the Commissioner of Land, Assessed & Property Tax', 'Superintendent Registrar', and as a hedge against any possibility of hard times, he held the agency for two insurance companies. He was soon to be secretary to the Faringdon Railway.

On the eve of the opening of the Faringdon branch, there were twenty-two advertised services of carts plying from the town. John Kent, the Great Western Railway agent in the town, sent a cart to Swindon daily, another to Highworth, while a third went as far as Cirencester, taking two days for the round trip. From outside the Salutation, carts went out to Bampton, Broadwell (pronounced Braddell), and Witney on Tuesdays, while from the Red Lion on the same day, you could find a cart bound for Highworth, Swindon, Kingston Lisle or Uffington. John Hayle drove a cart 'from his own home' (you had to know where he lived as no address was given in the advertisement!) to Abingdon on Mondays and Thursdays; Mr Bradfield drove from his own home to Oxford on Wednesdays and Saturdays, and on Saturdays only Mr Hazel drove to Wantage. No common carts were allowed to use the courtyard of the Bell, which still accommodated a daily stagecoach service to Fairford. A service of 'fast coaches in connection with the London trains under the supervision of Mr John Kent'

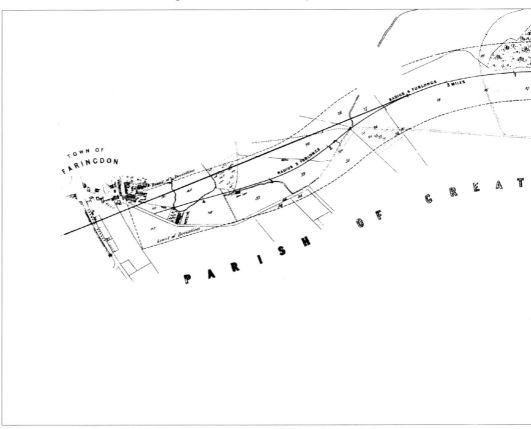

Above and below: Plan survey of the Faringdon Railway, 1860.

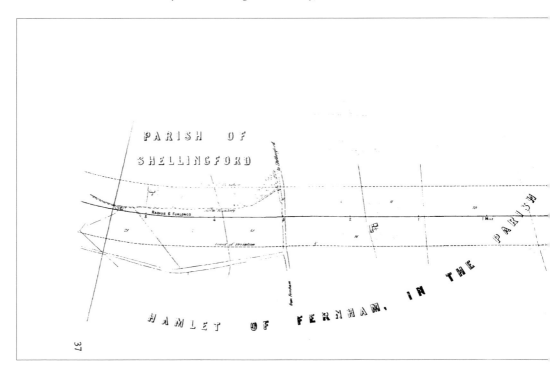

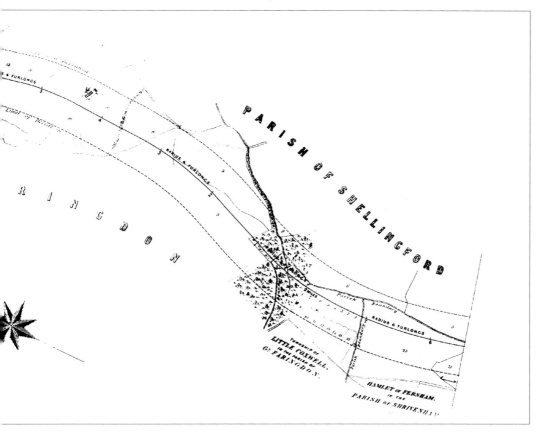

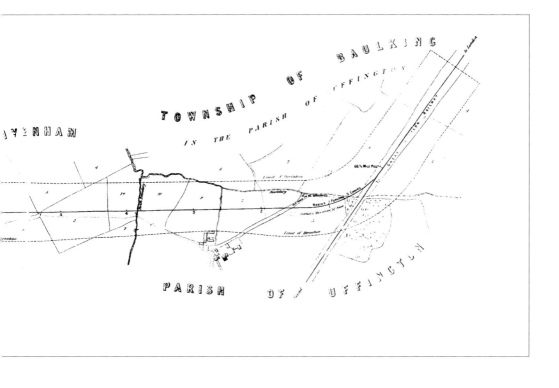

used the same yard. Carts and coaches from other towns called at Faringdon, so that if one knew the service, most places could be reached without walking. The town seems to have been well organised through local trading initiative and one wonders what extra blessings the exponents of the branch railway thought would be brought to the town by the construction of the line. The feeling was that railways were the ultimate modernity, no self-respecting town should be without one, even if, actually, it was not that much needed. Indeed, the carriers' carts were popular, and by 1869, five years after the opening of the branch line, only six of them had stopped operating. Because the branch railway would finish its course from Faringdon 1½ to 2 miles, by road, from the village of Uffington, the horse-drawn, Faringdon–Uffington village service survived until 1903. Those horse-drawn carters that survived to 1914, and there were a few, became mechanised after the Great War.

The ancient village of Uffington stands one mile, as the crow flies, south of the Great Western main line from London to Bristol and four and a half miles south of Faringdon. In 1860, the village was entirely self-sufficient though its population was declining; during the period 1861–81, it fell from 1,061 to 556, and with all farm work being carried out by hand, there was a decrease in the acreage under cultivation from 6,500 to 3,500. The branch railway was going to serve a declining economy. The only item that did not decline during those years was the rateable value of the parish, which rose by no less than £1,000. The beautiful thirteenth-century church with its octagonal tower was supervised by a vicar, Henry Gurney, MA (Cantab), who had held the living, worth £330 per annum, since 1855, the gift of Charles Eyre. Mr Gurney kept his post for at least forty-five years, though by the end of that time its value had dropped to £295. The village school for boys had an endowment to enable twelve lads to attend free, and as many more attended whose parents could afford 6d as payment to the schoolmaster, James Yates. The girls' school was maintained out of public donations and supervised by Mrs Elizabeth Deacon, whose husband might have been Joseph, a retailer of ale.

Many craftsmen lived within the bounds of the village, including wheelwrights, shoemakers and brick burners. Thomas Goodman was the village draper, grocer, veterinary surgeon and manufacturer of 'the celebrated White Horse Sauce'. Beer was in great demand, of course, and there were at least three retailers in the village: John Adams, also agent for the Wilts & Berks Canal, Joseph Cook, farmer and maltster, and Joseph Deacon.

The village blacksmith was John Mattingley. He had served in the Crimean War as an artilleryman and had survived all the hazards of war, only to suffer the tragedy of being kicked by a wounded horse during the last few days of the war, resulting in the amputation of his leg. He was discharged from the army and allowed to draw a weekly pension for eighteen months, during which time he bravely learned the art of smithing – on crutches!

Though John Mattingley is, perhaps, an extreme example, most of the men and women who watched the construction of the Faringdon Railway were cast in similar moulds. They had to be tough to withstand the grind of twelve or fourteen hours a day at work, six days a week. The women took their turn in the fields at harvest and otherwise engaged in the Herculean task of looking after their menfolk and keeping their homes clean by sheer elbow grease. They were, of necessity, less squeamish than we are today. Who of us nowadays could kill the pig as they did? This animal, first in the economy of cottage people, was fed on kitchen scraps and some meal, to be killed just before Christmas in the back garden.

Children could leave school and start work whenever their parents – or the child – wanted. It was common to leave at eleven and highly unlikely that any village child was still at school after he or she turned fourteen. A girl would enter service in a local magnate's house, if she were lucky, or she might have to go many miles from home to find her first 'place'. A boy who was blessed with thrifty parents just might have been

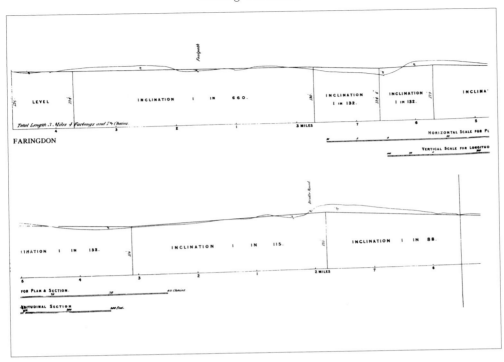

Above and below: Sectional survey of Faringdon Railway, 1860.

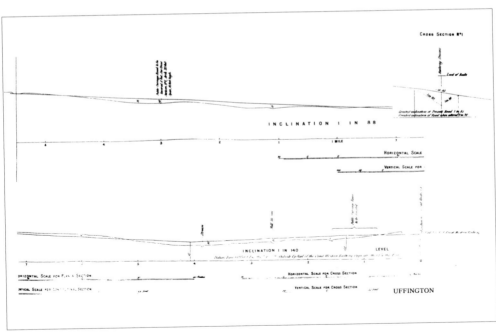

able to buy himself into an apprenticeship with a tradesman, but otherwise he would become a servant, either in a large house or on a farm. If he had a relation on the Great Western Railway, a place might have been found for him within the company's organisation, and failing all, the army and navy offered, in those Imperial days, an extremely hazardous career.

But they were not a miserable people, and if their pastimes seem rough and painful to us, it is only because their lives were so much rougher and more painful than our own. Tom Hughes, Squire of Uffington and author of *The Scouring of the White Horse*, published in 1859, describes their amusements. Backsword fighting was a popular entertainment. Using a wooden staff, the opponents squared up to each other and did their very best to knock the other's head off, the first to draw blood being declared the winner. Shin kicking was played in the intervals while the backsword players were being carried out. All this was quite above board, was played at any large gathering and properly refereed, for there were rules. Unofficial games were often played on the village green after the pubs had shut, because neighbouring villages often imagined that they had a deadly feud between them. There was the memorable occasion when the Ashbury men went over to Longcot intent on stealing a fine, old Maypole that had been planted in the green for centuries and was the sole surviving example in the county. Under cover of darkness and much brown beer, the Ashbury men dug up the treasured relic and carried it back to a ready-made hole outside the Rose and Crown. It towered above the pub's thatched roof and the Ashbury men sat round it proudly, drinking their ale and admiring themselves and their trophy. Soon, the whole neighbourhood was 'on fire' at the daring deed, and that Maypole became the most sought-after totem since the Holy Grail. So it was that, well stoked up on John Adams' beer, the men of Uffington crept along the road to Ashbury, dug up the pole and took it back to their village. Now, of course, the Maypole was more sought after than the Golden Fleece and several hundred honours had to be satisfied. One afternoon, the green at Uffington took on the appearance of the field at Waterloo as the men of Longcot, Ashbury and Uffington met in pitched battle, with backswords, hobnailed boots and massive fists in an attempt to decide the ownership of the magic totem. When hardly a man was left standing, they all felt a lot better and adjourned for the night but on the morrow discovered that the Maypole had vanished – Henry Gurney had taken it down and sawn it up for firewood!

This, then, is the background to the construction of the Faringdon Railway, which became possible in August 1860, when Her Majesty Queen Victoria, Empress of India, graciously gave her consent to the Faringdon Railway Company Act, which then became law.

CHAPTER 2

Construction

1860–61

The Act gave the Faringdon Railway Company powers of compulsory purchase over a two-year period for the purpose of constructing a broad gauge railway from a place called 'The Butts' on the southern outskirts of Faringdon to an area called 'Moor Mill', through which passed the main line of the Great Western Railway, one mile north of the village of Uffington. The junction between the company's lines was at the 66¼ mile post of the GWR. The Faringdon Railway Company was given three years to complete the work by the Legislature, which also directed that passengers were to be carried on the railway at 3*d* a mile, while freight, from dung to iron ore, was to be conveyed at 2*d* per mile or 3*d* if carried in wagons owned by the Faringdon company.

The public were very slow to invest money in the proposed Faringdon Railway and not even the passing of the Act melted the icy indifference most people felt towards the scheme. The year 1860 was a time when dozens of small railways were being proposed, filling in the gaps left by the great trunk routes completed twenty years previously, so that an investor could take his pick of the most credit-worthy proposals. Faringdon, with no particular industry, was not the sort of place to attract money from the great banking and insurance houses, and eventually the line was built largely with the cash and credit-worthy reputations of its eight directors, chief of whom were Daniel Bennett and Robert Tertius Campbell. The former was the elderly Lord of the Manor of Faringdon. The latter was a phenomenon. He arrived from Australia in 1859 as a very wealthy businessman and bought the semi-derelict Buscot Park estate. He used his own wealth and large amounts of borrowed money to develop the land into a mechanised, industrial farm. He built a huge, factory-like distillery on an island in the Thames, which formed the northern boundary of his land. Steam and water power was used as well as the very latest, even unheard-of, ideas on farming. Water-driven pumps lifted water up to a hillside reservoir where it was used for irrigation and a 2-foot 8-inch gauge railway with three steam engines carried manure and produce around the farmland and down to the Thames – six route miles – where Campbell built a wharf at the end of a short canal to enable barges to load and unload.

The other directors were Robert Charlwood, mill owner and brewer, Thomas Belcher, shopkeeper, Edwin Ballard, chemist, oil and paint merchant, Jeremiah Smith, newspaper proprietor, George Bevington, gentleman, and George Haines, solicitor. They acted to improve the town and trade of Faringdon, modernise it and bring it back into the mainstream of business life, but there was also the interesting possibility that the Midland Railway might want the line as a link in a route from Cheltenham to Southampton. Furthermore, GWR would be very keen to see that this did not happen; the line, once

The seal of the Faringdon Railway
Company. (British Rail)

built, might be worth a lot if sold to either great railway company. One might say that the
directors acted for the good of everyone in the town through the medium of self-interest.

The first meeting of the directors after the passing of the Act took place on
31 October 1860. Mr Dyke, the company's surveyor, was instructed to draw up
contracts for the purchase of the necessary land and the company's engineer, Mr
Brodie, of Carmarthen, was ordered to invite tenders from contractors interested in
building the line. Brodie set to work with considerable despatch, for within ten days of
the meeting he had received ten replies and these he set before his employers for their
mature consideration. Mr Scott offered to do the work for £24,900, Mr Treadwell
offered £20,000, Messrs Rennie & Lyon tendered for £17,500, and a certain Mr
Lewis, who by some happy coincidence came from Carmarthen, tendered £14,900.
As the company's engineer, Brodie had to advise the directors on all technical matters
and recommended the cheapest offer. The gentlemen of the board readily agreed to
this, and two weeks later, Lewis had been retained as contractor.

The first meeting of shareholders took place the next day, 13 November. The
rhetoric adopted by the chairman, Daniel Bennett, became the standard for all future
gatherings, a mixture of cajolery and euphemism as he squeezed the last drops of
cheer from the stone of despondency. Hiding all the facts, Bennett's words were full
of confidence and brisk competence, soothing to the nerves of timid shareholders, who
were not, in fact, coming up with the cash they had agreed to supply and therefore the
situation was anything but rosy. Mr Bennett's statements are all beautiful examples
of 'spin'. 'Your directors, with the able assistance of your engineer, Mr Brodie, have
gone carefully into all the tenders submitted by various contractors and are happy to
say that with such results as makes the speedy formation of the line a matter of little
doubt and enables your directors to express a confident belief that a sound investment
will be fully realised and the shareholders put in receipt of a remunerative dividend.
The cash situation has improved since the passing of the Act and I earnestly request
that all those holding shares should answer the call for payment, as very few have
done so.' Many were the 'earnest requests' that Mr Chairman would make before the
line was built.

At the next shareholders' meeting on the 27th, the chairman said he had no news but
noted with approval the 'evident signs of progress in the town, spirited improvements
are being made to houses and places of business', and he seemed to think that this was

A share certificate impressed with the company seal. (Author's collection)

due to the construction of the railway. Although at that moment it did not have a rail or a sleeper in its possession. Mr Lewis begged them to order these essentials quickly before prices rose or he would not be able to build the line for his estimated sum. His prayer was heard and approved, together with another, that GWR be requested to excavate the sides of Baulking cutting at the Moor Mill site to make room for the junction station and sidings. Robert Campbell volunteered to make the rounds of the iron foundries for rails and to go to Paddington to see about the junction site. He acted energetically, for within a month, Brodie had written to GWR's engineer asking him to come to Moor Mill to inspect the rails and sleepers and see if they were up to GWR standards.

Mr Chairman was very definite on one point: there was too much money going out and not enough coming in. 'The Scholars and Fellows of Oriel College have taken their price in company bonds which has been of great assistance to your company', and he thought that other landowners should do likewise. Lord Barrington, a director of the Great Western Railway who had lost some land to the Faringdon company, preferred hard cash and took it at the rate of £150 an acre, receiving £212. Numerous owners had to be compensated. One Mr Frampton, a tenant of Lord Barrington's, was particularly anxious to receive his portion and offered violence to the contractor's men when they tried to gain access to his land, driving them from the field, but on receiving £14, he became as 'quiet as a lamb'. The 'Charitable Trust for the Poor of Little Coxwell' was paid £150, as was the Earl of Craven, who owned the Moor Mill site. John Reade received no less than £746, and at every meeting of the directors, cheques were written for materials and compensation whilst very little construction work took place.

On 8 April 1861, the Faringdon directors, always keen to spur others to action, decided to ask GWR to build the junction station, and a deputation went to Paddington, where they were met by Captain Bulkeley, to whom they made out their case. They impressed upon him 'the great benefits which must necessarily accrue to the Great Western Railway' if that company were to build the station for the Faringdon Railway – and in support of their case, the Faringdon men gave Captain Bulkeley the traffic statistics for *his* station at Faringdon Road. This seems less than diplomatic, as the implication was that this traffic would be diverted to the Faringdon Railway when the junction opened. Bulkeley heard them out with no interruptions and then cooled their ardour by telling them to go back to Faringdon and submit their application in writing for consideration by the directors of GWR.

A few days later, before the letter had gone from Faringdon to Paddington, the shareholders of the Faringdon Railway were called to a meeting and informed, '... we have every reason to believe that GWR will build the junction station as they are fully alive to the advantages to be derived from the formation of a junction with your line.' Mr Chairman went on to say that 'you will get a station to be proud of', and left those simple souls to imagine the spires and turrets of Moor Mill station, which the Great Western was going to build out of gratitude for being allowed to have a connection with the Faringdon line. The chairman had to push the truth to its furthest limits to promote confidence amongst his shareholders in the hope that they would become more inclined to part with their cash. It was largely due to this poker-faced nerve that the line was constructed.

In view of the Faringdon chairman's 'station to be proud of' remark, it is amusing to note that GWR was seriously considering the closure of the Faringdon Road station and the removal of its office building to Moor Mill. If that had been done, the Faringdon people would have had a second-hand, timber building of rectangular ground plan. Only when the GWR engineer reported that the plan was not feasible did the directors of that company authorise the construction of a new station at Moor Mill and ordered that it should be given the name of the nearest village; hence it became known as Uffington Station, Junction for Faringdon. The Faringdon Road station was not closed, but its name changed to Challow to avoid any confusion with the station to be constructed at Faringdon.

The work of constructing the branch was carried on throughout the summer in a half-hearted manner because Mr Lewis was kept short of money by the directors – as they had hardly any to give. Materials, the men's wages and Lewis's personal expenses were all in short supply; he 'had private resources' to enable him to live between the directors' promises, but the labour force deserted at haymaking time and again at harvest, seasonal occupations which provided them with wages at the end of each week, beer during the work, and the chance of a harvest-home supper when the job was done.

On 17 September, a letter arrived at George Haines's office addressed to the directors of the Faringdon Railway Company. It came from the directors of the East Gloucestershire Railway and was just what the Faringdon board had been hoping for, the answer, so they thought, to all their financial problems. The letter 'begged to inform' that a mixed-gauge railway line was projected from Cheltenham to Faringdon, which scheme had the support of most of the inhabitants of Cheltenham and several of the great landowners along the way. The line would go via Andoversford, Coln St Aldwyn and Quenington to Fairford and Faringdon. At Fairford, a standard gauge line was to be constructed to an end-on junction with the Witney Railway at Witney. Such a railway, the letter said, would form a through route from South Wales to London with the Faringdon line making the final link to the Great Western Railway. The letter suggested that the Faringdon Railway amalgamate with the East Gloucestershire and asked what the Faringdon company's terms would be. The final paragraph was a threat, just in case the Faringdon directors considered their railway indispensable to the plan and felt inclined to ask a high price: '... should your Company not fall in with this idea this company will by-pass Faringdon and build its own line to a junction with the Great Western Railway at Wantage Road.'

Thus did the gentlemen of Cheltenham make diplomatic overtures to the hayseeds of Faringdon, never for a moment thinking that it was a comic situation. With no Act of Parliament, no money, no land or running powers over established lines, they wrote letters to near-bankrupt concerns, laying down paper railways and airily constructing trunk routes in competition with those which had been in service for twenty-five years. Putting aside the urgent notes from Lewis concerning the wholesale desertion of his labour force owing to lack of wages, the Faringdon directors composed for the EGR a reply that appears to have been written under the intoxicating influence of avarice. It laid out the terms of amalgamation as follows:

1. That the Faringdon Company pay the EGR £12,000. [FR did not have £5,000 in the bank at that time – Author's note]

2. That EGR pay the FR 4% interest on this money.

3. That the EGR take over the construction of the Faringdon line at their (EGR) own expense and finish the work as quickly as possible without any alterations to the levels of that railway or to the siting of its stations.

On 24 September, the shareholders were 'apprised' of the 'lucrative offer' of amalgamation that had been received from the EGR, though, in fact, the EGR had not mentioned a price. Mr Chairman did not bother to 'apprise' the floor as to the contents of the Faringdon reply to EGR or someone might have asked where the £12,000 was to be found. As it was, the shareholders were simply assured that 'the offer cannot fail to materially increase the value of your property' – which was not yet built! Director Robert Campbell was quite content with the value of *his* property and did not wish to improve it; he had approached the engineer of the EGR and persuaded him to make a deviation in the route so that it would not cut across his land at Step Farm. The meeting of shareholders broke up full of enthusiasm and confident of a prosperous future, not noticing the irony of Mr Chairman's final appeal: 'At such an important time in the company's affairs, I would ask all who have taken up shares to answer calls for cash.'

The directors of EGR were far from pleased with the reply from Faringdon but were resourceful and so now approached GWR with their scheme. Their approach was entirely typical of dozens of such schemes. The idea was to think up a scheme of connecting railways between various great companies, and then threaten those companies with the scheme and see which big fish might take the bait – feeling threatened by the proposal or else feeling that the proposal would be good as an attack on a rival. The EGR pointed out to the GWR Board that the planned EGR line from Andoversford to Witney could allow the LNWR access – through the Witney Railway junction with the LNWR at Yarnton – to Cheltenham, while the Midland Railway at Cheltenham could be allowed by the proposed EGR route through to Faringdon and maybe, eventually, to Uffington. Having received the correct impressions from these observations, the GWR directors offered to contribute a large part of the EGR capital and guarantee the interest on the rest, but only if the EGR would build its branch from Fairford to Bourton-on-the-Water. In consideration of this kind offer, the East Gloucestershire nobly gave up Witney as its goal and set its corporate heart on Bourton instead! In this form, EGR almost obtained its Act of Parliament* and, but for some disagreement over the effect the line would have on the wells in Cheltenham, an Act would have been obtained for a mixed-gauge railway from Uffington to Cheltenham via Faringdon and Fairford – with a branch to Bourton-on-the-Water.

From writing to the EGR in mid-September until 3 December 1861, the Faringdon directors apparently gave no time to the railway, but on the latter date, Lewis managed to gather them all together and begged them for £2,500 to pay wages and

---

* See page 13 *History of GWR*, Vol. 2 by E. T. McDermott for full details

buy materials. As they had not got such a large sum, they gave him some debenture bonds of the company and told him to take them to his bank, which establishment would, on seeing these securities, immediately advance the required sum in cash. Lewis went out with the bonds, doubtless feeling rather like a drowning man who has been given a sieve to cling to, and interviewed his bank manager, who refused to advance any cash against such doubtful security. When the Faringdon directors were told the result of this interview, they were puzzled by the ungentlemanly attitude of Lewis's bank manager and took the same bonds to their own man at the Bank of Gloucester. Here they received the same reply as Lewis: 'No!' After some discussion, the manager agreed to advance £2,500 against two promissory notes for £1,250 signed by two directors, and to cover the failure of these men, the bank also took the rails, sleepers and fixed plant of the railway into the mortgage. This was careful, even mistrustful, treatment, and it ought to have given the directors a clear picture of what impartial outsiders thought of the chances of their railway. They went home happy, themselves and their railway mortgaged for a bucketful of money that would only pay the backlog of bills, and they looked forward to the New Year convinced that the East Gloucestershire sun would shine and make them all a fortune.

1862

In January, Lewis was instructed by the directors 'to proceed leisurely with the work because when EGR obtains its Act the levels of the entire Faringdon Railway will have to be altered to conform to the standards of a through route'. Lewis probably felt like framing the letter and hanging it on the wall. He had done nothing but 'proceed leisurely with the works' since he came to Faringdon, and apart from that, he was well aware that the line might become a through route and did not need to be told about gradients by such a collection of amateurs as his directors. Where the latter had obtained this highly technical piece of information is not known; five months earlier, they had told the EGR that under no circumstances were the levels of the Faringdon Railway to be altered, but being now aware of the problems ahead, they exercised their shrewd judgement and put the brakes on their rapidly expanding empire, thus avoiding a nasty trap into which men of lesser ability would have fallen.

At the half-yearly meeting of shareholders in April, it was announced that work on the line had ceased until EGR obtained its Act, a statement which, having a pinch of truth, served as an excellent smokescreen to hide the real reason behind the cessation. Mr Chairman also announced that, as no one was taking up the company's preference shares, they would now carry 5½ per cent interest as an extra inducement for their purchase.

Lewis and Brodie retired, offended, to Carmarthen as a result of the stoppage of work and spent the next six months in a postal argument with the directors, even opening an action in the courts for breach of contract. But they knew that even if the verdict went in their favour they would never actually receive any damages from the impoverished railway company, so they took positive action as well and sold a quantity of new rails and sleepers that were lying at Gloucester en route for Faringdon. They then found themselves on the receiving end of a writ for theft; relations between them and the Faringdon directors could not possibly have been worse. The letters ceased to pass, and an icy silence descended as both parties awaited the verdict of the courts.

The shareholders met again on 30 September when the chairman of the board announced that work was to be resumed on the line, as it now seemed unlikely that EGR would get its Bill through Parliament, and he finished the announcement with the airy statement 'the levels of the two companies can easily be altered should EGR obtain its Act after your line has been built'. He then went on to offer what he called 'a wonderful bargain'. There was still £10,000 of the authorised capital to be subscribed, and this he now offered as preference shares at 5½ per cent and urged the shareholders to avail themselves of the bargain, 'as your company is dangerously short of money'.

That is not all it was short of. It lacked an engineer and a contractor, for Lewis and Brodie declined to come up from Carmarthen and restart the works. In October, the EGR Bill was thrown out of Parliament, and the Faringdon Railway's fate as a short branch was sealed. Circumstances were extremely grim. Even if it had a contractor and engineer, there was no money and there was less than twelve months to go before August 1863, the date at which the Parliamentary powers, conferred by the Act, to build the line would expire. However, the directors kept calm and wisely did absolutely nothing for another six weeks, until 10 December, when they wrote to their reluctant contractor, offered to drop their action against him and promised the £1,000 they owed him if he would come back to Faringdon and restart the works. So it was that, on 20 December, an aggrieved and sulky Lewis, backed up by his friend Brodie, sat down with the Faringdon directors in Haines's office to discuss the future. The season of goodwill had no influence upon the lordlings of Faringdon, for having lured their men up from West Wales, they promptly went back on their written promise and, instead of money, offered Lewis two promissory notes for £500 each, 'which would be honoured with cash whenever he presented them'. That being so, one wonders why they didn't just give him the money and have done. Nor was this the end of Faringdon's duplicity. The directors refused to hand over even those worthless bits of paper until Lewis signed an undertaking to start work within three months and by 3 March 1863 at the latest. For a while, a state of *impasse* existed, the directors holding out their promissory notes with one hand and the undertaking with the other while Brodie made 'earnest pleading' noises in Lewis's ear to hold out for hard cash. One wonders if Brodie's rent was dependent on Lewis being paid. In the end, Lewis took the directors' pieces of paper and signed the undertaking to resume work on 1 March, and with that, the two friends returned to Carmarthen for the Christmas festivities.

1863

Lewis resumed work at the date he promised, and in April, the half-yearly meeting of shareholders took place. The chairman announced the final abandonment of the East Gloucestershire Railway, and while regretting the loss of an opportunity to turn the Faringdon branch into a through route, he was quick to add that the loss of that opportunity would not adversely affect the prosperity of the branch. Mr Chairman continued, saying that after delays – caused solely by waiting for EGR to obtain its Act – work had now resumed 'vigorously', and an unbroken line of earthworks existed from The Butts to Moor Mill. If the Faringdon Railway Company Minutes are to be believed, not once in the twenty-six-year history of the company did an angry, or even puzzled, shareholder ask a question, otherwise, at this point, one of them might have asked why, if EGR was abandoned in October 1862, as reported in the local newspaper, was it March 1863 before work began again on the Faringdon line?

No murmur of protest has been recorded when the chairman told his shareholders that GWR had been offered 47½ per cent of the gross annual receipts if they would build the station and sidings at Moor Mill. Out of the remaining 52½ per cent, the Faringdon company would have to pay GWR for the use of engines, rolling stock and men to work the line so that the residue available for the dividends would be very small indeed – and there were thousands of shares issued bearing a promise of 5½ per cent. Luckily for the shareholders, the directors of GWR declined the offer. Last of all, the shareholders were told that £8,320 of capital was still needed even after its conversion to preference status at 5½ per cent. Mr Chairman hastened to add that this was not an adverse reflection upon the reputation of the company, rather it was because the market was depressed. Actually, at the very moment he spoke, the money markets were lending money at a great rate to railway construction. It was essential to raise the final share capital, because until the entire amount of authorised capital had been collected, the company could not raise the additional loan of £7,500 authorised by the Act of 1860. The directors therefore asked the shareholders 'to vote to your directors, power to dispose of the remaining shares in other quarters on terms which, under the circumstances, your directors fully believe you will consider satisfactory'. Though the directors did not know to whom or at what discount they would sell the shares, they were absolutely right in telling the shareholders that *they* would agree with whatever their directors did.

The remaining £8,320 was hawked around the country carrying 5½ per cent interest, which was backed by the personal guarantee of the eight directors, and when this failed to sell the shares, they were offered at 5 per cent discount into the bargain. Soon after the April meeting, a curious little paragraph appeared in the *North Wilts Herald* which stated that a Mr Beattie of Surrey had taken up £4,500 worth of the shares and the Maharajah Duleep Singh another £10,000 worth, which was strange in view of the amount available for sale. No such people appear in the company's books, and one wonders where the *North Wilts Herald* got its information from; could director Jeremiah Smith, owner of the *Faringdon Free Press*, have exercised a little poetic licence with his friends on the Swindon-based paper?

Throughout the summer, spoil wagons lurched and rattled over their makeshift tracks as they took earth from cuttings or from wagons in temporary sidings leading from GWR at Moor Mill and tipped the material to make embankments. Even on this small undertaking, there were several deaths. A young man who made a habit of riding on the spoil wagons as they ran down hill was thrown off, owing to his precarious hold and a bad jolt in the track. His legs were crushed between the rails and the iron wheels, and he died during the amputation operation. Another man who was working in a badly supported trench had his ribs and collarbone crushed when the sides of the trench caved in. He was carried home and died there a few days later. The minute mentions nothing about compensation to the bereaved families.

In August, a deputation, consisting of Messrs Campbell, Bennett and Brodie, went to see the representatives of the GWR board at Paddington and were met by Captain Bulkeley. The Faringdon company's proposal was that GWR should work the branch at cost for the first two years and that thereafter they should receive 55 per cent of the gross receipts unless that sum exceeded £3,500 when GWR should get 50 per cent. The proposal was accepted and the deputation returned to Faringdon to write a formal application for the consideration of the whole of the GWR board. Three weeks after the application had been sent to Paddington, the Faringdon directors had a change of heart and wrote again asking the GWR board to accept 52 per cent of the gross annual receipts and this was rejected.

Shortly after the rejection was received at the Faringdon company's offices, the September half-yearly meeting of shareholders took place. They were informed that GWR had been asked to work the line, 'but their terms are not as favourable as one could have wished though they are not unusually excessive and in some respects more favourable than those negotiated by the directors of the Calne Railway'. A remarkably vague statement. The chairman went on to 'regret' that the line would not be finished that autumn because 'so many men had gone to get the harvest in', which does not say much for the wages Lewis was able to pay. However, the chairman 'noted with satisfaction that the new Corn Exchange is now open', and with this rather irrelevant crumb of comfort and the chairman's pious hope that the line would be ready in January, the meeting breathed a silent 'Amen' and broke up.

There was a slight stir in November when someone wrote to the *North Wilts Herald* and suggested that a railway be built from Little Faringdon, a mile north of Great Faringdon on the flat river plain, to Witney and Northleach, but these notions soon died a natural death and the fourth Christmas since the line commenced construction came along to sweep everyone up in its spirit of festivity and good will.

1864

At a meeting of shareholders in February, it was announced that another attempt was to be made to build the East Gloucestershire Railway from Cheltenham to Faringdon with a branch from Fairford to Witney. The GWR shareholders had taken offence at the EGR blackmail attempt a year or so previously and had voted against their board, thus preventing any GWR money from reaching EGR. Having lost the support of one powerful company, EGR looked for other supporters. To attract the London & North Western and the Midland Railways, EGR reintroduced their scheme for a line from Cheltenham to Fairford and Witney. The chairman of the Faringdon company asked his shareholders to vote support for EGR, which had again become a 'life saver' in the eyes of the Faringdon directors. The shareholders obediently voted for the new scheme, and while they were all in a happy mood, Mr Chairman took the opportunity to wheedle a vote of £100 out of them in order to install an electric telegraph between the Faringdon terminus and the junction at Uffington. He said, 'It will only cost £100 and no railway should be without one.' Delighted to have secured respectability for such a paltry sum, they voted for the telegraph with enthusiasm.

In March, the *North Wilts Herald* carried the following report: 'Our branch railway [i.e. the Faringdon branch] really looks like a railway now. The rails are fixed, the passenger and goods stations at the terminus and junction are completed and during the week one of the Great Western Railway engines has been running ballast wagons.' The directors shared the reporter's excitement and, at the end of the month, sent word to the Board of Trade that the line was ready for inspection, and it was arranged that the inspector should come to Faringdon as soon as he had finished his business in Scotland.

Captain F. H. Rich, RE, came on 13 April to see if the line was safe for the use of the public and found so many faults that he was unable to recommend its opening. While the directors and the newspaper reporter can be forgiven for thinking that a line of rails and some buildings constitute a railway, the same cannot be said for Lewis and Brodie. The line was not constructed in a workmanlike manner nor constructed with the best materials, and for the past four years, Brodie had been assuring the directors that the contract was being adhered to and recommending payments to Lewis. Some of the bridges were actually dangerous, and at the junction, where the Uffington to Faringdon road crossed the line on the level, elementary safety precautions had been ignored. The Captain's report stated:

1. The new line joins the GWR about 2½ miles west of Faringdon Road station at a place called Uffington. The station and passenger platform have been constructed between the GWR and the new line to Faringdon, there being no junction for passenger traffic with the main line. The only other station is at Faringdon.

2. The line is 3 miles 46 chains long, is single throughout with sidings at the terminal stations. The gauge is 7'0¼" using flat bottomed rails 72 lb per yard in 21' lengths. The rails are fastened to transverse sleepers with dog spikes and fang bolts. The sleepers are 10" x 5" section and laid 3' apart save at joints where they are 2' apart, the rail joint occurring above a sleeper. The line is well ballasted.*

3. There are four under-bridges. One has wrought iron girders with Barlow rails laid transversely to carry the Permanent Way. The others consist of Barlow rail on masonry piers spanning the gap. The [Barlow] rails are not tied and the weight is not distributed evenly except by the cross and longitudinal sleepers and these being timber do not do so satisfactorily. I recommend that iron ties be added every 4'.

---

* Ballasting had been done under GWR supervision.

4. There is one brick overbridge which requires something more than the slight wire fencing which runs up the wing walls.

5. The following remain to be completed. Clocks at stations. Mile and gradient posts. Some fencing near Faringdon and that to bridge wing walls of under-bridges. Indicators to all facing points – of which there are four at Faringdon – some of them should be done away with by removing all siding points to the loop. Points require a double connecting rod and the station (at Faringdon) requires a starting signal.

6. There will be no turntables so that an undertaking to work tank engines only will be necessary, in addition to an undertaking specifying the manner in which it is proposed to work this line.

7. The public road at Moor Mill crosses the Gt. W. Rly. on the level. The goods shed for the Faringdon Rly. and the line of rails for goods have been laid across the public road making the crossing over the rails about 70' wide without any protection for passengers or carriages. There are no gates across the railway and no lodge for the man in charge. This extensive level crossing is most objectionable. Herds of sheep are driven across it on market days and there is nothing to stop them taking fright and running away down either line of rails.

8. The approach for passengers to the junction station is also over this crossing which is most objectionable and if not removed altogether should be enclosed and defined with gates and fencing so that they may have some protection and guide to the platforms.

9. The public footpath near Faringdon station, reported by the Highways Board, is also very objectionable and I urge on the Co. the desirability for a footbridge which might be erected at a very moderate expense.

10. The handles of point and signal levers at the end of the loop near the junction should be brought closer together.

I submit that the line cannot be opened owing to the incompleteness of the works above enumerated.

F. H. Rich. (Capt. RE)

Captain Rich returned to Faringdon on 13 May, and though all was not exactly as he would have wished, he seemingly gave the Faringdon company the benefit of the doubt and passed the line as fit for passenger traffic in the following report:

> The two additional lines of rails which were laid across the public road at Uffington have been taken up on the crossing and the fencing of the public road is continued nearly up to tile GWR which are now the only ones crossing the public road. The approach to the junction station is now arranged to be on the north side of the GWR from the outside of the gate, across the public road and it is fenced off from both lines of rails. This fencing was not quite finished but the men were at work on it and would probably complete it by this evening.
>   A second platform has been constructed at Faringdon and the several other points referred to in my former report have been completed.
>   I beg to submit that the Faringdon Railway may be opened for passenger traffic without danger to the public using same.

F. H. Rich (Capt. RE)

This seems very fair, especially as the footpath footbridge that both Captain Rich and the Berkshire Highways Committee had recommended at Faringdon had not been installed. The good news that the line had been passed for passenger traffic was officially communicated to the shareholders at a meeting in May. After four years of gloomy gatherings when nothing that was cheering could be reported, this must have been an exciting occasion. Furthermore, Mr Chairman, Daniel Bennett, could also report that the company and the board of GWR had reached an agreement over the costs of the latter supplying engines and rolling stock with which to work the line. But this was not strictly true. The working agreement was not signed by the Faringdon directors until early June and not until the end of that month by the GWR board. Daniel Bennett's ability to stretch a point, or bluff, had without a doubt kept the shareholders of the little company together when their business seemed to have disappeared into the mud. It was his 'nerve' and leadership that had brought the Faringdon Railway Company to the threshold of success. At this meeting, he was able to heap good news upon good news, for his next announcement was that GWR had written to say that they would be closing Faringdon Road station once Uffington commenced business, and of course the Faringdon directors felt that this would have a very good effect upon the takings at the junction station. By now, the mood in the hall must have been one bordering upon intoxication, so Mr Chairman asked the shareholders to vote more money for 'a double line of telegraph wires which will be supplied by a contractor at an under-rate.' The shareholders voted with gusto.

THE OPENING OF THE LINE, 1 JUNE 1864

The day of the Opening was declared a public holiday in the Faringdon area and a director of the line, Mr E. Ballard, displayed outside his shop a banner which bore the legend 'Success to the Faringdon Railway' and underneath this stood a few evergreen shrubs. In the Market Place, the band of the 11th Battalion Wiltshire (New Swindon) Yeomanry 'gave colour to an otherwise dull scene'. The *North Wilts Herald*, which had always tried to say something kind about the branch, could find nothing else to comment on concerning the town's decorations or demonstrations, while the *Reading Mercury* ignored these trifling displays and instead wrote sourly,

> Faringdon was once a centre of roads ... then the GWR came through the Vale and had a bad effect upon the trade of the town and took away important traffic. The leading men of the town felt that a railway to link their town to this artery would improve trade but the town is still a by-way, traffic will not flow up to it, the world of commerce has passed it by.

This was an unkind thing to say when reporting Faringdon's happy day, but nevertheless it was very true.

The *North Wilts Herald* reported that 'a number of people went up the hill to witness the arrival and departure of trains' but mentions no opening ceremony. All that appears to have been done to mark the occasion was to run a shuttle service of trains to the junction. At 3.30 p.m., the directors arrived at the terminus and took a train up to Uffington station but, apparently, not even this train was given any distinguished treatment. It soon arrived back at Faringdon, and without comment to the bystanders, the directors hurried off to 'partake of a cold collation at the Corn Hall'. Though it was only to be expected that a cold buffet would be served at mid-summer, one cannot help feeling that the consumption of 'cold collations' as part of the opening festivities was a foretaste of the cold comfort the shareholders were to receive in the years ahead.

During the meal, several speeches were made and toasts proposed, but these proceedings were only sketchily reported, probably because it was felt to be in everyone's interest that they be forgotten as quickly as possible. The chairman of the company, Daniel Bennett, was reported by the very scornful *Reading Mercury* to have proposed the toast 'Success to the Faringdon Railway'. He said,

> We are all perfectly aware how under the best auspices under which the railway was commenced we have been delayed in an affair which might have been completed in a few months [for] over two years. This was not the fault of the Directors, nor that of the shareholders, nor of anyone save that they had been foolish enough to listen to the voice of a great company which had professed to be interested in a scheme which we imagined would benefit our small line and in consequence of that great company we delayed finishing the railway for over two years. The great railway then threw over the scheme and the Faringdon Railway found themselves in the same position they had occupied over two years earlier with no one to look to but themselves for the completion of the line.

It was a rash speech to make when the working agreement with GWR was not yet sealed, for Mr Chairman had grossly distorted the history of the previous four years, and there was a little whine of self-pity too; after all, who else but the Faringdon shareholders should be responsible for the construction of the Faringdon Railway? The last sentence of the toast concluded thus: '... trust that there will be some return to the directors for their outlay, what the shareholders will receive is of course dubious.' This was greeted by 'laughter', but he was not joking. That was how the *Reading Mercury* reported the speech, and it is amusing to read how the ever-loyal *North Wilts Herald* reported it. For instance, Bennett's brutally honest concluding sentence was rendered as '... and the line is finished only through the exertions of local people. Now it is finished and I hope we shall reap the reward. (Rapturous applause.)'

Not everyone joined in the applause, and at least one man grew hot under his cravat as the travesty of the truth was rolled out. John Kent, chief carrier in the town and agent for GWR, now rose and proposed 'The Town and Trade of Faringdon' beginning, 'My family have traded in Faringdon for one hundred years and I would be very pleased to see the line taken over completely by the Great Western Railway ...' Except that he received no applause, nothing more is reported, but one feels that he was about to launch into an attack on the Faringdon Railway management while tension rose in the hall. A pro-GWR group, heavily outnumbered, formed around John Kent, and the next speech, by Edwin Ballard, director, replying to Kent, was 'listened to with impatience and many amusing quotes were made from those trying to put him down'. Unfortunately, nothing else concerning Ballard's speech or the heckling is recorded, but afterwards the floor was hastily cleared for dancing and revelry, which continued into the small hours of the next day.

The working agreement between the Faringdon Railway and GWR was ratified by the latter company at a meeting of GWR shareholders and directors, chaired by Sir Daniel Gooch, in the boardroom at Paddington on 4 June 1864. The GWR shareholders were anxious not to give any GWR money to the East Gloucestershire Railway, whose new Bill was soon to be debated in Parliament. In the past, they had managed to beat the directors in a vote on the subject but were always fearful that on a future occasion a vote might go the other way. Thus mistrustful, they saw the present ratifications of the Faringdon working agreement as a step towards helping the EGR, and therefore the Midland Railway, to Uffington. The meeting became very noisy, and the vote on the Faringdon Railway working agreement was taken and passed in a totally unconstitutional manner. The two most aggressive members of 'the floor' were Mr Darby-Griffiths, who constantly interrupted all the proceeding by jumping to his feet with the cry of 'I demand a poll!', and Mr Adams, who was just bad-tempered. Sir Daniel Gooch said, 'The Faringdon branch is a short branch running out from the main line about mid-way between Didcot and Swindon and into that line the

East Gloucestershire, of somewhat famous memory, was projected. The line shall be worked at cost for the first year, we charging not less than a certain sum per mile, I believe £1,040 per mile and after the first year we shall receive 55% of gross receipts provided that if the said receipts attain £1,040 per mile the rent shall be reduced to 50% of the gross. This arrangement is advantageous to us.' The motion was put to the floor by Sir Daniel Gooch and seconded by Captain Bulkeley. The following clash then occurred.

> *Mr Adams.* This is connected with a railway which you would rather we would say nothing about – the East Gloucestershire.
> *Daniel Gooch.* You can say what you like about it.
> *Adams.* Sooner or later the subject will arise of the junction between EGR and the Faringdon Railway and it will have to be discussed. Will the proxies you hold in your hand be used to defeat the shareholders should they want nothing to do with EGR?

There followed some arguments about the correct use of proxy votes. It was obvious that Gooch was getting very tired of Mr Adams, and without more ado, and quite forgetting that the meeting had not yet voted, he said,

> 'Carried unanimously.'
> *Darby-Griffith.* Not unanimously.
> *Gooch.* The resolution is carried and your single vote will not prevent it being carried.
> *Darby-Griffith.* I demand a poll!
> *Gooch.* I have made a note of it. Now gentlemen, the next item is …

So the motion was carried without the formality of a vote, and the Great Western Railway became the operator of the Faringdon branch.

The First Timetable for the Branch
June 1864

Faringdon Railway. Broad Gauge single line worked by Train Staff.
Colour: Varnished Oak. Shape: Triangular.

		a.m.	a.m.	a.m.	p.m.	Sundays p.m.	p.m.	p.m.
Faringdon	dep.	8.10	9.00	11.50 noon	1.55	12.25	3.40	8.15
Uffington	arr.	8.20	9.10	12.00	2.05	12.35	3.50	8.25
Uffington	dep.	8.40	11.20	12.45	5.30	12.55	5.15	8.45
Faringdon	arr.	8.50	11.30	12.55	5.40	1.05	5.25	8.55

The First Full Timetable for the Branch
July 1864

		a.m.	a.m.	a.m.	a.m.	p.m.	p.m.	p.m.
Faringdon	dep.	8.10	9.00	9L+45	11.50	1.55	5.00	6.15
Uffington	arr.	8.25	9.14	10L+00	12.05	2.10	5.15	6.30
Uffington	dep.	8.40	9L20	11.15	12.40	2.25	5.20	8.00
Faringdon	arr.	8.55	9L35	11.30	12.55	2.40	5.45	8.15

Sunday service
as for June.

L = First Monday of each month only.
+ = Empty coaches.

It is interesting to note that the journey time on weekdays was fourteen or fifteen minutes and on Sundays it was ten, the weekday average speed being therefore 14 mph against the Sunday speed of 21 mph. The slowness of the weekday trains may be due to allowances made for any freight traffic coupled additionally to the branch set of coaches, which consisted of three four-wheel carriages.

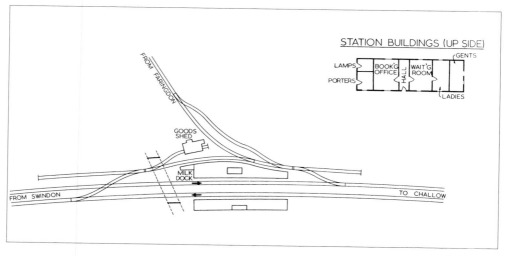

Layout at Uffington, 1864.

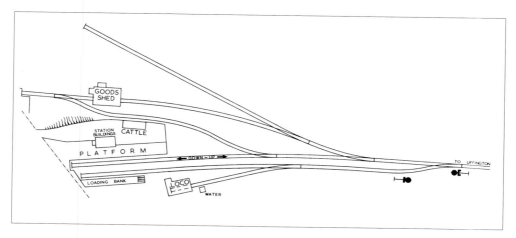

Layout at Faringdon, 1864.

CHAPTER 3

Trains on Barrowbush Hill

The original main line of the Great Western Railway turns north-west at Reading and holds that approximate bearing for seventeen miles through the Thames valley, the line rising at about 1 in 1,320 until a point between Didcot and Steventon is reached. Here, the railway is at its furthest point north and now turns almost due west into the Vale of White Horse on a general gradient of 1 in 880. At Wantage Road station, the line turns slightly south of west and continues over moderate embankments and through shallow cuttings for six miles until half a mile before Uffington station. There, the rolling farmland rises up in the path of the line forcing a short, deep cutting to be made, a quarter of a mile long with a maximum depth of sixty feet, the greatest earthwork on the Didcot–Swindon section. A fine, red-brick arch at the deepest point existed from 1840 and still carries the Uffington–Baulking road. Where the cutting petered out to level ground, the Uffington–Fernham road crossed the railway on the level and the new station's platforms ran up to the level crossing.

From there, the 66½ mile post from Paddington (originally 66¼ miles from Paddington but the terminus was rebuilt a quarter of a mile east of the earlier site in 1854) to the 69 mile post at Knighton Crossing, the line rides on a tall embankment, and the gradient, at 1 in 660, is the steepest between Didcot and Swindon. Brunel made a superb track for his railway, swinging the line in a great arc, using then the westerly rising White Horse Vale to bring the tracks gently to the summit of the London–Bristol route at Swindon, where the tracks are 310 feet 6 inches above sea level. The average gradient is seven feet per mile.

The Faringdon branch trackbed had no earthworks of any magnitude – the greatest embankment was only seventeen feet tall and the deepest cutting was no greater figure – while the bridges were distinguished only by their fragility. The greatest features of the line were its steep gradients and sharp curves. Leaving Faringdon on level track 350 feet above sea level, it headed south-east. It entered a cutting a quarter of a mile long 300 yards from the terminal buffers and, on leaving this, began to climb at 1 in 660, curving towards the south to 'contour' around Barrowbush Hill. After half a mile, the line encountered a small cleft in the hillside, dipped and rose across it at 1 in 132. Having topped that short climb, it promptly *fell* at 1 in 132 for about 350 yards, at the foot of which slope the southward curve reversed to the south-east and the line began to climb at 1 in 115. This was of nearly a half-mile duration, and the summit of the bank was also the summit of the branch, slightly to the east of Ringdale Manor. The line was in a cutting on both sides of the summit, and the cutting ran through a wood, the worst possible conditions for heavily laden locomotives coming from either direction, particularly in the autumn. Coming out of this cutting, the line was approximately one and three-quarter miles from and one hundred feet above the junction station, and finishing its south-easterly curve, the track straightened and headed down the face of Barrowbush Hill on a gradient of 1 in 88. Three-eighths of a mile from the cutting, the rails crossed the Fernham to Shellingford road on a bridge of wrought-iron girders. The earth road beneath was lowered to give laden wagons headroom, but the resulting slopes in the road, 1 in 20, were very trying for the flesh and blood haulage of the nineteenth century. In winter, the hollow under the bridge flooded regularly to make a near-impassable barrier to loaded carts as the heavy earth was churned into a morass by the struggling hooves of teams of draught horses. Further towards the junction, the little River Ock was spanned by a bridge of Barlow rails, and a smaller stream a quarter of a mile further on was dealt with in a similar manner. It was at this point that the gradient changed to 1 in 88, rising as the rails were brought straight up the valley side for a quarter of a mile before levelling off and entering the junction station on a flange-squealing curve of sixty-six chains radius. Faringdon Railway metals continued through the station to make a trailing connection with the Great Western Railway up main line exactly opposite the (then) 66¼ mile post.

The station buildings at Faringdon were built by Mr Malachi Bartlett, a Witney craftsman builder and naturally a champion of all local railway projects. He had given evidence for the East Gloucestershire Railway before a Parliamentary committee in 1862 when he referred to 'the appalling condition of the parish roads' and the difficulties he, as a builder, experienced in transporting materials to his sites of work. He stated that he had been obliged to send the 600 tons of stone needed to build the station at Faringdon by rail from Witney to Oxford and from there to Uffington via Didcot and that this was quicker and cheaper than sending it by road the thirteen miles from Witney to Faringdon. From his evidence, it would appear that the GWR had temporary sidings at Uffington to cater for this sort of traffic before the permanent station was built. The stone he used was limestone, which has weathered to a mild grey colour. The Faringdon station building was unusual in that it had a double roof. The two roofs met over the centre of the building. One roof edge extended beyond the walls on the public entrance side to form an awning, while the other formed an awning over the platform. Throughout the working life of the station, it possessed two platforms: one was just over one hundred yards long (extended around 1878) upon which stood the station buildings, while the other was about twenty yards long, two lines of rails intervening. The short platform was added at the recommendation of Captain Rich, who criticised the lack in his first report, and in his second he says, '... a second platform has been constructed at Faringdon and the several other points referred to in my last report have been completed.'

Cattle pens on a raised platform were provided from the outset, but the short spur that terminated against the wall of the pens for end-on loading was not part of the original layout and may well have been added when the main platform was lengthened. One track away from the pens stood the goods shed. It was built cheaply in stone, with a timber weather screen forming an arch over the single track that passed through the building. In an old catalogue of plans held at the Chief Civil Engineer's office at Paddington, there is a reference to drawings for 'Faringdon Goods Shed, Drawn I.K. Brunel 1857'. It does not seem credible that almost at the end of his life, when he was engrossed in the launch of his great ship, he should have troubled with such a detail, but the drawings are lost so we will never know if this modest station had a building – or buildings – designed by the Master. More likely that an assistant made the designs and Mr Brunel signed them to authorise construction. At some undetermined date, a large timber yard and sawmill was built on the west side of the engine shed. This was rail connected. A 'dairy' siding was also added. The 'dairy' being more a depot for the collection of milk from the locality and getting it onto trains. Until roads and road lorries became improved, in the later 1920s, the branch railway had a good income from this freight.

A 1950 view of the timber yard and sawmill, rail-connected to the Faringdon station goods yard. In 1926, the assistant superintendent of the GWR recommended the closure of the branch line, but the GWR directors said it could not be shut, because so much business in Faringdon depended on it. (Courtesy Jim Brown)

The original Faringdon station layout was curious in that no running-round facility was provided at the station, and the branch engine must have got around its train at the end of its journey by taking the carriages to the Goods Shed sidings where there was a run-round facility. By 1879, a 'run-round' had been provided at the station.

The station buildings at Uffington were in red brick with limestone quoins and window surrounds. The main building stood on the up main/branch island platform and measured approximately 50 feet x 16 feet 6 inches. An awning extended all round the building to the edge of each platform, making the interior of the building fully in the tradition of what one might term 'gloomy Gothic'. For a station built in a cutting to have narrow windows, shaded by a very efficient awning, was the worst possible design. Brunel's erstwhile assistants were still turning out fairly accurate copies of the Great Man's style, but the designs lacked the illumination of his genius. The goods shed was in a matching style of red brick and limestone and had high gables, the eastern one being surmounted by a diamond-shaped chimney, which rose from the 'lean-to'-type office – a typical 'Brunellian' construction. The shed's western wall was bordered by the Fernham Road and was entered by the siding to which Captain Rich had objected in April 1864. This the Faringdon company had lifted at his command and re-laid as soon as he had departed. This siding along with the up and down main lines cut through the Fernham Road, making the level crossing forty-eight yards wide. Its dangerously unfenced condition remained, a hazard not only when herds of animals were crossing the open line but when carters were working at the milk dock, for then they were inside the gates and horses could, and did, run under passing trains.

The operation of the branch trains was simple. One engine only was allowed to be in steam on the line, the only way two locomotives could be at work was if they were coupled together. This arrangement would tend to insure against head-on collisions, but as an extra safeguard, a Train Staff was provided. The Faringdon Staff was a piece of varnished oak about fourteen inches long, triangular in section, fitted with a brass plate engraved 'Uffington–Faringdon' and with a ring at one end to enable the guard, who carried it when the train was in motion, to hang it in his van. When not on a train, the Staff was laid on its own shelf on an outside wall at one of the stations. The important point was that there was only one Staff, no train could leave a station unless the guard was in possession of the Staff and the driver had seen that this was so, and if everyone did their job honestly, no collisions could take place. Details of signalling for 1864 are not known beyond the fact that there was a disc and crossbar signal protecting the entrance to Uffington station against up-branch trains. Faringdon had no signals at all. The guard could wave the Staff in the air from his van and the driver could start.

In November 1865, the rule was changed and the driver, or rear driver where there was more than one engine, carried the Staff. The train having left, it is very probable that the policeman let the station at the other end of the line know by means of the single-needle electric telegraph instrument and then entered the departure times in his occurrence book.

Details of signalling on the main line at Uffington in 1864 are not known. There were two policemen stationed there. Perhaps one was responsible for the east end of the station and the branch train and the other for the level crossing and west end of the station. These men were properly sworn-in constables charged with maintaining all the company's bye-laws at the station, including the signalling and manoeuvring of trains. It seems likely that up and down line disc and crossbar signals were erected at Uffington on each side of the level crossing because of sighting difficulties on the down line. An Auxiliary – or Distant – signal was probably placed on the east side of Baulking bridge and half a mile to the west of the level crossing so as to give drivers of trains an early warning of the 'aspect' of the 'Danger/All Right' signal at the crossing. The level crossing signals, level crossing gates and all points were hand operated, but the Auxiliary signals were probably worked by lever and wire from the station. If the level crossing gates were opened and shut by a gateman – as they were at Wantage Road – that man would have worked under the policeman's instructions. The signals stood normally in the 'All Clear' position. Each set of points at Uffington was switched by a lever at the side of the track by the points, so the policeman had a good deal of walking to do, especially during shunting, and had to remember how he had left each set of points. On dark winter mornings, in the pouring rain or on hot, dusty, summer evenings, he stumbled over the ballast, altering points, turning signals, allowing herds of cattle across the line. There was no information of the whereabouts of the main line trains – apart from the whistle of an approaching train – and the policemen were obliged to act on what was *timetabled* to happen. When a train was due, he cleared the main line of any shunting, closed the crossing and waited until the train had passed – if the train did not appear, he waited until it did. The worst scenario was if the train ran early. Trains in those days had no power brakes and took a long distance to stop.

They worked two twelve-hour shifts from 7 a.m. to 7 p.m. and from 7 p.m. to 7 a.m., and as if that was not hard enough, on Sundays the night turn man, finishing at 7 a.m., returned at 1 p.m. to allow his mate to go home for a short rest and to return to take up the night shift at 7 p.m. the same day. The other man then went home and came back at 7 a.m. on Monday for his week of day shifts. There were mechanical safety devices to save the policemen – or the passengers – if their memories failed for a moment. Candidates for jobs as porters, switchmen or policemen on the Great Western Railway had to fulfil the following specifications: 'Under 35 years of age, minimum height 5'8" without shoes, to be able to read and write, generally intelligent, free from bodily complaint and of a strong constitution in the opinion of the surgeon who will examine-him.' To have stood those killing hours, they would have needed the constitution of a first-class cart horse. Men working as policemen were not paid as much as 'switchmen' – men operating points – but at Uffington, the jobs were combined and the policemen's wages were 22 shillings per week. Sunday work was not considered as overtime until at least 1880. The company issued them with the following items of apparel: annually – 1 hat; 1 stock; 1 dress coat; 2 pairs of trousers; 2 pairs of boots; biannually – 1 great-coat; 1 cape.

Opening the Faringdon branch resulted in the renaming of Faringdon Road station as 'Challow'. Nothing so startling happened to the train service, which continued generally undisturbed. Uffington shared the available service of slow trains with Challow, except that the 8.10 p.m. Paddington did not call at Uffington and the 10 a.m. Paddington, which had been 'all stations' now became 'main stations and Uffington' to Bristol. The 8.55 a.m. Swindon–Paddington transferred its semi-fast service to Uffington and ceased to call at Challow. The service was constantly under revision, monthly timetables were issued so that unprofitable runs could be retimed or discontinued, and as the timetables were published weekly in the local newspapers, there was no fear that intending passengers would be ignorant of the services available. Such frequent tinkering with the service would not have made life easy for the operating staff in those days of poor communications between stations, but it seems the Great Western Railway ran trains for the benefit of the public rather than the Operating Department.

The branch line service remained in this state of flux for the next twenty-two years, according to the extravagant desires of the Faringdon company and what they could wheedle out of the economically minded GWR management. During the opening month in 1864, four trains ran daily in each direction, but in July, two more trips entered the schedules with some specials. On the first Tuesday of each month an extra cattle train ran down to Faringdon with empty cattle wagons to cater for the 'Great Cattle Fair', and on the first Monday and second Tuesdays of each month, special passenger trips connected with main line trains to take passengers to Swindon and Chippenham markets respectively. These 'away' trips did not receive much patronage, for they were withdrawn early in 1865. All six regular trains connected with a main line service. The 8.10 a.m. Faringdon met the 6 a.m. Paddington–Plymouth 'Cheap' which arrived at Uffington at 8.35 a.m. and got to Swindon, after a stop at Shrivenham, at 9 a.m. Here one could change to the 9.25 a.m. to Cardiff or remain with the 'Cheap' for all stations to Plymouth.

The 9 a.m. ex-Faringdon connected at 9.16 a.m. with the 8.55 a.m. Swindon. This train arrived at Didcot at 9.50, where northern passengers changed and caught the 10.30 a.m. to Wolverhampton. At Reading (reached at 10.30), there was no real connection; the Basingstoke train left at 11.50 and that to Trowbridge at 12.5 p.m. The 9 a.m. Faringdon remained at Uffington until 11.15 a.m. when it returned to Faringdon with the people from the 11.12 a.m. main line arrival, but on the first Tuesday of each month, an extra trip was made to take passengers off the 8.55 a.m. Swindon. That trip could have taken empty cattle wagons behind the passenger coaches. The branch locomotive then returned with the empty coaches, according to the working timetable, but of course it may well have brought loaded cattle trucks with it.

An up fast train, 10.20 a.m. from Bristol, was scheduled to call at 12.10 and could exchange passengers with the 11.50 a.m. Faringdon. The Bristol arrived at Didcot at 12.37 for a very quick connection to Wolverhampton but made no further connections at Reading, its only stop between Didcot and London. Soon after the 10.20 a.m. Bristol left Uffington – if all was working according to plan – the 10 a.m. from Paddington arrived, so that the 11.50 Faringdon was a particularly important train if branch services are to be judged by their connections! The 10 a.m. Paddington arrived at Swindon at 1.07 p.m. and left for Bristol at 1.30 p.m. calling at Chippenham, Bath and Bristol, reaching there at 2.50 p.m.

CHAPTER 4

The Faringdon Management

The business of managing the railway's affairs was conducted in a curious manner, characterised by long periods of indecision – or perhaps 'pig-headedness' – punctuated by short periods of fierce activity. During one of these rare moments, the directors would make an agreement with another party and then, overcome by indecisiveness again, they would allow the agreement to lapse or even repudiate it, saying that they wanted fresh negotiations. Several important matters and dozens of lesser ones were, in this way, dragged through the years. For example, two gentlemen, one from Oxford and the other from Cambridge, spent ten years writing to George Haines asking for money that the company owed them. The letters (which I saw in the Berkshire Record Office) go through the whole spectrum of human emotions from the first, cheerful, confident missive of 1868 to the last, furious, frustrated letter of 1878; and then they got no satisfaction. Neither did some bankers, like Bolitho of Cornwall, whose submissions the company saw fit to ignore for as long as possible. On the other hand, GWR was constantly pestered for favours. One can imagine Frederick Saunders, and later on Grierson, groaning quietly when they saw yet another letter on the desk from Faringdon, but both men remained unfailingly polite, even when, at the eleventh hour, Faringdon would go back on its word. At the start of any negotiations, Paddington was even friendly and encouraging, though the officials must have known that it would be to no avail, and one wonders how far the poor reputation of the Faringdon management affected public confidence in the line. After the opening of the railway, with takings rising steadily each half year, the shares of the company could find few buyers and the directors had to ask the Board of Trade for permission to borrow £5,000 to pay off debts. In August 1864, there was a mild flutter of interest when someone proposed to build a railway called 'The Andover, Hungerford & Faringdon' and someone else proposed for the fourth (and last) time the 'East Gloucestershire Railway' in its original form, but both schemes died quietly and quickly, leaving the Faringdon shareholders in their solitary and unprofitable position. The telegraph, that installation 'which no railway should be without', brought no happiness to the Faringdon line. The directors had had the system installed 'at an under-rate' and in 1864 concluded an agreement with the installers, the Electric Telegraph Company, for the poles, wires and single-needle instruments on the branch to be maintained at a special, cheap rate, in the enigmatic words of the ETCo., 'owing to the exceptional circumstances of the case'. This was one agreement the Faringdon management did not back out of, but unfortunately they omitted to pay even the cut rates so that, in July 1867, the Electric Telegraph Co. were obliged to sue them for £200.

Some of the telegraph circuits between Uffington and Faringdon were for public use, and about £15 per annum was raised from this source between 1864 and 1868. Now, the agreement whereby the Great Western Railway worked the Faringdon line allowed the

Above and below: Broad gauge 2-4-0 locomotive *Aries* at Faringdon *c*. 1868. This engine was built by Rothwell in 1841, to the order, designs and templates supplied by Daniel Gooch. It was one of the Leo class of goods engine – hence the four driving wheels. The Leo class were the first coupled-driving-wheel engines for the GWR. When loads became too heavy for the Leo's, they had their tenders removed and were converted to saddle tanks for light work. *Aries* was withdrawn from service in 1871. The man with the oil can is engine cleaner George Haliday. (Courtesy Jim Brown)

former 55 per cent of the gross earnings, so that company took 55 per cent of £15 leaving the Faringdon management with residue and the cost of maintenance – to say nothing of solicitors' fees. This was a source of great anguish to the directors at Faringdon, and in 1867, they took some positive action: they sent their maintenance bill to Paddington and told Saunders that in future his company could foot the bill since they were taking the lion's share of the telegraph revenue. This started an argument that was to last five years, and in the meantime, the Postmaster General took over all railway telegraph circuits not used directly for traffic operating purposes. In return, the PMG paid a wayleave of 15 shillings per mile of wire. Powers for this derived from the Telegraph Act 1868, which directed that, when a small line was worked by a larger company, the latter should receive the wayleave payments due to the smaller line. Thus the Great Western Railway got £5 12s 6d p.a. for the Faringdon Railway – something the former did not trouble to tell the latter. It was May 1871 before the Faringdon management woke up to the situation, and with no legal claims, wrote a furious letter to Paddington demanding a share of the wayleave and a settlement of the old problem of the maintenance bill. Having only an imperfect understanding of the situation, they threatened to sell to the PMG the telegraph circuits yet remaining in railway hands. Paddington's reply, its customary politeness slipping a little, concluded thus: 'I must remind you that the telegraph on your railway was erected as part of the appliances for working the line and as such it will be necessary for it to remain. You will see, therefore, that it is not competent for you to dispose of it to the PMG – even if he wanted it, which is unlikely as there are already two wires belonging to him on the line.' One feels that Grierson's temper was just beginning to heat as he wrote that last sentence! But having put the Faringdon directors firmly in their place, Grierson made an agreement with them whereby GWR undertook to pay half of the maintenance bill incurred between 1864 and 1868.

But the question of the wayleave money had not been resolved, and in June 1875, Haines wrote to Saunders asking if an agreement could be reached. Back from Paddington came the generous reply that they were willing to credit the gross receipts of the Faringdon line with £5 12s 6d p.a. when they heard that this was acceptable. This seems decent when the GWR had no need to credit the line with a penny from this source. But there came no reply; the Faringdon management were in a huddle. If the wayleave went to gross receipts, the awful GWR would take back 55 per cent. What a hard life! Saunders wrote again at the end of August to ask what they were doing, whereupon Haines was galvanised into action and sent off a telegram informing him of Faringdon's momentous decision to accept the offer. But Paddington wanted a proper letter of acceptance, for they suspected the Faringdon people of wanting to 'wriggle'. Back came a note from Paddington, very bland, very firm: 'Glad to hear you accept, but do you understand that the money will be credited to gross receipts? When I hear from you affirming your understanding of this point, I will authorise payment.' Doubtless very annoyed at being understood by Saunders, the Faringdon directors sent no more telegrams and never again did they raise the subject of the telegraph wayleave.

The year 1868 found the takings of the Faringdon Railway on the increase, though they were nowhere near the expectation of £1,040 per mile and the directors were desperately looking for ways of making more money. They never looked into the possibility of getting more traffic for their line but only for ways of squeezing cash from other concerns. In May of that year, they sent a letter to Paddington informing the directors of GWR that the Faringdon Railway would require a toll on each Great Western train calling at Uffington station. As GWR had built the place and only stopped trains there for the benefit of the Faringdon Railway, the letter may well have been considered insolent, and unfortunately no reply survives giving GWR's answer – perhaps Haines thought it better burnt. However, the GWR's reply to a request for a crane at Faringdon station does survive.

In September 1868, Faringdon wrote to Paddington asking if the GWR would install a heavier crane at Faringdon station, at no charge to the Faringdon Railway Company, in return for which favour GWR would receive £10 per annum and hand the crane over to the Faringdon company in 1874 when the GWR lease of the branch expired. Astonished, Saunders wrote to Haines:

> You surely do not intend that this Co. shall provide a crane costing £150 for a consideration equivalent to £90? The £10 p.a. would realise £60 between now and the expiry of our lease and the value of the crane you offer us is £30 – having cost only £40 when new. If the heavier crane were to belong to you at the end of the lease we should lose £60 in providing accommodation which you ought to have done for yourselves.

Having thus mowed down Haines, Saunders held out a friendly, helping hand, 'If you agree to pay the cost of the crane we will install it free and will not object to it belonging to your company at the end of the lease.' Haines wrote back almost at once to refuse this very reasonable and co-operative idea, and on 29 September, a letter came back from Paddington regretting Faringdon's refusal to co-operate, 'which will be to the detriment of both Companies'. Receipts reached a peak at the end of 1870 when £2,320 came in – and £1,176 went out to GWR. Never again was this total achieved by the railway under Faringdon management. Dividing the meagre takings was profitable to neither party. The shareholders of the Faringdon Railway had never seen a dividend and many creditors of the line had not yet seen their money back. The 'remunerative dividend' of 1860 had become a legend, and the only true words ever spoken by Mr Chairman, concerning the railway, made at the 'cold collation' for the opening of the line, had been forgotten. The news that GWR was seeking Parliamentary permission to buy the line was therefore greeted with enthusiasm by Faringdon Railway shareholders and creditors alike though the directors were not so eager. The terms offered by GWR were £6,000 of Great Western stock – earning 6 per cent per annum – for distribution among the Faringdon shareholders – and GWR to take over the Faringdon Railway debts and liabilities. This seems a very fair offer of gold-plated securities to people who had never received a penny from the shares.

Unfortunately, the Faringdon directors fancied themselves as tycoons and thought that for the GWR to make such a generous offer showed that 'something was in the wind', though just at that moment they could not think what that might be. Then Brodie wrote from Carmarthen urging the directors to 'stand out for better terms, perhaps a 50% increase'. He went on to say, 'The projected extension of the SMAR, which looks an easy line (to build) from the map, may ultimately lead to increased traffic on your line.' He was referring to the northwards extension of the Swindon, Marlborough & Andover Railway, from Swindon (Town). This had to descend into the Thames valley on a 1 in 75 incline from Swindon and then climb the 800-foot Cotswolds and descend to Cheltenham over miles of 1 in 50 gradients. How Brodie could look at the tight-packed contour lines around Cheltenham and assert that the line was an easy one, or how it was to benefit the Faringdon line is difficult to say. At any rate, the directors at Faringdon felt that their business acumen had been vindicated by these superficial observations of Brodie's and wrote confidently to Paddington refusing the offer. So it was the chairman's painful duty, at the next shareholders' meeting, to read a letter from Paddington informing the Faringdon Company that the takeover was 'off', as there seemed no likelihood of the negotiations reaching a satisfactory conclusion. The shareholders must have been very upset by this, for one of them asked what the stumbling point was in the talks, and Mr Chairman had the cheek to say that he didn't know and that he would write to Paddington and ask!

While the Faringdon directors' businesslike vision roved to the impoverished SMAR and its schemes, they overlooked what was happening at Uffington. The mixed gauge had been laid from Paddington to Bristol, and broad gauge freight trains to take traffic away from the branch were becoming fewer. The inconvenience of the change of gauge at the junction made itself felt in the number of consignments that had to be reloaded into standard gauge wagons at Uffington. Traffic was being sent by road to Challow station, and the Great Western instructed John Kent to do this 'whenever possible to avoid re-loading delays'. The Faringdon line's receipts fell to £1,680 by June 1874. John Kent was a shareholder in the Faringdon line and must have been very unpopular with his partners in the misfortune. One wonders if he ever took the trouble to go to shareholders' meetings. He had never made any secret of his dislike of the Faringdon management and may have been behind a movement of shareholders who tried to get up their own Bill to put before Parliament in 1873, which would have given the Great Western Railway the power to take over the line. Nothing came of this, and a few months after the proposal was first put forward, a petition was sent to the Faringdon directors by their shareholders that they should sell to GWR upon WHATEVER TERMS that company cared to offer.

Saunders called Haines to Paddington early in 1874 and told him that GWR was no longer willing to work the Faringdon line unless the lease was in perpetuity. In order to take the line over, they intended to put a Bill before Parliament in the autumn and buy the company out on the 1872 terms, as this 'would be in the best interests of everyone concerned'. The proposal was put to the Faringdon shareholders at their March meeting and warmly approved but not by the directors. At the September meeting, the shareholders were informed that 'acceptance of the Great Western Railway's terms has been delayed owing to the absence in Scotland of Mr Saunders'.

From the £1,680 of June 1874, takings rose to £1,980 at the end of twelve months, only to fall to an all-time low of £1,560 by June 1878. The directors blamed the change of gauge at Uffington and the consequent diversion of traffic to Challow. This was true to a certain extent, but even after the standard gauge had been laid on the branch, earnings only improved very slowly and, under Faringdon management at any rate, never rose above £1,740.

Coming to an agreement for the conversion of the Faringdon line from the broad to the standard gauge is the usual one of delays and haggling on the part of the Faringdon directors and the firm refusal of GWR to give an inch from the perfectly fair position they originally adopted. Letters came in from various sources, even from Brodie, urging the directors to 'narrow' the gauge. They should not have needed any urging; they knew conversion was essential and yet they wheedled and drivelled on for four years before the dwindling earnings of the line forced them to take the action everyone knew was necessary. One letter Haines received on the subject was from Robert Charlwood, who had been deputy chairman of the Faringdon Company in 1873 and who died in 1875. He wrote in a sprawling, spidery hand, which suggested a tired, querulous old man, using the eighteenth-century long 's', which I translate here with an 'f':

To the GWR Directors. 18.9.74.

We have had so *very* many complaints of the lofs and very great inconvenience for the want of the narrow gauge on our line.

Our next half yearly meeting will be held on Tuesday next, 29th Sept. The Directors strongly urge and will be very much obliged if you will furnish some information for the Directors guidance to publish in their report on Tuesday 29th Sept.

R. Charlwood.

(To Mr Haines. Dear Sir, Will you kindly look over this and see if you think it advisable to send it. I do.)

The letter is still tied up in the bundle where Haines left it 102 years ago. In June 1877, Haines wrote to ask the Great Western if they would 'narrow' the gauge on the line and to ask how much they would charge. A few days later, back came the reply from Saunders: '... undertake the gauge conversion for £1,020. If your Directors think it desirable to incur this outlay and will make a definite proposal as to the terms upon which they would ask this Company to advance the money, I shall be happy to submit same to the Directors of this Company.' The directors were aghast at the cost and hurried up to Paddington to force a reduction out of GWR. But all to no avail, for, they were told, 'you have overlooked the fact that the Board of Trade will require a locking gear box at the terminus'. Back at Faringdon, they wrote to Brodie and asked him to sort the matter out for them. Brodie wrote to Grierson for an explanation and got the following reply: 'In every case of gauge conversion the Board of Trade considers it to be New Works and as such it must comply with all modern requirements. All our stations on the Wilts & Somerset have had to be altered, facing points taken out and platforms lengthened, tracks locked and signalled.' It seems that Brodie knew no more about legislation governing railway construction than his friends at Faringdon, which, for a railway engineer, appears a little strange. The letter from Grierson was dated 6 August 1877, and eight months later Faringdon was still querying the figures. On 30 April 1878, Saunders wrote to Haines: 'Mr Owen (the GWR Chief Civil Engineer) has estimated that the cost of locking Faringdon station will be £400 and of narrowing the line will be £620.' As it became known that the gauge was to be changed, a small upsurge of local interest occurred. People even bought shares in the line, and the directors, encouraged by these signs, increased their outpourings against the broad gauge at the various meetings of shareholders. But still they choked over the awful problem of the cost of the operation. In June, it appears that they had nearly swallowed the price tag but still considered the 'locking gear box' a dreadful imposition. A Mr R. H. Barefoot came out from the Civil Engineer's Office at Reading to meet the Faringdon directors and inspected the layout at Faringdon with them to see what needed doing to modernise it. Every mention of a 'locking gear box' was met with non-committal replies or just a sudden change of subject to such an extent that Barefoot, on his return to Reading, wrote a tactful little note to the Faringdon directors in order to have written proof that he had properly explained the situation to them. He wrote:

18.6.78. GWR Engineer's Office, Reading.

Dear Mr Haines,
    Since I saw you at Faringdon it has been arranged to alter the sidings so as to have fewer facing points and to lock the station. I think it better to mention this as I was under the impression when I saw you that the line was to be narrowed in its present state and not locked, and perhaps it would be better if you were to explain this to them.

Once again, the directors had been put firmly but politely in their place by a member of GWR's staff! The gauge was changed during 26/27 July 1878, and an account of this is given in the next chapter.
    Takings at Faringdon began to increase after the conversion, though as they had been at an unprecedented low, this is hardly surprising. The directors were jubilant, buoyed up by the success of their shrewd judgement, and at the very next meeting of shareholders, Mr Chairman made a speech wherein he referred to 'embracing new opportunities', a cosy, cuddly phrase he had not used for many years and one that he would not use again. The slow rise in the line's fortune continued until June 1879, when the revenue for the preceding twelve months totalled £1,740, then a decline set in. The directors saw their new task, in the face of this alarming trend, as finding fresh excuses and justifications for the fall, and urgent messages began to fly to Paddington requesting a better service to the west, to the north, to London … Very lame replies came back; one, the height of ambiguity, said, 'The time bills are at the printers.' At three consecutive meetings of shareholders, Mr Chairman gave the following excuses for low receipts: 'The statement of receipts shows a deficiency of £50 7s 11d when compared to the same period last year. It is *satisfactory* to note that this deficiency arises only on passenger traffic and despite the depression in trade and agriculture generally, the receipts from freight are £14 8s 4d up on last year.' That was September 1883. One year later, he was obliged to report, 'Receipts are down £126 1s 7d, which is not in excess of your

directors' anticipations …' And in 1885, he reported, 'The deficiency is solely in freight traffic due to the depressed state of trade and agriculture generally.'

The financial state of the company was now so bad that, on 20 February 1885, Haines wrote to Grierson and asked

> whether the present does not seem a desirable time for resuming negotiations for the transfer of the Faringdon Railway to your Company? Since the idea was first ventilated in 1875 [*sic*] we have, as you know, altered the gauge and our outstanding liabilities have been reduced to, say, £1,500. I am inclined to think that there would be a disposition on the part of our shareholders to take in cash £50% for Preference Shares and £25% for Ordinary Shares, your Company adopting our debenture debt, the rent charge of £70 to Oriel College and paying £1,000 towards our floating debt. I shall be glad to be favoured with an expression of your opinion.

Saunders replied saying that his company looked favourably upon the proposal, except that they would not contribute to the floating debt. There followed the usual flurry of correspondence wherein the Faringdon directors tried to shift the entire responsibility of the line onto the Great Western, but at last Paddington grew tired of them and finally wrote,

> I have looked into the 1875 correspondence and cannot find anything there to justify the conclusion that we are offering less by 14% now compared to 1875. Times and circumstances change and the present is not a good time for this company to be incurring new liabilities. The tendency of railway competition in your area does not lead me to suppose that traffic will increase on your line. We would like to carry out the merger but cannot offer any increase.

Apparently, Haines had been pulling out all the stops in an effort to get a better deal from Paddington, even referring to Brodie's old SMAR chestnut of 1873.

One month later, the board of GWR authorised the merger on the terms sent to Faringdon in 1872, and in February 1885, everything stood ready for the takeover except the directors of the Faringdon Railway Company.

While that company's debts mounted throughout 1885 and 1886, its board held back from sealing the agreement with GWR. They had even to borrow £70 to pay Oriel College, but still they would not come to terms with Paddington. The shareholders of the Faringdon company now took matters into their own hands. For years, they had fumed away in silence during the meetings, but now, goaded beyond endurance at the incessant delays, they acted for their own interest against their directors. They laboured under a disadvantage, for they were just ordinary townspeople while the directors were their 'betters', people they normally respected. However, they were driven to revolt by the thought of delaying for another day the exchange of the worthless bits of paper that were the Faringdon share certificates for those almost gilt-edged securities offered by the Great Western Railway. At the May 1886 meeting, they absolutely refused to vote for, or discuss, anything, but instead demanded that the agreement with GWR should be sealed forthwith. All the astounded directors could do was to adjourn the meeting for a month to allow for that favourite pastime of theirs, 'further consideration'. But the heat generated over the years and at the May meeting could not be dissipated in a month, and at the meeting in June, the shareholders actually took over and hammered out a form of words for an agreement with GWR, voted for it unanimously, and told their chairman to send it away to Paddington. Stonewalling to the end, Mr Chairman asked for 'five days reconsideration', though it is impossible to say what he thought would change in that time. However, he had exercised his last little bit of authority, and five days later, the document had the seal of the Faringdon Railway Company attached and was sent to Paddington on 17 June 1886. One month later, GWR put their seal to the agreement and the Faringdon Railway ceased to exist.

CHAPTER 5

The Train Service 1870–96

Commencing in 1870, the branch Sunday service was increased from three to four round trips, and there were eight round trips on weekdays. All these trains found one or more main line connections at Uffington. The first mention of a goods train on the branch was made in June 1871 with the introduction of the 10.40 a.m. and 4.45 p.m. 'runs if required' trains. In June 1873, they were abolished when the first 'passenger and goods' trains were introduced, soon to be known as 'mixed trains', the freight vehicles being coupled behind the passenger coaches. The branch made it easy for local farmers to send milk to the great market of London, and the annual quantity carried quickly rose as local men took advantage of the opportunity. During 1869, 50–60 churns a week left Faringdon to join Uffington's 100 or so. In 1873, Faringdon was sending 150–180 to Uffington's 180–200. By comparison, Challow sent 360 a week in summer and 460 a week during the winter – one third less than Chippenham or Swindon.

Faringdon Branch Train Service
July 1870

	a.m.	a.m.	a.m.	a.m.	p.m.	p.m.	p.m.	p.m.	
Faringdon	8.00	8.35	9.55	11.55	1.50	5.00	6.05	7.55	
		L	M.O.	p.m.					
Uffington	8.10	8.45	10.10	12.10	2.05	5.16	6.20	8.10	Weekdays
Uffington	8.20	8.57	10.20	12.45	2.20	5.35	6.30	8.45	
		L	M.O.						
Faringdon	8.30	9.10	10.35	1.00	2.35	5.45	6.45	8.40	

L = First Tuesday of each month.
M.O. = Mondays only.

	a.m.	p.m.	p.m.	p.m.	
Faringdon	7.05	12.40	3.40	7.30	
Uffington	7.20	12.55	3.53	7.45	Sundays
Uffington	9.45	1.05	5.12	7.55	
Faringdon	10.00	1.20	5.25	8.10	

GWR carried the full churns and returned the empties at the rate of 1½d per gallon. The traffic grew very popular and generated a considerable amount of paperwork, some of which was concerned with pilfering. Men working on the stations for twelve hours a day, six days a week sometimes found the temptation to have a surreptitious pint of fresh milk irresistible; two or three men along the line feeling the same way would then result in the churn becoming considerably lighter by the time it reached Paddington. This complaint, made to the station inspector at Uffington, is typical:

Whitfield's Farm,
Uffington.
26th May 1870.

Dear Sir,
　　We have had several complaints that the milk don't reach London with the full amount as loaded at your station. Please see that it isn't tampered with at your end,
　　and oblige,

J. Whitfield

The handwriting was as blunt as the message!

In addition to its undoubted advantages for local farmers, the branch also contributed an addition to the diet of the area. Because of the comparatively rapid transit times of the rail-roads, fish could be brought up from the coast to hitherto remote, inland towns and Faringdon got its first fishmonger soon after the opening of the branch.

In 1873, sixty-nine main line trains were scheduled to pass Uffington during a weekday twenty-four-hour period, but this is a minimum figure, for the working timetable refers to 'the specials that are frequently run'. Some express trains were timed to reach 55 mph, while the speed of goods trains varied from 20 to 40 mph, yet they were separated by nothing more than a time interval – and they were not equipped with power brakes. After the passing of a passenger train, Uffington's policeman turned his disc and crossbar signal to 'Danger' for ten minutes or for fifteen minutes in the case of a freight train. To make matters even worse, the braking distance between the Auxiliary signal and the stop signal was insufficient, a deficiency which was well demonstrated on a drizzly November day in 1873 when a goods train of forty-seven wagons overran the Up stop signal at Uffington. No damage was done, and the driver was fined 'a mitigated penalty' of 5s in view of 'the weight of the train, the greasy rail and the high speed of the train'.

There was a limit to the number of trains that could safely be run under the time-interval system, and in March 1874, the Didcot–Swindon line came under the control of the electric block telegraph. The line was divided into sections, each under the control of a signalman in a 'locking gear box', or signal box as they soon became known. Uffington box was a timber structure about thirty feet high containing the block telegraph instruments, a frame of levers numbered from 1 to 28 all interlocked by the Great Western Railway's patent 'single twist' mechanism. It is not known how many levers the frame actually contained – frames usually contained some spaces for future developments – but there may have been twenty-four made up as follows:

Signals	12
Points	7
Level crossing gate and wicket gate bolts	4
Interlocking lever with ground frame	1
Spaces	4
	——
	28

The signals at Uffington, under the electric block telegraph system were a mixture of the disc and crossbar signals peculiar to the GWR, although of much smaller and lighter construction to enable them to be turned by lever and wire, and the new – to the GWR – semaphore signals. The signalman at Uffington was in communication with Challow box, 2½ miles to the east, and Knighton Crossing box, the same distance westwards, by means of his electrical signalling indicators and signal bells. The former gave an indication as to whether it was safe for the train to pass along and bells were for the transmission of the standard messages in the routine of signalling a train; for other messages, he had a single-needle telegraph instrument. This acted in the place of telephones and passed complicated messages by means of Morse code converted to deflections, left and right, of the instrument's needle. The letter 'S' in Morse is 'dot, dot, dot', which became three deflections thus \\\ and 'O' would have been ///. Men became so expert in sending and reading on the instruments that they were able to 'talk' to the man in the next box with speed and ease.

The principle of signalling trains was opposite to that in use today. Under the 1874 rules, the line was considered clear unless stated otherwise. The routine of signalling was as follows. Supposing there were no trains at Uffington station, main line, and none in the block sections to Challow or Knighton Crossing, the block indicators at Uffington would display 'Line Clear' and the main line signals would be lowered to show 'All Right'. This was very similar to the old, time-interval system. When an up train passed Knighton Crossing, the signalman there sent one beat on the block bell to Uffington. The signalman there acknowledged the signal by repetition, unpegged his 'Line Clear' key, and pegged down the 'Train on Line' key, which altered the display on his own and Knighton's indicator. When the train passed Uffington, the signalman there sent one beat to Challow, placed his signals to 'Danger' behind the train and, if he had seen the train's tail lamp, would send three beats back to Knighton. This meant 'Line Clear', and Uffington would reverse the display on the Uffington/Knighton indicator. Uffington maintained his Up signals at 'Danger' until he received the three beats from Challow and saw the 'Line Clear' display appear in the Uffington/Challow instrument; the Up signals at Uffington were then lowered to show 'All Right'. The great advance in safety of this system over the time-interval system was that there was now a definite minimum distance maintained between each train that was not to be encroached upon. However, the rules did not require the signalman to have a clear space of a quarter of a mile between the last vehicle of a train and the protecting Home signal. Three beats could be sent to the box in rear as soon as the train arrived within the protection of the Home signal complete with tail lamp. But under this system, a driver finding a Distant signal showing 'Danger' was supposed to stop at it or as soon as possible after passing it and then pull cautiously up to the Home.

On the branch, the Up Distant signal was only 403 yards from the 'Danger' signal protecting access to the station. Supposedly, the planners felt that the 1 in 80 rising gradient would be very helpful in braking. In November 1875, an up train came down Barrowbush Hill so fast that it ran up the hill out of control, through the branch platform at Uffington and crashed into two horseboxes in the headshunt.

At the end of January 1875, the Sunday passenger service on the branch was abolished in favour of a morning engine and van, which worked down from Uffington for freight and milk. With only a short break in 1934, this remained the Sunday service on the branch until 1951. The new Sunday service of 1875 was operated by the 2.30 a.m. Bristol to Paddington goods, which called at the junction at 7.20 a.m., and having stabled its train in the up refuge siding, the engine with a guard's van ran down to the terminus whence it returned at 8 a.m. as 'Milk, goods and cattle'. The clerk at Faringdon had the duty of telegraphing Swindon yard inspector, giving the load that was waiting to be collected, then, if the Bristol were fully laden, Swindon yard staff would 'knock off' some wagons to make room for the Faringdon traffic and thus avoid overloading east of Uffington. The 2.30 a.m. Bristol was a broad gauge train and re-established a through service for Faringdon cattle. Since early 1872, when the Great Western main line had been converted to the mixed gauge, the number of

broad gauge goods trains had dwindled, so that traffic from Faringdon had either to
be trans-shipped at Uffington or taken by road to Challow.

While the directors at Faringdon were, in 1877, gripped by their dilemma over the
cost of 'narrowing' their railway and the continuing loss of trade if they didn't, the
Paddington management was making plans for the change of gauge, which they felt
could not be delayed for much longer – even by the men of Faringdon. An important
feature of any changeover from broad to narrow gauge was the additional wagons
needed on the line. An average of ten goods vehicles went over the branch each day
and this would treble just to keep the same carrying capacity, and the question arose,
therefore, of siding accommodation at Uffington and Faringdon. This was answered to
the satisfaction of both railway companies – it was not increased – though the strain
on existing facilities must have been great. The passenger stock on the line remained
the same, consisting of a first/second composite coach, a brake third, a carriage truck
and a horsebox. Indeed, this was the allocation in 1912 and in 1932, though then
without the last two vehicles. Goods traffic was ever the strong point of the branch.

The cost of 'narrowing' the branch was kept down by the happy fact that the
sleepers had originally been laid at right angles to the rails, unlike most broad gauge
road where the sleepers formed a continuous strip beneath each rail. However, a
considerable amount of time was saved 'on the day' by being able to pre-place a new
chair on each sleeper at the 4 feet 8½ inches position, so that when the time came,
all that was necessary to alter the gauge was to lever the rail out of one chair and
into the other. This preparation was not possible at points and crossings, which had
to be taken to pieces and reconstructed to the standard gauge. During June and July,
a signal box was built at Faringdon. This contained a frame of ten interlocked levers,
three working points, two for bolting facing points, three for working signals and two
spares. Communication with Uffington signal box was by means of a single-needle
telegraph instrument. The branch was closed for the narrowing on 26/27 July 1878
and two stagecoaches ran in place of the branch trains, doubtless an uncomfortable
reminder of the old days. They took an hour for a single journey.

The years 1876–84 were difficult for GWR, and reductions were made in the
passenger service; a total of fifty-five trains were scheduled to pass Uffington in 1878
compared with sixty-nine four years earlier, but the cuts did not affect goods trains,
which still called at Uffington or passed through as frequently as ever. The goods'
schedules were distinguished by the close running of trains between 3 a.m. and
6 a.m.

The down 'Irish Express Goods' passed at 12.05 a.m. There was half an hour
before the next train – time for uninterrupted supper, provided no late-night farmer
wanted the level crossing gates opened to take his horse and cart across the line.
At 12.30 a.m. the up 'Plymouth Limited Goods' was due. This was a curious train,
broad gauge, whose entry in the working book is endorsed, 'One wagon only from
Plymouth, Exeter and Bristol'. At 1 a.m., a standard gauge coal train from Cardiff
went rumbling by, taking the regulation fifty minutes running time between Swindon
and Didcot. The night shift had its 'crack' trains: one was the 'Plymouth Limited', the
next was the broad gauge 'Up Mail', 3.50 p.m. from Penzance, which passed Uffington
at 2.05 a.m. running at nearly 60 mph behind a Gooch '8' single' locomotive. Mail
bags were picked up and put off this train at speed when passing Challow by means
of the special lineside apparatus. This 'Mail' train was divided at Bristol, the mail vans
and passenger vehicles running up to London as separate trains, and at 2.35 a.m., the
passenger portion of the train went past the tall signal box by the level crossing in
the Vale.

Unless something unusual happened, such as a special train to be passed, the
signalman now had nearly an hour before the next train and the first on the down
line since 12.05 a.m. This was the 12.05 a.m. Paddington bound for West Wales with
Irish traffic, which ran through Uffington station at 3.40 a.m., just as a Bristol to

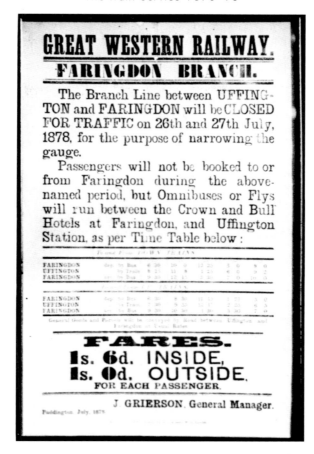

The broad gauge track of the Faringdon branch was not constructed in the Brunellian manner. The Faringdon track had the sleepers at right angles to the rails, which were of 'I' section. The rails were held in cast-iron 'chairs', which were bolted or spiked to the sleepers, and 'fishplates' were used to clamp each rail to the one next to it. This made the job of narrowing the gauge from 7 feet o¼ inches to 4 feet 8½ inches very much easier. One new chair was spiked down at the correct distance within the 7-foot gauge onto each sleeper, and on the appointed day, one rail had to be lifted out of the wide gauge chair and dropped into the standard gauge chair. Point work would have been more difficult, but the whole change was easily made over a weekend.

The timings of the horse-drawn buses and the trains with which they connect are given on the poster as follows:

To and from DOWN TRAINS

FARINGDON	dep. by Bus	6.30	10.0	12.25	5.0	8.0
UFFINGTON	″ by Train	8.25	11.8	1.25	6.0	9.2
FARINGDON	arr. by Bus	9.30	12.15	2.30	7.0	10.0

To and From UP TRAINS

FARINGDON	dep. by Bus	6.30	8.30	11.15	1.25	5.0
UFFINGTON	″ by Train	7.30	9.33	12.17	2.25	6.5
FARINGDON	arr. by Bus	9.30	10.30	1.30	3.30	7.0

General Goods and Parcels will be conveyed by Road between Uffington and Faringdon at Usual Rates.

(The poster is in the collection of Mr David Castle.)

Paddington 'narrow gauge' goods train was pulling up to perform a little shunting. First the wagons for Uffington and Faringdon were berthed in the up siding and then the engine went forward, onto the branch, running past the goods shed, so that it could set back into the shed and push out the loaded wagons that had been waiting there from the previous evening. Having coupled these to its train and perhaps taken water, the locomotive was worked away hard, for the driver would have known that a New Milford to Paddington express goods was due to pass Swindon just at that time, followed by several long drags of coal from Aberdare going to Reading, Southall, Basingstoke and Paddington. These passed behind standard gauge saddle tanks, or the occasional tender engine, while strings of empties rolled past on the down road at about 20 mph. The last up train of the twelve-hour night shift was a Gloucester to Didcot standard gauge freight that 'called if required' at Uffington to pick up anything that the Bristol, owing to overloading, had been obliged to leave behind. Thus, it is very likely that the day-turn signalman walking along the lane to the station through the greying dawn would have heard the shunts and clangs of the Gloucester clearing the yard and walked up the long staircase of the signal box in time to see the train steaming off into Baulking Cutting.

The first job of the day-turn man was to shunt the 12.45 a.m. Birmingham to Bristol goods, which arrived at 6.10 a.m. to put off traffic. The train was left standing on the down main, there being no siding on the downside, while the engine drew forward and set back into the goods shed with the local wagons. Only a few minutes were allowed in the working timetable, so that the trucks would simply have been dropped off clear of any points – the branch engine would position them to the liking of the station staff later on. There was now a gap in the traffic, which would have allowed the signalman to take his breakfast.

The meal over, the first train to pass was the 5.30 a.m. Paddington to Plymouth broad gauge 'Mail and Passengers'. Doubtless hauled by a Gooch '8ft' single-wheeler, the train came storming through Uffington at around 60 mph, due in Swindon at 7.25. Hard on the heels of the 'Mail' – 'block and block' as signalmen would have said – was another broad gauge train, the 4.55 a.m. Paddington to Penzance 'Meat and Fish Empties', an important train that carried the highest priority possible for a freight. As the 'Fish Empties' went through, the first train from Faringdon came steaming round the corner and two minutes later the 7 a.m. from Swindon drew to a stand at the up main platform. An exchange of passengers now took place, with the Faringdon people joining the main line train for Didcot, where there was a connection for Oxford and the north. At Reading, trains for Basingstoke and Trowbridge were waiting, while those wishing to go to Slough or Windsor travelled in the slip coach. The Swindon left at 7.30 a.m., leaving the branch engine one hour in which to shunt round the station, putting the yard and goods shed in order and marshalling as many freight wagons at the rear of its passenger coaches as could be conveyed up Barrowbush Hill to the terminus. While the branch engine shunted, sometimes coming out onto the up main line to perform running-round movements, a succession of freight trains ran through on the down and up mains. At 8.05 a.m., another Gloucester to Didcot goods arrived to detach traffic. Now, the 5.50 a.m. Paddington to Plymouth 'all stations' was due at 8.23 a.m. and the branch trip to Faringdon had to leave at 8.30 a.m., so there was no time to lose. The driver of the Gloucester shunted the wagons onto the up siding smartly and got out of the way to allow the branch engine to go onto the string and pull out any for Faringdon and maybe put them on the passenger train. Everyone had to work quickly, porters, signalman and train guards, to ensure a punctual departure for the branch train. At 8.32, silence had descended upon Uffington station, the porters could go into their room and the signalman could sit down after two and a half hours steady work, the Up and Down signals at 'All Right' ready for the next train, the 10 p.m. from Penzance, due at 8.55 a.m.

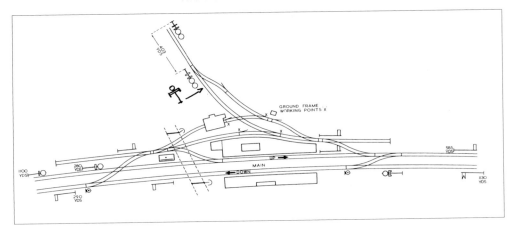

Layout at Uffington, 1875.

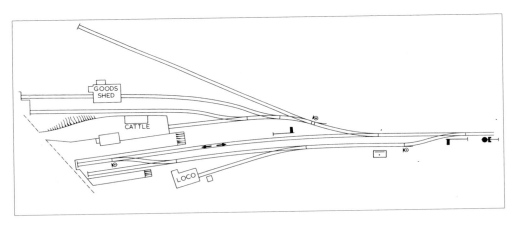

Layout at Faringdon, 1879.

Faringdon Branch Train Service
July 1878

	a.m.	a.m.	a.m.	noon	p.m.	p.m.	p.m.	p.m.	
Faringdon	7.15	9.20	10.50	12.00	1.10	2.05	5.45	8.45	
Uffington	7.25	9.30	11.00	12.10	1.20	2.15	5.55	8.55	Weekdays
Uffington	8.30	9.40	11.15	12.20	1.30	2.30	6.20	9.10	
Faringdon	8.40	9.50	11.25	12.30	1.40	2.40	6.30	9.20	

		a.m.		
Uffington	dep.	7.35	Engine and van ex-main line goods	
Faringdon	arr.	7.45		Sunday
Faringdon	dep.	8.00	Milk, goods and cattle	
Uffington	arr.	8.10		

Faringdon Branch Sunday Service
March 1883

		a.m.		p.m.	
Uffington	dep.	6.22	Engine and van ex-main line goods	5.30	Engine and van ex-main line goods
Faringdon	arr.	6.29		5.40	
Faringdon	dep.	6.36	Milk	5.55	Milk, goods and cattle
Uffington	arr.	6.43		6.05	

Faringdon Branch Train Service
June 1887

Narrow gauge, single line. Worked by Train Staff and Ticket.
Staff: Triangular, varnished oak. Ticket: Square, buff.

	a.m.	a.m.	noon	p.m.	p.m.	p.m.	
Faringdon	7.15	9.25P	12.00	1.10	5.45	8.45	
	M	ST 52	P	P	M	P	
Uffington	7.25	9.35	12.10	1.20	5.55	8.55	
							Weekdays
Uffington	8.00	10.15	12.20	2.15	6.20	9.15	
	M	P	P	P	M	P	
Faringdon	8.10	10.25	12.30	2.25	6.30	9.25	

M = Mixed train.
P = Passenger train.
ST 52 = Station truck 52 conveyed by this train.

		a.m.	p.m.	
Uffington	arr.	6.15	4.33	
		N	K	
Uffington	dep.	6.22	4.40	
Faringdon	arr.	6.29	4.50	Sundays
Faringdon	dep.	6.36	5.05	
Uffington	arr.	6.43	5.15	
Uffington	dep.	6.50	5.25	

N = Worked by engine and brake van ex-5.45 a.m. Swindon–Brentford goods. Brings out milk from Faringdon.
K = Worked by engine and brake van ex-3.50 p.m. Swindon–Paddington ordinary goods. Brings out milk, goods and cattle, also ST 52 from Faringdon.

The pattern of local passenger trains was established by 1878 and was to continue along very similar timings until November 1964 when the Didcot–Swindon stopping trains were withdrawn. The route was treated like a branch in this respect, its passengers taking a slow train to Didcot or Swindon and there changing into a fast train. Uffington had one fast train to Paddington in the mornings, but this was later transferred to Challow. Wantage Road, serving the most important place on the section, does not appear ever to have had an up express calling regularly, though in some timetables the up morning express that called at Challow called also at Wantage Road 'if required'. The latter station did have a morning express service from Paddington by means of a slip coach off the 9 a.m., which was otherwise non-stop to Swindon. The slip arrived at Wantage at 10.15 a.m. where passengers de-trained and the coach was towed into the siding by the station shunting horse – a very heavy duty for any horse – and sometimes, when the slip guard brought the coach to a stand too far up the platform, making too great a labour for the horse, the Wantage tramway locomotive was used, although it was not authorised to go onto GWR rails. This service ran daily from at least 1878 and was suspended in 1914, never to be reinstated. It was the only down line morning express ever to give a service on the Didcot–Swindon local route.

The 11.25 a.m. Reading–Bristol 'stopper' connected with a Faringdon branch train at 1.23 p.m. and arrived on the down branch platform at Swindon at 1.50 p.m., ten minutes before the '12 noon Paddington to South Wales and Weymouth' express drew in on the main line platform. Separated by the width of the platform was an 'all stations' to Bristol, an express for Trowbridge, Somerset and Dorset, and another for Gloucester, Chepstow and South Wales.

The Train Staff and Ticket method of working the line was adopted from June 1882 to allow a greater frequency of trains over the line – and also, I hope, to make life easier for the porter at Faringdon. The problem on the Uffington to Faringdon line, worked on the 'One Engine in Steam' principle, was that the last down train, from Uffington to Faringdon, was obliged to take the Train Staff. The Staff was then at Faringdon with the engine and coaches and was in the right place because the first train next day left from Faringdon. But as from January 1875, the branch line Sunday passenger service was abolished and only a Sunday morning 'Goods and Milk' ran, using an engine and van from a main line goods. That engine and van could not go to Faringdon without the Staff and so someone at Faringdon had to walk with it to Uffington in time to meet the main line train – and then, when that train had returned to Uffington, the same person had to walk the Staff back to Faringdon, ready for the Monday morning passenger service.

By the addition of the Ticket to the Staff working, the last train down on a Saturday evening went away with a Ticket and the Staff remained at Uffington, ready for Sunday Morning. The Tickets were kept in a very strong, locked, steel box. The box could only be opened by a key, which was fitted to the end of the wooden Train Staff. The Sunday engine and van went down with the Staff and came back to Uffington on a Ticket, leaving the Staff at Faringdon for the start of the Monday service. The first milk (only) train service to run between Bristol and Paddington was started from Chippenham in June 1882. In March 1883, a Sunday evening 'Milk, goods and cattle' train was put on on the branch. It is known that military specials worked over the line during 1883, which would have been impossible without the Train Staff and Ticket system.

The Staff Tickets on the Faringdon branch were pieces of buff-coloured card, about 4 inches x 4 inches and carried the words, 'To the driver of — train. You are authorised to proceed to Faringdon (or Uffington) and the Train Staff will follow.' The card was signed by the station master and given to the driver, who could then take his train away, provided that he had been shown the Train Staff to prove that it was still at that end of the line, provided that the signals were 'off' for him to proceed and that his guard had given the 'Right Away' with flag and whistle. Under this system, as many trains could leave Uffington for Faringdon as could be accommodated at Faringdon, but no train could leave Faringdon for Uffington until the Train Staff had arrived. The signalman would not allow a train to follow another until the first had run within the protection of stop signals at the other end of the line, a fact that would, on the Faringdon line, have been communicated by means of the single-needle telegraph instrument. Clearly this system was a great advance on the earlier system.

In 1885, the method of block signalling on the main line underwent a profound change. The principle upon which the system was founded was reversed, and from 1885, the running lines were considered blocked until stated to be clear. Signal box routine altered drastically, as signalmen now had to keep their signals at 'Danger' and lower them for a train to pass only when they had asked, and received, permission to do so from the signalman towards whom the train was running. This is the basis of block signalling used in the British Isles to this day. The old rule concerning distant signals altered, and drivers passing a distant at 'Danger' had now to shut off steam and bring their train under control in order to stop at the Home signal if required. The Distant signals for Faringdon and Uffington (on the branch) were 'worked' until 1904, when 'Fixed at Danger' Distants became the rule in such situations. Between 1885 and 1890, there were three or four cases of drivers arriving at Faringdon with their trains out of control and crashing into the buffers. A 'fixed distant' could not prevent a driver from crashing if he were so inclined, but it could act as a reminder, to anyone less determined, of the need to slow down. This five-year period was a particularly trying one for the branch so far as accidents were concerned, and there were several incidents of locomotives failing, big ends running hot, and drivers getting their locomotives 'off the road' for one careless reason or another.

After the trade depression of the 1870s, when the annual dividend of GWR was 2 or 3 per cent lower than that to which the shareholders had become accustomed, 1880 and the succeeding years were increasingly like old times, and the dividend to Ordinary shareholders returned 6 or 7 per cent annually. Having weathered the storm and considerably modernised the railway into the bargain, the directors were content to let the company settle down to a long period of steady work, free from any heroics. This attitude is clearly seen in the train services of the Didcot–Swindon line, which had a direct effect upon those of the Faringdon branch. In July 1885, the branch service, which had lasted since January 1882, was modified. The 'RR' goods was withdrawn together with the 1.55 p.m. passenger from Faringdon, and of the remaining six trips, the 7.15 a.m. and 5.45 p.m. services from Faringdon were authorised to run as 'mixed' trains. This arrangement was very successful and ran without significant alteration until October 1894.

The stability of the main line train service is shown by the fact that, in 1885, eighty-five trains passed Uffington in a weekday twenty-four hours and only seven were added to the schedules during the next nine years. In spite of the branch reductions, all main line trains were met, there was a very reasonable service and the 2.30 p.m. from Paddington was reinstated. In the up direction, some trains calling at Uffington, which had been 'all stations' to Paddington, now ran 'fast' from Reading. The 10 a.m. from Bristol was such a one and had a slip coach for Slough too. The opening throughout of the Didcot, Newbury & Southampton Railway in May 1885 added another service to those available at Didcot. Train speeds increased – there was plenty of room for improvement. Stopping trains had a few minutes cut out of their tortoise-like 'running' times and several up and down express and mail trains were accelerated by three, five or even eight minutes between Paddington and Swindon, though the 'crack' broad gauge 'Flying Dutchman' continued to run from London to Swindon in eighty-seven minutes. The GWR was content with these gentle improvements and worked in this manner from one royal jubilee to the next, when the advent of very much more powerful locomotives enabled radical changes to take place in the schedules.

Various innovations were brought about during the 1880s. Faringdon's milk exports were not conveyed by coal train after 1883. The engine and van of the Sunday goods thereafter brought only the milk vans to the junction where they were left to be collected by an early, up stopping passenger train. The Royal Mail continued to

Broad gauge Swindon-class 0-6-0 heads a down fish empties past Uffington *c.* 1885. The tall signal box can be glimpsed to the rear of the train. The goods shed is covered by the bulk of the engine. The infamous level crossing lay between the signal box and the station. Three horseboxes stand on the up siding and between them and the engine is the single-storey brick office, which survived the rebuilding in 1896–97 to the present day. The signal in front of the building is the earliest type of GWR semaphore, where the arm goes into a slot in the post to give the 'Proceed' aspect. The arm has a red spectacle only in front of the lens of the lamp. At night, the 'Proceed' aspect is given by a white light. (Jack Slinn Collection)

Uffington station shortly after its enlargement and re-signalling in 1896. The view looks east from the new bridge, which replaced the level crossing. (Oxford City Library)

be carried by goods train, at least until 1887, the 11.45 p.m. Paddington to New Milford goods being a case in point. Mail for Faringdon was unloaded from this train at Swindon. The practice of running 'Station Trucks' began in the 1880s. Faringdon's station truck was No. 52 until about 1910 when it was renumbered 60 and remained so until withdrawn, probably in 1934. The station truck was an important part of railway service. It was a covered vehicle, painted – 'branded' as the railway said – with its daily working circuit, thus ensuring that perishable or other urgent traffic had a direct and recognisable service. Several hundred stations, large and small, had their own truck – or trucks – conveying the special manufactures of the district, sausages from Calne factory to various destinations, or simply luxury perishable food from a London department store to a high-class grocer's shop in a country market town like Faringdon. In total, the marshalling of these hundreds of trucks made a considerable increase in the daily work of the railway, but the company reckoned that any traffic was worth having and undertook the complicated organisation accordingly. The title 'Perishables' was first applied to a train (the 4.40 a.m. Bristol–Paddington) in 1887, though this type of traffic had been running under the title of 'General and Fast Market Goods' since 1874.

A very important innovation was made in October 1888 with the first headlamp codes for locomotives. These codes were an arrangement of lamps at the front of a locomotive to indicate to signalmen the type of train that was approaching. The lamps had a glass bullseye lens and on one side of the lamp case was a white diamond and on the other a white 'S' on a black background. By arranging the symbols or the lens to face forward, the class of train, 'A' to 'F', was indicated. Each class of train had a maximum permitted speed and each had its distinguishing bell code for signal box use. Any kind of passenger train on a main line was then a class A train and carried a lamp at the base of the engine's chimney. This applied to the 'Faringdon Johnny' or the 'Flying Dutchman'. The branch goods became D headcode, 'Ordinary or local goods', and carried a lamp over the locomotive's right-hand buffer by day; at night the lamp showed a green light forward.

Commencing in October 1890, two 'Saturdays Only' trains ran over the branch, starting from Faringdon at 8.20 a.m. and 7.30 p.m. but apparently they were not successful, being withdrawn the following March and since then no 'SO' trains ran on the line. An ancient practice was restored to the line in July 1891 when the 'First Tuesday of the Month' goods train began running on an 'if required' basis. The following May, a passenger train commenced running under the same conditions until October 1894, when it became a regular daily trip, and in June 1895, the first daily goods train on the branch for twenty-two years was put into service. Curiously enough, just as the branch timetable was beginning to grow, the Train Staff and Ticket system on the branch was abolished, leaving only the awkward Train Staff. This must have been very inconvenient, especially on Sundays when two trains required to travel over the line. But this was a period when questions were being asked in Parliament about safety at Uffington (see Chapter 7) and the Board of Trade may have forbidden the use of the Ticket unless correct electrical signalling appliances were installed in connection with Ticket working.

January 1896 saw two more passenger trains and an extra daily freight enter the timetables to give the branch the busiest service to date. For a single engine to make so many journeys, it was necessary to shorten its journey times and some of the passenger trains were timed to make the journey in seven minutes, an average speed of 30 mph, which must have sounded impressive going up Barrowbush Hill. The schedules for the line had a pleasant sparkle, but the Paddington management were no longer content to sparkle, they wanted to dazzle! In May 1896, another passenger train entered the time book and yet another in July. Twelve round trips a day plus two cattle fair trains once a month! The 'Great Awakening', to which E. T. McDermott refers in volume 2 of his *History of the Great Western Railway*, was not confined to the main lines; even the Faringdon branch shared the benefits owing to the new attitude at Paddington and the greater prosperity of England as the country reached the climax of Victoria's reign and the zenith of Imperial power.

Faringdon Branch Train Service
July 1896

Single line worked by Train Staff and only one engine in steam.
Staff: Triangular, varnished oak.

	A	D	A	A	A	A	A	A	A	D	A
	a.m.	a.m.	a.m.	a.m.	a.m.	a.m.	p.m.	p.m.	p.m.	p.m.	p.m.
Faringdon	6.50	7.30	8.17	9.25	10.00	11.05	12.10	1.55	3.30	4.20	6.00
					ECS:L						
Uffington	6.58	7.40	8.25	9.33	10.08	11.13	12.18	2.03	3.38	4.30	6.08
Uffington	7.15	7.55	8.43	9.45	10.13	11.25	12.36	2.28	3.51	4.45	6.20
				L							L
Faringdon	7.22	8.05	8.50	9.52	10.20	11.32	12.43	2.35	3.58	4.55	6.27

	A	D	Mxd
	p.m.	p.m.	p.m.
Faringdon	6.35	7.10	8.45
	ECS:L		
Uffington	6.42	7.20	8.53
Uffington	6.48	7.48	9.10
Faringdon	6.55	7.55	9.17

A = A headcode
D = D headcode
Mxd = Mixed train
ECS = Empty coaching stock
L = First Tuesday of each month

Sundays

		a.m.	p.m.
Uffington	dep.	6.10	7.55
		N	K
Faringdon	arr.	6.17	8.02
Faringdon	dep.	6.48	8.15
Uffington	arr.	6.55	8.22

N = Working by engine and van ex-5.15 a.m. Swindon goods. Brings out milk to Uffington.
K = Worked by engine and van of 6.45 p.m. Swindon goods. Milk, goods and cattle to Uffington and beyond.

CHAPTER 6

Men on the Line

The year 1897 was an optimistic jubilee year in Britain with the people full of enthusiasm for their country's achievements. Optimism welled up just as strongly at parochial level. In March, the landowners of the Fairford district took a petition to Paddington: that GWR would extend the Fairford line to Kemble or Cirencester. Local produce, they said, had difficulty leaving the area, while coal via Oxford was expensive and a link with the Swindon–Gloucester line would allow Forest of Dean coal to come in at a cheaper rate. Viscount Emlyn, Chairman of GWR, (who became First Lord of the Admiralty in 1905) replied with a certain informed irony, telling the petitioners that his company must be assured of a reasonable return on its outlay and asking if the landowners 'who presumably require this line to be built will give the necessary land free or at a nominal sum as this would reduce our building costs and make us proportionately more willing to construct the extension'. The deputation, who were probably hoping to make some money through the sale of land to GWR, were unable to answer that shrewd question immediately and retired to Gloucestershire 'for further discussion'. Of course, the lines were never built.

The branch railway's influence for good in Faringdon was considerable, although, paradoxically, the town's population declined steadily from 3,700 in 1864 to 2,900 in 1903. England suffered a series of trade depressions in 1864–65, 1878–83 and 1890–94, yet despite these, business enterprise in Faringdon increased steadily. The *Post Office Gazette* for 1864 listed eighteen trades in Faringdon, all the expected occupations of a country town with the exception of the gasworks, which was in operation *before* the coming of the branch railway. In 1880, the *Gazette* listed nine new trades, one, the fishmonger, requiring the speed of rail transport to convey the wares from distant seaports, and four depending on a railway's heavy haulage capacity: an iron foundry, an agricultural machinery manufactory, a sawmill and timber merchant, and a steam plough hire firm. Other improvements seen by the year 1880, which may have been in some part due to the new railway, were the introduction of an architect's office, an estate agent and a cabinet-maker, while the bare title of the 'Gas Works' had now become 'The Faringdon Gas Light & Coke Company'. The 1897 *Gazette* shows no additions to the inventory of the town's trades, though an increase in the number of one-man businesses is indicated. The only occupation to be shown in decline was that of carrier. In 1864, there had been twenty-one men licensed to convey parcels and people, but by 1897, the number had dwindled to six, obviously the result of improved rail communications. The determined survivors worked from Faringdon to Oxford, Abingdon, Wantage, Highworth, Stanford-in-the-Vale and, strange to say, Uffington.

If a man in the employment of GWR had a son or brother or nephew approaching school-leaving age, he would keep a sharp lookout for impending vacancies and ensure that his relation applied for them, hence the legend that it was essential to have a relation working on the line if one was to secure employment. This was not strictly true, but having a family connection was an advantage in the competition to join the company's ranks. Apart from higher wages, railway employment offered any bright lad the chance of a career, which was a rare thing for a working-class boy in those days. It was usual to start as a porter, or lad porter if less than eighteen, and progress from that level. If one was lucky, it was possible to start as a signal-porter and earn an extra shilling a week for the added responsibility of working part of one's time in a small signal box, but this was not at all usual for a beginner. No formal training was given to newcomers to the service; they were expected to learn from reading the Rule Book and Signalling Regulations, from the example of more experienced men and from their own mistakes.

GWR was a paternalistic employer using a 'carrot and stick' method of government sparingly so that neither punishment nor reward became commonplace and therefore despised; both required a certain amount of effort to achieve, so that the recipient probably felt that he deserved whatever he received. A man could earn a week's wage for a particularly quick piece of thinking in an emergency and all signalmen stood to gain five weeks' wages if they could work for half a year without being found out in an irregularity – not easy but certainly not impossible. Conversely, one could be fined a quarter or even half a week's wages for a piece of appalling negligence, drunkenness or bad timekeeping, while conviction for theft entailed then, as now, instant dismissal. However, dismissal was the ultimate punishment and used sparingly, the company obviously valuing trained men and not wishing to lose them for some ordinary human failing. An example of the extraordinarily chivalrous approach of GWR to offenders is that of a travelling porter who threw a case of fish out of an express train as it was passing Twyford one dark night, causing a strolling passenger to fall bruised and winded to the platform. At Paddington, the culprit was cautioned by the on-duty inspector and there the matter rested. A few weeks later, the porter was seen by a railway policeman acting in a furtive manner with a crate of fish at Paddington and was duly escorted to the inspector's office. Here, he was given the choice of arguing the matter with a magistrate, or leaving the service immediately with a reference suitable for obtaining further employment elsewhere. He left.

A member of the company's police force was fined several times for being drunk on duty but was not asked for his resignation. When no improving effect was forthcoming after several changes of scenery, he apparently became aware of his conscience and resigned voluntarily. A stableman who 'gave a horse a bath when it had a cold' was fined 2s 6d, though by his action the company stood to lose a valuable animal. It is interesting that those men who did suffer any punishment usually did so during the first ten years of their career, whereafter they lived blameless lives.

In 1897, trade union activity was vigorous throughout the country, accompanied by many strikes, but this was not quite the case on GWR, where union men wrote 'prayers' to the directors and occasionally received favourable replies. Prayers for two and subsequently three days paid holiday per annum had been made during 1895–96, and the prayer had been granted, but when the union tried to increase the indulgence of the board to six days per annum they were rebuffed. The directors had 'sympathetically considered but reluctantly refused your request owing to the cost to the shareholders. You should bear in mind that recently you were granted three days holiday per annum. However the request is noted and will be borne in mind for a future occasion.' In January 1897, the gentlemen of the board of directors had voted £60,000 to make a birthday/jubilee present for Queen Victoria: a new station for her personal and private use at Windsor adjoining the public station she had used for over forty years.

During the hundred years of the branch line's existence, it gave well-paid employment to scores of men, most of whom have been forgotten, but a few, because of their virtues or exploits, have become legends that were then handed down through generations of railwaymen. Faringdon station had two such heroes, both of whom had worked on the line in the days of the Faringdon management: John Campbell, station master, and Thomas Cane, train guard. Campbell was a Scot whose natural thrift and regard for economy had earned him the reputation of being the largest shareholder in the old Faringdon company. Possibly to discourage any attempt at burglary, he worked only at night at his office with his best friend, a large, sandy-coloured cat. Campbell left his office when the early-turn porter arrived to open the station and went back to his house in Bromsgrove Place for breakfast. At about 10 a.m., he would return for the previous day's takings, which he carried to the bank, and would not be seen again at the station until it was time to close it down for the night. He was quite bald and herein lay his only conceit, for he covered his shiny cranium with a blonde wig. In his desire for economy he bowed to no man, so that when the Bristol Divisional Superintendent arrived at the station one day – for which special visit Campbell had altered his usual routine – and told the Scot that the station nameboards were of an obsolete design and would have to be renewed, Campbell snapped, 'It is an unnecessary expense and if ye send them I'll no hae them put up.' The new signs duly arrived, and true to his word, Campbell had them stowed away in a store where they mouldered until after his retirement, when they were erected – obsolete. Campbell never allowed any claim against the Faringdon Railway made by a member of the public to go beyond his office but paid them all from his own pocket. Having obtained a receipt from the claimant, he pinned claim and receipt together and put them away in a drawer. When he retired, he presented this considerable accumulation to the company and asked to be reimbursed. The GWR management, recognising a businessman, allowed his claim and paid him by instalments as an addition to his weekly pension, which is doubtless what the canny man had intended all along. He valued hard-working members of his staff, though this was by no means an advantage to a favourite clerk or porter, for if one was to apply to Head Office for a promotion, Campbell simply wrote 'Not Recommended' on the form and that was the end of the matter. One porter, valued for his excellent grasp of station accountancy, who had applied for a position worth 2s a week more than the one he held at Faringdon, had his chances ruined by Campbell in the manner described – *but* for two years the man's wages were made up by an extra 2s a week from Campbell's own pocket. Eventually, he had to let the porter go; it was not simply a matter of the 2s but steps up the promotional ladder. The necessity of obtaining one's station master's approval for a promotion often meant that a useful man was kept back while a poor one was 'Recommended' – just to get rid of him. John Campbell retired about 1893 and was replaced by Walter King, who held the post until about 1903 when H. W. Tidsbury took over.

Tom Cane's claim to fame springs simply from his long service unblemished by any accident or carelessness. He came to Faringdon in 1872, when he was twenty-seven, and took a porter's job earning 16s per week. He carried on this occupation, twelve hours a day, six days a week, with a short turn of duty on Sundays for the next seventeen years – until 1889 – when the branch train's guard retired and Tom got the job. His wages at that time had been £1 per week and now rose to one guinea. He supervised the branch train for thirteen years, cleaning the carriages inside and out, with assistance from the lad porter, looking for mechanical defects, stowing luggage, parcels, milk and passengers. He retired early when he was fifty-seven, earning 23s per week.

For other men, Faringdon was simply a step in the promotion ladder. They came and left for better-paid jobs, spending only a year or eighteen months at the terminus, and others came and found the place a stumbling block. Bill C. had been a lad porter at Banbury earning 11s per week, but on attaining adult status at the age of twenty, in March 1882, he had to find an entry into the grade of porter or leave the service. There were no vacancies at his home station, so he was obliged to move and came to Faringdon where he received 12s per week. Within the year, he had moved on to Challow for an extra 1s a week. He worked there blamelessly for five years, then began to collect a succession of fines, 2s or half a crown, for carelessness. He stuck it – and the company stuck with him – for two years; he came out of his bad patch and worked quietly for the next eighteen years, until 1906, when he damaged some wagons by 'rough shunting' and soon after blocked the up main line by derailing a milk wagon. The poor man must have been very upset over these latest lapses, for he resigned, losing 23s a week.

Richard K. came to Faringdon from Reading, 'shilling chasing', in August 1899. He got 2s a week more at Faringdon than at his previous post and remained two years. He was a young man and the town had its attractions. Once, while delivering parcels round the shops, he went absent without leave from 10 a.m. until the following day, but whatever attracted him was not worth missing an extra shilling a week, and in 1901, he returned to Reading and a better-paid job.

Occasionally, men did not come up to standard. One of these men had been posted to Faringdon from Savernake. He had started his career as the porter at Burbage Wharf goods station in 1893, but owing to his heavy sleeping, he was sent to nearby Savernake, where, as only one of several staff, he was not quite so vitally important to the station. He remained a liability of course, and one suspects that he may have been recommended for promotion. At any rate, he arrived at Faringdon in 1896, the worst place possible for a heavy sleeper, as it was the early-rising porter who opened the station for the day's work. Less than a year after his arrival, he was sacked for 'constantly over-sleeping, coming late to work and thereby delaying trains'.

The post of signal-porter at Faringdon earned £1 a week in 1901 when Harry J. came from his porter's job at Hermitage to the signal box at Faringdon. He appears to have found the job too difficult, for eighteen months after his arrival he derailed the branch locomotive by moving the points too soon and was punished by three days' suspension. Two months later, he did the same thing again and was dismissed.

Arthur Jennings had been a porter at Shrivenham for six months when, in May 1893, he transferred to Uffington for an extra 1s, making his basic wage 16s per week. He was the night-shift porter on 16/17 September, to deal with a freight or two which called in the small hours, a lonely and possibly uncomfortable job, as there was little for him to do except clean, trim and fill a few oil lamps to while away the dragging hours. But on this particular night, the signalman sent him to relight the lamp in the Down Main starting signal, three-quarters of a mile from the station. The lamp was on a thirty-foot-tall post, which stood on an embankment fifteen feet high. There were no guard rails around the platform upon which Jennings had to stand while he attended to the lamp; the night was dark, and possibly windy, with the result that he slipped, fell and died instantly. GWR was criticised by the coroner's jury, who asked why there was no lamp-hoisting gear at such a tall signal to which the company replied, 'We only fit this equipment to signals over thirty feet tall.' No one seems to have queried the lack of guard rails at the lamp platform and so the matter rested. But the signalman did not get off so lightly. When Arthur Jennings did not return and the lamp was not relit, he took no further action and only mentioned the matter to his mate as he was taking over duty at 6 a.m. It was then that the alarm was raised and Jennings's body was discovered. GWR reported to the coroner, 'This signalman committed a serious error in allowing the lamp to remain unlighted. He should have put his signals to 'Danger', 'Blocked Back' and called the station master so that a search could have been made for the porter. Suitable notice has been taken of this.' But no one took any 'notice' of GWR's lack of guard rails on signal lamp platforms.

For nine months, from March to December 1890, Uffington station rang with crashing sounds as Jim J. taught himself the porter's trade at the company's expense – smashed buffers, crushed sleepers and mangled pointwork. Uffington was his first station, and it is only surprising that it was not his last, but GWR tolerated his clumsiness. He earned the honourable nickname 'Slammer', and at the end of the year, he transferred to Reading as a shunter. In this role he was, if not successful, then at least energetic and caused damage to many wagons through rough shunting, on one occasion reducing the contents of a furniture van to matchwood. Having devoted his energies to Reading Yard for two years, he went to Oxford as a shunter and after three years became a brakesman at Didcot, which seems a little ironic in view of the little use he had had for wagon brakes in the past. His job was to ride on freight trains and pin down wagon brakes before the train descended steep inclines, a function he performed for four years, much of his time being spent on the Didcot–Winchester section. This riding around on trains gave him the taste for a guard's job which he found back at Reading. Undismayed by a variety of fines and suspensions for offences like 'going home with the crossing keys in his pocket', he served out his time and retired with a pension in 1935.

Uffington signal box was well known locally for its long-serving signalmen. Bill Norton, Walt Thomas and Alf Joyce are three men who deserve to be remembered for their constant work. Bill joined GWR in January 1881 and worked in both signal boxes (see Chapter 7) from 1885 until his retirement in January 1928, a total of forty-seven years' service, forty-four at Uffington, during which time he had only six weeks off duty owing to illness. In 1910, Alf Joyce joined Bill in the box, and in 1914, Walt Thomas arrived. The former completed forty-six years' service, thirty-two at Uffington; the latter fifty-one years' service, thirty-eight of them at the station (see Appendix 3). Such long periods of employment were quite common on GWR, but perhaps that length of service in one box is unusual. In 1914, Thomas and Joyce, in common with hundreds of other signalmen, worked a twelve-hour day with (except in emergencies) a minimum of nine hours' rest between shifts. Bank holidays were worked without any increase in pay except that if a man worked on Good Friday and Christmas Day he was paid double time for the latter day only. Normal overtime rates then were time and a quarter for weekday hours over twelve each day and time and a half for Sundays. In 1919, working hours were reduced to eight per day. Uffington was a Class 3 signal box in 1923, a classification it retained until 1968, and in 1923 was possibly the best-paid job between the junctions at Highworth (Swindon) and Foxhall (Didcot). These classifications were arrived at through a 'marks system'. Each movement the signalman made during a twenty-four-hour period – pushing or pulling a lever, ringing a bell or taking the staff out to a train, putting a reminder collar on a lever – was worth a certain number of marks, and at the end of the day, all the marks were added up and divided by twenty-four to give an hourly rate. 150 to 224 marks per hour justified Class 3 pay, £3 a week, and Uffington box fell into this category by thirteen marks. Challow missed it by eleven; the Faringdon branch added twenty-four marks an hour to Uffington's marks for the main line, making Uffington Class 3, 'a very nice little number'.

Before 1900, 400 small stations on GWR were under the supervision of a station inspector, a rank below that of station master, and Uffington formed one of this number. There had been some prayers, during 1897, from the station inspectors to the Board of Directors for upgrading to station master, but whether the upgrading of Uffington's inspector was due to this praying or to the rebuilding and enlargement of the premises is not known. What is certain is that the ponderously named Cornelius Joseph Crook was the first man to hold the office of 'Station Master, Uffington'. Crook commenced his railway career at fourteen, serving as a weighbridge lad in the goods depot at Salisbury. Five years later, in 1872, he had to find adult employment and was lucky enough to get a parcels porter job at the passenger station. This was treble promotion, to move to the passenger side, to miss the grade of porter and go straight to parcels work. This may indicate that C.J.C. was recognised as one with a flair for paperwork, for his new job had nothing to do with carrying luggage but involved waybills, invoicing and ledger work. This he stuck at for fully thirteen years;

Faringdon station and goods yard about 1906. No. 541 shunting. The little hut – 5 feet by 7 feet – at centre of view was the signal box, accommodating eight or ten levers to operate the signals, points and point bolts. Also in the signalling hut were the block telegraph instruments and a single-strike bell communicating with Uffington. (Author's Collection)

No. 541 at Faringdon. Driver Arthur Taylor, fireman Ted Glanville. (Courtesy Jim Brown)

indeed, he may have been a victim of the system mentioned earlier and had fallen into the category of 'useful'. However, in April 1885, he was sent to the soon-to-be-opened Whitchurch station on the Didcot, Newbury & Southampton Railway where he was to perform as a booking clerk for 26s a week. Although this was a step up the promotional ladder, he had to work harder than many porters, for he had responsibility for the sale and accountancy of all sorts of tickets, passenger and goods, and for the operation of the station yard, shunting and loading. He obviously worked very hard for his money, but characteristically he stuck to the grindstone and, after four years, was able to move to the booking clerk's job at Uffington with no increase in salary. He would not have had any responsibility for 'outside work' however, so he had an easier time. He may have been the first occupant of the station house, which was built on the north side of the main line and completed late in 1888. The company's minutes note that 'the house has been built for the Booking Porter by Samuel Robertson, contractor, at a cost to this Company of £258'. Crook lived in the house for twenty-one years, enjoying a low rent, cheap coal and firewood (supplied by the company to all employees who were householders whether or not the house was company owned) and if he needed more garden space there was plenty of land available on the northern bank of Baulking Cutting near the station. Indeed, railwaymen had allotments there until the early 1960s. Joseph Crook became station inspector in 1890, just in time to take responsibility for an engine's derailment at the ground frame points, but the incident was not held against him, so when the station was upgraded to the dignity of supervision by a station master, he was appointed to the post. In this capacity, he continued for thirteen years until an early retirement in 1910 when he was fifty-seven.

One gets the distinct impression that C. J. Crook was a very conscientious, very patient man. His replacement was a very different man whose rise from the bottom to the top of his profession had only taken a little longer than it had taken the tireless Crook to pass from one grade of porter to another. The new man, whom I shall call Charles Sharp, though that was not his name, began his career in 1884 at the age of fourteen as a lad porter at Montacute on the Taunton–Yeovil line. At nineteen, he got his portering job and went quickly through all six grades of signalman and relief signalman, collecting on the way several 'cautions' for disobedience and irregular signalling, none of which stopped him from becoming an assistant inspector in the divisional superintendent's office at Paddington before he was thirty and assistant to the chief inspector of signalmen by his thirtieth birthday. Two years later, he became chief inspector of signalmen. In those days, when promotion was often referred to as 'waiting for dead men's shoes', such rapid progress must have been made at the expense of other more senior and probably more competent men, railway work being largely a matter of experience, so that one is left with a nagging suspicion that Sharp enjoyed the patronage of a higher official. His transfer to Uffington in 1910, after eight years at the top of his particular profession seems strange – one wonders if it were really promotion or whether his patron had retired, leaving him vulnerable to attack from some well-placed enemy. Then again, the company had a practice of punishing its more senior officers by sending them to outstations whose obscurity was carefully chosen and graded according to the magnitude of the offence. If Sharp was in disgrace, he ought to have been reassured when he arrived at Uffington Junction – it was hardly GWR's equivalent of Siberia. But it appears he was unhappy at the station. Elderly people in the village recall that Sharp spent so much time in the bar of the Junction Hotel that the station staff followed his example, leaving the place quite deserted at times and obliging intended travellers to go to the hotel in order to winkle out a porter who would sell them a ticket. This state of affairs lasted four years, but in 1914, Paddington became aware of the dereliction of duty that was continuing at Uffington, and Sharp was transferred – or banished – to Upton & Blewbury station, the Outer Mongolia of the GWR.

Faringdon station staff, *c.* 1910. From the left, standing: Eric Bonner, carman; 'Mac' McKenzie, porter; Bert Vaughan, porter-signalman; another; Fred Dibden, goods shed foreman; the Didcot lampman; Jack Berryman, parcels porter at Faringdon; Ted Glanville, fireman of branch engine; Arthur Taylor, engine driver; Jack Hammond, a porter from Uffington. Seated: Stan Norton, junior clerk at Faringdon; H. W. Tidsbury, station master; Lewis Crook, booking clerk.

H. W. Tidsbury was a very friendly station master, popular with his staff and the public. Bert Vaughan had been a porter at Henley. He travelled home on a tender engine which was running tender first in mid-winter ice and snow. He died from the effects of his exposure. (Mrs K. Singleton)

Uffington station staff, *c.* 1910. Left to right, standing: Alf Joyce, signalman; Mr Norton, signalman; Jack Grace, porter; Ernie Essex, porter. Seated: Miss Hancock, booking clerk and station master's daughter; Mr Hancock; Walt Thomas, signalman.

Jack Grace served the Great Western Railway and the public from 1904 to March 1946. He spent thirty-nine years at Uffington. When he retired from railway service, a public subscription was made and a cheque presented to him at a meeting in Uffington. The then station master, Arthur Westcott, presented the cheque. Then the retired station master of Uffington, Mr H. Westcott and Signalman Walt Thomas each gave their tribute to a fine railwayman. Several civilians also spoke of their very high regard for Jack. In reply, Jack thanked one and all, and in moments he was well launched into regaling the assembly with many amusing anecdotes of his railway career.

This is a copy of a picture belonging to Walt Thomas's son-in-law, Signalman Bill Mattingley, and loaned for use in this book by Jim Baldwin.

Uffington permanent-way gang, *c.* 1910. From left to right: Joe Bailey, -?-, -?-, -?-, -?-, -?-, Iles, Harry Bailey, -?-, Ganger Edward Hodges.
(Courtesy Jim Brown)

The permanent-way department had two 'gangs' at Uffington, one for the main line, the other for the branch. They were responsible under their 'ganger' for maintaining the track, footpaths, ditches, drains, fences, hedges and grass in perfect order. This they did with great care and no mechanical aids – unless one counts their shovels and ballast forks – and all the line looked very handsome as a result. The men did not have August Bank Holiday Monday off duty before 1919, but the ganger, usually a very strict man, would unbend a little and allow them to take the day off providing everything on the 'length' was in perfect order on the day of the District Engineer's annual inspection. This took place during July – because the DE was a humane man who understood local customs. If every detail, from well-packed rail joints to tightly cut thorn hedges, was in 'apple pie' order, he would express his approval. The ganger had his men lined up on parade after the engineer's inspection, and he would compliment them on their work and show his appreciation by giving each man a cigar – and two to the ganger.

CHAPTER 7

Reconstruction at Uffington

The dangerous level crossing at Uffington claimed its first life in 1884 and was to be the death of four men by June 1894. In November 1891, a carter left his horse and wagon standing at the milk dock while he went across to the bar of the Junction Hotel. After waiting half an hour, the horse decided to follow and walked slowly out from the shade of the signal box into the path of a train. The horse was killed and the cart smashed to bits.

The Old Berks hounds were hunting on 1 April 1893, and their quest led them over the level crossing, which remained open long enough for the hounds and huntsmen to cross but closed before the 'field' could pass, so that they came to a milling, impatient stand, bunched around the gate. At that moment, a cart horse that had been left unattended along the road became excited by the hounds and so many horses. It galloped into the mounted throng, still dragging its cart, and knocked a well-known farmer, Mr Jefferies, from his horse, killing him.

At 7.20 a.m. on a fine June day in 1894, a young lad called Gerald Ritchings was rolling a churn down the platform ramp to take it across to the upside for loading into the 6.55 a.m. Swindon to Paddington stopping passenger train (see Appendix 4). The rolling, ringing sound of the churn drowned the noise of the passenger train as the locomotive coasted into the station. Gerald walked directly under the engine and was killed. His death, so soon after Jefferies, and his youthful age shocked the coroner and all the local people. The coroner wrote to GWR saying, more or less, that he was getting tired of investigating deaths at Uffington, that the station was generally a dangerous place 'with hair-breadth escapes freely talked about' and ended by asking what the company was going to do about the situation. The reply from Paddington was disdainful; they did not care to comment on airy generalities such as 'generally dangerous' and asked for details. As for local gossip, that was no concern of theirs. GWR's case was that they were willing to build an underbridge on the line of the crossing but the highways board of Berkshire County Council would not allow them to do this, because such a passage would flood each winter. The county council wanted a detour to be made over land not owned by GWR. 'If the Highways Board will help defray the expenses incurred on land other than Company owned we will be pleased to do this.' Such was the reply handed out to several enquirers over the years. Of course, the highways board had no power to grant money to the company, so the matter rested. However, the local people were very angry with the situation at the crossing and wrote a letter of complaint to the Board of Trade. The letter made four points:

1. The length of the crossing and its unprotected condition.

2. Danger to men in charge of carts carrying milk churns, coal, corn etc., owing to inadequate siding and loading accommodation.

3. Delay to road users owing to constant passage of trains over crossing, either on the main lines or shunting.

4. Danger in so many tracks crossing the road.

No mention was made of the illegality of the sidings over the crossing; apparently everyone had forgotten Captain Rich's directions of 1864. Major York, RE, came down to inspect the crossing in July 1894 and part of his report ran thus:

> I may say that, from my inspection of the place, these complaints are entirely reasonable and in no way exaggerated. There is no fencing across the tracks when the line is open to road users and 120 trains a day pass through, three-quarters of them between 6 a.m. and 6 p.m. which is an average of one every eight minutes. On 21 July the gates were closed by shunting for a total of 101 minutes and to this delay must be added that arising from the passage of the main line trains. Sometimes the crossing was shut for twenty minutes. [See Appendix 5.] Moreover, it sometimes happens that a farm cart is allowed onto the crossing only to find its exit barred owing to some necessity having arisen in the meantime for closing the gates. Part of the rating agreement is that carters help load the churns but then their horses are left unattended. Empty carts often cannot get out of the crossing to let loaded carts in because the gates are shut for a main line train or for shunting. Passengers at the station have to cross and recross the tracks as there is no footbridge provided. Captain Rich had objected to the sidings and these were removed but someone replaced them and even added a third, so the level crossing has been restored to the same dangerous condition which Captain Rich refused to sanction, if anything it is worse now than when he inspected it in 1864.

This devastating exposure had an immediate effect upon GWR, and the company got a Bill into Parliament in time for the August session of 1894. Parliament passed the Bill willingly and gave GWR powers of compulsory purchase to obtain the land necessary to build a new road, a bridge and to abandon the original highway over the railway. These powers became operative in August 1895 but no use was made of them and ten months later the countryside around Uffington was still waiting for a start to be made on the work. In order to put pressure on the company, Mr Lloyd, Member of Parliament for the area, tabled the following questions to be asked in the House on 10 May 1896, to be answered by the President of the Board of Trade.

> *Question.* Has the Great Western Railway assured the Board of Trade of their intention to remedy the danger and obstruction caused for many years past from the sidings across the highway at Uffington station?

> *Question.* Whether the danger and obstruction complained of has now been continued for more than nine years in spite of repeated remonstrance by the Highways Board and the condemnation of the Board of Trade?

> *Question.* Whether any similar instance has occurred of work condemned by the Board of Trade in the public interest and required by the Department to be removed before sanctioning the opening of the line being replaced after such sanction had been obtained?

The general manager of GWR, Mr Wilkinson, gave the following reply on 16 May: 'We do all in our power to reduce inconvenience, staff at Uffington are instructed to cease shunting when the crossing is required and if delays occur the local staff is to blame.' Having shifted the burden of responsibility onto Fred and George at Uffington and made them the targets for parochial anger, the company expressed innocent bewilderment concerning the illegal sidings. 'We are unable – after repeated searches – to explain the circumstances whereby the sidings were replaced over the crossing.' But the company could hold out no longer, their blatant disregard of the law and public safety had been shown up for all to see and it now set about putting matters to rights.

Tenders were invited from civil engineering contractors for the construction of a bridge over the railway and approach embankments, the metalling of the road and provision of iron railings around the station. Excavations in Baulking Cutting necessary to accommodate new sidings and the ballasting of new track were also the subject of contract. GWR used their own men to construct platform extensions, erect a footbridge, demolish the goods shed and horse-loading platform and build, to the west of the new road bridge, a new loading platform with 'lock-up' and 1½-ton crane. A milk platform was constructed in the 'V' between the branch platform and the branch line. In consequence of the latter, it was necessary to demolish the coal merchant's office which stood by the branch line and rebuild it close to the station master's house A new signal box was required, the old one demolished, signals had to be erected and a revised scheme of tracks laid. This work was carried out by the company's men who worked side by side with those of the successful contractor Jackman of Slough; the work commenced in January 1897 and took a year to complete, during which time there was a strike and two men were killed.

The new bridge was of 'bow and string' construction in steel, riveted plates to cross a gap of 99 feet with a skew span of 109 feet. The bridge was built without incident, though subsequently one of the approach embankments slipped, destroying some land drains, which Jackman made good at his own expense of £450. His men went on strike for higher wages, their demands were met with a compromise increase, and all but one of them returned to work. One of the two fatalities mentioned earlier was a man working for Jackman. He had been at the east end of the station, helping to excavate land in the cutting. It was lunchtime and payday. He was seen by some locals, who were standing on the new footbridge, to walk along the up platform and pass under their vantage point to the barrow crossing at the west end of the station. He waited at the foot of the new platform ramp on the crossing, close to the steps of the old signal box, while the train he had been helping to load cleared the down line, and then he stepped out from the shelter of the signal box to cross the tracks. All this was visible to the watchers on the bridge, who also saw the rapid approach of an up express. They shouted to the man, but he did not hear them and walked out into the path of the train. His last words had been something to the effect that a 'pint' would be welcome after a long morning at work. He left a widow and three children.

The up and down main line platforms were extended westwards about fifty yards, burying the old crossing beneath a bank of clay, making the new platform about 150 yards long. No increase was made to the length of platform available to branch trains. It is possible that the height of the platforms was increased at this time; most stations had this done during their life, and at Uffington, one had to go down two steps to reach the booking hall. It does not seem likely that this would have been the original arrangement. GWR had, in the 1890s, evolved a standard design for small- and medium-sized stations, and it is a little surprising that the old 'Brunel-type' buildings were not demolished in favour of the new style. The GWR did not seem greatly concerned with Uffington – anything serviceable would do. The footbridge that had given a grandstand view of the tragedy just mentioned came second-hand from Langley (Bucks) and was erected on the site of the western ends of the old platforms at a total cost of £150. Apart from its wooden floorboards, the entire structure was made of cast iron. It looked fragile. It had no roof and its walls were something less than knee height, to an average adult, surmounted by a light hand rail.

Eastwards, from the platform ends to the abutments of Baulking bridge, the cutting sides were excavated to make room for up and down sidings. On the upside, the old shunt spur from the branch, about 120 yards long, was extended a further 420 yards and a hand-operated point on the site of the old spur buffer led to another parallel siding, 300 yards long. A very badly needed siding was laid on the downside from trailing points at the eastern end of the down platform to buffers 230 yards into the cutting. This formed a down refuge and could hold forty-five wagons, the engine and guard's van. Since 1864, there had been a siding on the upside west of the station, and this was now extended to 330 yards, to form a refuge for a 60-wagon goods train. A connection from this led to a new goods-loading platform and on, to the buffers fifty yards beyond. The platform was surmounted by a small, brick-walled, iron-roofed 'lock-up'. There was a crane of 1½ tons lifting capacity and 360 degrees traverse just to the west of the building. The only tracks lost in the reorganisation were those from the branch run-round loop to down main, and the old loading dock siding. The track from facing points in the branch which passed by the old goods shed now passed the milk-loading platform.

This was massively constructed, its walls being several rows of brick with 'bull-nosed blues' at all corners to prevent damage to horses or vehicles and was paved with the same material in the form of tiles whose surface was deeply impressed with a diamond pattern. To fit its situation the platform was 'V' shaped, the arms being of unequal length, that facing the branch was twenty-five yards, the other forty-five yards. Carts could be backed into the hollow of the figure, which was the terminus, so to speak, of the station approach road and quite sealed off from the tracks by stout fencing. There were no buildings on the platform, which was simply an aid in the transfer of cans from farm cart to railway wagon and a place to stack the returned empties while they awaited farmers' collection.

The old signal box was no longer big enough to operate the new layout and a new box with a lever frame of nearly double the size was installed within the bounds of the up platform, east of the station buildings. It was a handsome, timber structure. The interlocking room was below platform level, giving the building a pleasing, long, low outline capped by a hipped roof decorated with earthenware pinnacles at each

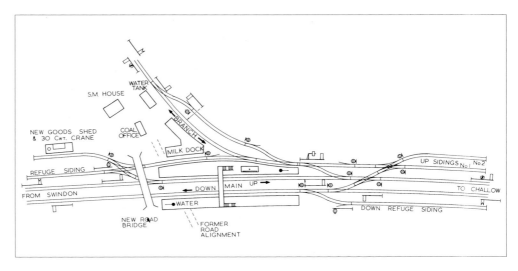

Layout at Uffington, 1897: after reconstruction.

end. Access to the locking room was down steps protected by a wooden pale fence and wicket gate, while immediately above rose the outside stairs to a landing and door which opened into an interior porch and thence through another door to the operating room. Coming through that door, one was faced with a large, triangular sink fitting into the corner of the building and to one side of the sink was a large wooden box for coal. Next to this was an open fireplace complete with domestic-style mantelpiece. The fire grate was raised two feet above the floor in an iron basket and to one side there was a small oven. Children delivering food to signalmen in the days of a regular twelve-hour shift were authorised persons in the eyes of the company and allowed to enter the signal box for that purpose. At a later date, probably in the early 1920s after the eight-hour day had become standard, the old fireplace was bricked up and replaced with a small, cast-iron stove, which stood out from the wall and which was also provided with an oven. Their grates were small, burned less fuel and were therefore quite useless against the icy draughts to which a signal box must inevitably be subjected and successive signalmen shivered their winters away until 1962 when a really good slow-burning stove was installed.

No lavatory was originally provided in the box because the public lavatory – as part of the station building – was close, too close said some. During the 1939–45 war, a water closet was installed at the station end of the box but the flimsy, wartime-shortages nature of its *cardboard* walls were a disadvantage. The signalman's armchair was parked right against the cubicle into which would sink any visitor – official or otherwise – and during the time that he was there the signalman felt embarrassed to use the facilities.

At night, the box interior was illuminated by three paraffin lamps, each having a brass tank or vessel surmounted by a circular wick burning at the foot of a glass funnel about fourteen inches tall. The concentrated heat that rose from the funnel was sufficient to ignite paper spills should the signalman want to light the fire or a Woodbine cigarette. Two of these lamps hung from the ceiling, one at each end of the lever frame and a third illuminated the Train Register. This sat in a cast-iron basket and carried a white, opalescent glass globe to soften the harsh glare so close to the signalman's eyes. With or without these globes, the light given out would seem very dim to modern eyes and with the glow of a warm fire could have had a soporific effect that a man might have difficulty in resisting unless he was kept very busy. Pressurised paraffin light – the Tilley lamp – of 300 candle power was introduced after 1926, the box having two ceiling-hung lamps while retaining the wick-type illumination over the register. Electric light was not installed until 1962 but still the old wick lamp over the Train Register remained in case of a power cut. In passing, it is interesting to note that the Tilley pressure lamp was taken into Great Western service after trials at Challow where a saving of £2 10s 0d a year was made as a result of needing fewer lamps. The roof-hung Tilley was named 'The Challow' by the firm to mark the occasion. The interior walls of the signal box up to window sill level were painted dark brown; above this, cream paint was used, while the rafters, ties and ceiling boards (the ceiling conformed to the exterior shape of the roof) were painted white as were the window frames. Within this room, 33 feet 6 inches x 12 feet, the signalman worked forty-seven levers interlocked by GWR's double-twist locking apparatus, which took up the interlocking room beneath the operating room floor. On the block shelf, running the length of the lever frame, were the block telegraph instruments and bells working with Challow and Knighton Crossing signal boxes. These bells were of the 'single strike' variety: an induced magnet snapped a hammer over smartly to ring the bell, by which means bell codes conveying set messages could be sent. A bell was also provided to signal trains to and from Faringdon.

This last was a departure from the usual practice and was the result of over three months of letter-writing between Mr Wilkinson, general manager of GWR, and the Board of Trade. On 10 March 1897, Wilkinson asked the Board of Trade to sanction the use of Train Staff and Ticket working without the usual block telegraph instrument but with the bell only. The company intended to use the Ticket on a Sunday in connection with the milk traffic 'because at the present the Train Staff has to be walked to Uffington and back'. Colonel York did not approve of the proposals and in his reply on 19 March said, 'I do not think it advisable to sanction the use of bells in the place of block instruments, although in this case the objections would not be very great, but it would act as a precedent of which advantage would be taken.' Encouraged by this, GWR wrote back on the 23rd,

> ... the difficulty in the way of full block signalling would be the constant attendance in the signal box of one man and in the present circumstances this arrangement could not be made without extra staff. Moreover, the Faringdon branch is one that can normally be worked by the train staff and one engine in steam system. The special arrangement which has been made by this company to bring the milk out on Sundays is already unremunerative and would become more so if a signalman were to be employed on Sundays. In endeavouring to make arrangements which would adequately meet the requirements of Faringdon this company is animated by a desire to assist as far as possible the agricultural interest, in this district largely represented by dairy farmers who would be at a disadvantage if the special arrangements for conveying their milk to London on Sundays were to be discontinued. I would venture to hope that the Board of Trade will grant a relaxation in the special case of Faringdon.

This gentle blackmail had the desired effect, and on 5 April, the Board of Trade approved the arrangement and asked for a formal undertaking from the GWR. This was sent, over the Seal of the Company, on 24 June thus:

> The Great Western Railway, as owners of the single line branch railway from Uffington to Faringdon, hereby undertake to work the said railway on the Train Staff and Ticket system in conjunction with auxiliary block telegraph.

Six days later, Colonel York acknowledged this, saying, 'Satisfactory. But the relaxation granted in this case as to the use of a bell instrument in place of a proper block instrument must not be regarded as a precedent.'

Surveys of Uffington station prior to 1897 show no provision for locomotive water. This seems to be a curious situation but understandable in the case of the Faringdon Railway. Money was always short, and with water available at Faringdon, only three and a half miles away, pumping installations at Uffington were considered superfluous. However, part of the 1897 rebuilding included a supply of locomotive water. Two water cranes were erected, one at the eastern tip of the up platform to serve the branch and main line, while the other was located at the western end of the down platform. These were fed through 8-inch pipes from a storage tank, which stood slightly west of the milk dock and close to the branch line. The tank was rectangular, measuring 20 feet x 12 feet x 8 feet, had a capacity of 11,250 gallons when filled to within six inches of the brim and stood 19 feet above ground level on four columns. The tank was roofed over and water from the roof drained into the tank, but the main source of water came from two wells, sixty feet above the top of the tank and 1 5⁄8 miles to the north where Barrowbush Hill rose to the Faringdon Ridge. At this point, approximately a quarter of a mile north of the Fernham Road underbridge, where a farm track crossed the line – a place known locally as Reid's Crossing – the engineer of the GWR had the bores made, 12 feet in diameter and 18 feet deep. From them, the water flowed down to the tank through a 4-inch pipe effectively divided into 500-yard sections by means of stop valves. Thus a length of defective pipe could be isolated from the length above, emptied and replaced with no great loss of water. The arrangement came in handy on occasions.

The inlet valve on the tank was similar to that used on domestic cisterns, for it was opened and shut by a floating ball at the end of an arm but in the railway tank the valve was of the 'sleeve' variety much better able to withstand the weight of water standing on it. The inner tube of the sleeve valve had an upper and lower sealing ring of rubber and of course these were the subject of regular examination and replacement. A workman carrying out just such a replacement wanted to see if his handiwork had been successful, so he depressed the arm to allow water to enter, and as it did so freely, he let go of the arm and sure enough the flow of water was cut off. Pleased with his work, he went through this procedure several times, on each occasion, the valve springing shut with some violence, as it had been opened against the water level. He had started and stopped, suddenly, several tons of water but this did not occur to him until, as he climbed down the ladder, his head came below the bottom of the tank and then he saw a huge fountain roaring a glittering spray into the sunshine about a mile away. His abrupt stopping of the flow had caused such a peak pressure within the pipe that it had burst.

The second fatality can finish the story of the alterations at Uffington station. A blacksmith was working with a portable forge, which he had placed near a siding on the upside at the west end of the layout. Normally employed in shaping rodding for points and signals, he had been asked by the contractor's men to make a spanner to fit a bolt, which held a buffer to the headstock of one of their trucks. The wagon was in a line with some others and he walked across from his forge to try the fit of the new spanner. The buffer was on the far side of the vehicle and rather than go round he put his head between the nearest buffers as he stretched across with the spanner in his hand. It was a blithe morning up until then, with everybody minding their own business and getting on with various jobs – including a shunter who knew nothing of the blacksmith's errand between the trucks he was about to move. As the shunter called 'Ease up!' to the engine driver, the blacksmith moved his head between the buffers and was killed instantly.

When the alterations and extensions were complete, Uffington station possessed a layout and buildings that were to remain unaltered (though the signalling was changed) for the next sixty-five years. The cost of the work, in pounds, shillings and pence rather than life, was as follows:

Engineering work	£8,344
Locomotive costs	£40
Telegraph	£116
Locking and Signals	£896
	£9,396

Between 1864 and 1897, the Faringdon branch achieved several minor records. It was the last piece of purely broad gauge passenger-carrying railway east of Bristol, it was the only railway in the country to reinstate a layout condemned by the Board of Trade, and now, in 1897, it became the only single-track branch line to be signalled by Train Staff and Ticket assisted by auxiliary block telegraph – which actually meant a bell. There was no instrument to indicate the occupation or otherwise of the branch line.

CHAPTER 8

The Golden Age

Now that the improvements were complete, a new period opened in the history of the branch line and its junction station. It was as if the twentieth century had started three years early at Uffington station. Even before the improvements, the branch train service had taken on a close resemblance to its early-twentieth-century form; the replacement of the awkward little Victorian layout was the final break with the past, and the cramped miserly ghost of the Faringdon Railway Company was laid forever. The new era, which lasted from 1897 until 1934, might be called the line's 'Middle Period'.

Faringdon station earned more revenue in 1913 than in 1903, but the opposite was true of Uffington. In 1903, a staff of seven at Faringdon loaded 19,000 tons of freight and 259 cattle wagons while the booking office sold 18,000 tickets: total revenue was £15,678, and the year's wages bill was £515, one thirtieth of the income. Ten years later, nine men loaded 21,000 tons of freight and 491 cattle wagons, 19,000 people bought tickets and the total income was £17,667: the wages bill was £741, one twenty-third of revenue. This trend of wages against income was the only constant factor in otherwise fluctuating circumstances. December 1903 found Uffington station with a staff of six who brought in an income of £4,929 and got £412 for themselves – one twelfth of receipts. By 1913, eight men worked at Uffington and earned £662 in wages, one seventh of the station's total income. No cattle wagons were loaded during the period but the tonnage of other goods rose from 3,900 to 4,400 (see Appendix 6).

The branch depended for its prosperity on goods traffic. The 1913 total of 19,000 passengers buying tickets at Faringdon makes an average of five per day per train, not enough to fill one compartment in a coach. There would have been other passengers, people who were leaving Faringdon with return tickets bought elsewhere, but it seems very unlikely that the average train left Faringdon with sufficient people on board to fill a coach. On the other hand, 21,000 tons of freight leaving the station makes an average of 68 tons per day to be loaded, invoiced, labelled, sheeted and roped by two or at most three men – quite apart from the work involved with incoming goods and the embarkation of cattle into those 491 wagons. The last two items would have been largely handled by the traders but even so, it can easily be appreciated that the goods department had a hard day's work, every day.

Locomotive power in 1912 was stated to cost £1,007, excluding the further hidden charge against all the vehicles allocated to Faringdon, that of the interest on the capital they represented. Depreciation of these assets does not appear to have been taken directly into account, but to cover the cost of a 'stand-in' locomotive when the branch engine was away for repairs, the company reckoned its locomotive costs in terms of one and one third engines – and one and one third 517-class engines cost £2,133, which at the then Bank Rate of 4 per cent was £85 6s 8d, and this was duly charged against the engine. Similar calculations were also made for the carriage and wagon stock so that the entire 'running and maintenance' costs for the line amounted to £2,323. To this should be added the cost of wages at Faringdon and, say, half those at Uffington, which brings the total to £3,395. But many important costs are not known: cost of maintenance of buildings, local rates, cost of paraffin oil for dozens of lamps, maintenance of signal and telegraph equipment and capital charges on all these installations, and last, but by no means least, cost of upkeep of the track, including the men's wages. Taking all this into account, the annual outgoings must have been at least £5,000, while the annual income for Faringdon plus half Uffington was £19,000. Up to 1914, costs were rising slowly and income did not keep pace, but while the Great Western, with all the other railways, held a virtual monopoly of long-distance passenger and freight haulage, enough use was made of the tracks to produce worthwhile profit margins. Thus the period under scrutiny here was indeed a 'Golden Age', with money for the perfect upkeep of the tracks, buildings and vehicles. The 1920s were busier than the 'Golden Age' but then the schedules were full of trains not only to cater for an enormous demand for transport but also to provide a splendid service against competition from road haulage.

In January 1897, an extra cattle train began running on the first Tuesday of each month, leaving Faringdon at 2.43 p.m. and returning from Uffington 'engine and van'. The cattle had to wait for a main line goods to stop and pick them up, the arrangements for this being carried out by one of the station staff at Uffington by means of the single-needle telegraph instrument to Didcot or Swindon, depending on the destination of the animals. From July 1899, the 4.20 p.m. daily cattle train began to carry general merchandise in addition to livestock, and in June 1902, the 2.43 p.m. from Faringdon commenced running daily 'if required'. Six months later, the 6.55 p.m. from Faringdon was authorised to convey empty coaching stock with the freight wagons (the reason behind this is not known), and thus amended, the service ran unaltered until 1907. Then a new passenger train was put on, leaving Faringdon at 2.30 p.m., which resulted in the withdrawal of the 2.43 p.m. 'RR' cattle train. A new service for cattle from the monthly fair began at this time. An engine and brake van for Faringdon came up to Uffington coupled in front of the engine of the 12 noon Swindon to Old Oak Common locomotive coal train. This engine and van left Uffington at 12.45 p.m. and returned from Faringdon at 4.45 with the cattle wagons and took them all back to Swindon. Other trains were slightly altered to give an absolutely first-class service with no wasted effort. The 6.35 p.m. Faringdon 'ECS' became a mixed train, which allowed the 7.10 p.m. goods to be dropped and made possible an extra passenger trip, at 7.45 p.m. A bonus arising from this was that the 7.45 p.m. got back to Faringdon later and made the last trip of the evening start for the junction at 8.55 p.m. instead of 8.45. It is always good for the last train of the day to be at a reasonably late hour. The 1896 working timetables had now reached their fullest development and ran unchanged in frequency until January 1915, five months after the outbreak of the First World War.

The motive power for the branch Sunday trains was, as usual, provided by main line freights, which were frequently hauled, even as late as 1914, by the heaviest saddle tanks beside a variety of small tender engines. The problem of 'stabling' their wagons at Uffington has already been discussed, though the improved layout would have eased the difficulties, but in 1902, a fresh problem arose. The date is significant, as at that time the Dean/Churchward alliance at Swindon factory had been producing the biggest freight engines yet seen on the GWR – the 'Kruger' 4-6-0, then its 2-6-0 'Aberdate' derivatives. These were prohibited from travelling over the branch but that did not deter enginemen from going, and on arrival at Faringdon, they discovered the reason for the prohibition. The following letter tells the story.

Privately owned coal wagon. Uncharacteristically splendid in grey with white lettering shaded with black. Fresh from the manufacturers – the Gloucester Railway Carriage & Wagon Company. For their maintenance, these wagons had to rely on the tender mercies of their owner. As a result, they were often in bad order and caused the GWR a lot of inconvenience.

Shedmaster, Swindon Works, Swindon. 6th January, 1902

Dear Sir,

It has been necessary to use the tow rope at Faringdon in consequence of large tender engines going on the branch. There is only 49 feet between the stop blocks and the loop points. Please ensure that only ordinary tender engines work trains from Swindon, the engine of which works engine and brake van to Faringdon.

W. Waister, Works Manager.

An 'Aberdare' or 'Kruger', standing at the buffers of the Faringdon platform line, fouled the points to the run-round loop, in which case the only way to get the engine past the van was to use the tow rope. The engine with its guard's van arrived at the first set of points at Faringdon, tender first. The train stopped short of the points, the guard uncoupled his van and the engine then moved straight on, over the junction, towards the passenger platform. The guard then turned the points for the run-round loop, and the engine stopped. A rope was attached to the guard's van drawbar and to the locomotive, which would steam slowly along the platform line towing the van across the points onto the run-round loop. This operation incurred some risk of derailment to the van and took up valuable time. It had been used a lot in the past but various mishaps had caused the company to discourage the practice now. Once the van was on the loop, the points were turned and the engine came forward, set back into the yard, picked up its traffic and set it back onto the van. The guard coupled up, climbed into the van, waved 'Right Away' to his driver, and the short train steamed off to the junction. So a freight train arriving at Swindon hauled by a 'large' tender engine but booked to call at Uffington, for Faringdon, would require an engine change to a smaller type and that might then be overloaded for the onward journey.

The number of trains running through Uffington in a twenty-four-hour period had increased from the 45 of 1870 to 120 by 1897. The absence of any goods loops between Didcot and Swindon, the low speed of freight trains and the length of some of the block sections at that time (Challow–Wantage Road and Wantage Road–Steventon, three and three-eighths and four miles respectively) made 120 trains just about the full capacity of the route, leaving little room for the excursions and extra freights that had always to be run. In 1899, to cope with a growing weekend traffic, all the signal boxes normally closed between 10 p.m. Saturday and 6 a.m. Monday were scheduled to remain open. Challow was one of these; Uffington had been a 'continuous box' for years operating at weekends with Wantage Road 5⅞ miles away – a very long section when unbraked goods trains ran at 25 mph or less. In August 1900, expenditure was authorised for the quadrupling of the route from Didcot to Wootton Bassett but the plan petered out when only an up goods line had been laid from Ashbury Crossing to Knighton Crossing; earthworks were partially constructed for an extension of the loop to Uffington and may still be seen on the upside of the line between the 69 and 67½ mile posts. In 1903, the long sections between Challow, Wantage Road and Steventon were roughly halved by the installation of two four-lever signal boxes: one at 62 miles 49 chains, near Circourt Bridge, between Challow and Wantage Road, the other at 58 miles 51 chains. The former was called 'Circourt' and the latter 'Lockinge'. Their introduction had an immediate effect upon the timetables, for in the next issue after the installation of the boxes ten extra trains entered the schedules. The next goods lines to be built were laid in 1907 when up and down loops were provided between Foxhall Junction, Didcot and Steventon and an up loop – called the Up Avoiding Line – came into service between Challow and Wantage Road in November of that year. Thus enlarged, the Didcot–Swindon route remained virtually unaltered until 1932.

FARINGDON BRANCH.

Week Days only.

		a.m.		a.m.		a.m.		a.m. a.m.		p.m. p.m. p.m.			p.m. p.m. p.m. p.m.		
Uffington	dep	7 45	Mxd.	8 40	...	9 45	Q	10 13 11 30	...	12 36 2 30 3 59	Mxd.	6 40 7 23 8 8 9 38	Q—First Tuesday
Faringdon	arr	7 55		8 47	...	9 52		10 20 11 37	..	12 43 2 37 4 9		6 47 7 30 8 15 9 45	of each month only
		A.M.	...	a.m.		a.m.		a.m.		p.m. p.m. p.m. p.m.		p.m. p.m.	
Faringdon	dep	6 50		8 12	...	9 22	...	11 7	...	12 10 1 55 3 23 6 2	...	7 45 9 0	Mxd.
Uffington	arr	6 58		8 20		9 30	.	11 15	.	12 18 2 3 3 31 6 10	.	7 53 9 15	

Timetable, 1902.

Faringdon Branch June–December 1902

Single line worked by Train Staff and Ticket assisted by Block Telegraph.
Staff: triangular, varnished oak. Ticket: square, buff.

Weekdays

	Gds								Z		Y
					ECS						
	a.m.	a.m.	a.m.	a.m.	a.m.	a.m.	p.m.	p.m.	p.m.	p.m.	p.m.
Faringdon	6.50	7.30	8.17	9.27	10Lo	11.05	12.10	1.55	2.46 RR	3.30	4.40
Uffington	6.58	7.40	8.25	9.35	10L8	11.13	12.18	2.03	2.50 EBV	3.38	4.50 EBV
Uffington	7.15	7.55	8.43	9L49	10.15	11.25	12.36	2.28	3.00 RR	3.53	5.00
Faringdon	7.22	8.05	8.50	9L52	10.22	11.32	12.43	2.35	3.10	4.00	5.10

		ECS	Gds	Mxd
	p.m.	p.m.	p.m.	p.m.
Faringdon	6.00	6.35	7.10	8.45
Uffington	6.08	6.42	7.20	8.55

		Passr		
Uffington	6.22	6.51	7.50	9.15
Faringdon	6.29	6.58	8.00	9.22

ECS = Empty coaching stock
L = First Tuesday of each month
Z = Cattle train
Y = Cattle and goods
EBV = Engine and brake van

Sundays

	EBV	EBV
	a.m.	p.m.
Uffington	6.10	7.55
Faringdon	6.17	8.02
Faringdon	6K48	8N15
Uffington	6K55	8N22

K = Milk traffic worked by EBV off 5.15 a.m. Swindon
N = Milk, goods and cattle worked by EBV off 6.45 p.m. Swindon

By 1902, traffic over the branch had become considerable and there must have been times when the signalman was puzzled to know what to do with all the trains that required to call at his station. At Uffington, a climax, or crisis, would build up several times a day, the intervals between being of a straightforward nature. A typical example of one of these scrambles was scheduled to take place during the currency of the 1907 timetable between 2.20 and 2.35 p.m. if everything was running to time, and if it were not, the scramble would probably turn into a rout. The 11.42 a.m. Gloucester to Paddington stopping passenger train called at Uffington at 2.17 p.m., just as a Kingswear to Paddington express passed Swindon at around 65 mph. This train required Knighton Crossing's Up Distant to be showing 'All Right' at 2.23½ at the latest. There was no loop into which a *passenger* train could be sidetracked until Foxhall Junction, and the Gloucester had to stop at Challow, Wantage Road and Steventon. The timetable directed that it should be back-shunted to the branch. That would have been fine but for a train from Faringdon that was due to arrive at 2.20 p.m. The signalman could have put the 'stopper' into the up refuge, always supposing it was not occupied by wagons, but more likely he crossed it to the down main. This might cause delay to a down freight – no passenger trains were due – but that was better than stopping the Kingswear. The crossover and other trailing points, which became facing during the crossing movement, had to be secured by clamp and padlock so that the signalman did not move them prematurely – there being no regular device to ensure this – and some quick work was needed from the station staff, because until the up line at Uffington was clear, the signalman could not give permission for the Kingswear to approach from Knighton Crossing. The 'Warning' bell signal was authorised for use at Uffington but not when a passenger train was blocking the station. Should Challow 'ask Line Clear' for a down goods at about the time that the Gloucester was due, or while it was crossing to the down line, Uffington would refuse that because he was going to block the down main with the Gloucester. Supposing everything to have been carried out thoughtfully, the Kingswear would have flashed through Uffington on the up main at about 70 mph, hauled by a 'Star', passing the 2-4-0-hauled Gloucester on the down main and the 517-class branch engine taking water. Having replaced to 'Danger' the up signals behind the Kingswear, the signalman had now to get the Gloucester back to the up line, then accept the down goods waiting at Challow, run the branch engine round its coaches and, when the down goods arrived, shout to the driver that he wanted him to reverse into the down refuge. The 1.10 p.m. Paddington–Cardiff express was off Didcot and the down main had to be cleared for it.

A code of whistles was laid down for use at Uffington:

1 whistle. Set points branch to main.
2 whistles. Set points branch to Baulking sidings.
3 whistles. Set points branch to run-round loop.
4 whistles. Close loop points.

There was a great deal of whistling in September 1909 when the branch became vital to the success of large-scale army manoeuvres. The War Games, organised by Southern Command at Aldershot, were played over an area bounded by the Berkshire Downs in the south, the Cotswolds in the north, Swindon eastwards and Oxford in the west. A dozen regiments took part including the Coldstream, Grenadiers, Scots and Irish Guards, all of them arriving at and leaving the area by train, using Swindon, Shrivenham, Challow and Witney stations. Faringdon town was the control centre of the exercise, so the branch was exceptionally busy for a fortnight as all the food and equipment for thousands of men and horses was taken down to Faringdon for distribution and of course the empties came back. The Train Staff and Ticket system was not sufficiently flexible to deal with the expected volume of traffic and so electric Train Staff instruments were temporarily installed in Uffington and Faringdon signal boxes on 18 September until the exercise was finished. Thousands of troops with their artillery, blank ammunition, food for men and horses were conveyed over the line. The progress of the mock war was watched from the high knoll just to the east of the town by observers from several European armies and also the Japanese. Among the plumed and be-medalled was Frederick Wilhelm August Ernst Hohenzollern – the Crown Prince of Germany.

There were lengthy strikes by coal miners during 1911 and 1912, but only the 1912 strike resulted in service reductions on the Faringdon branch. A 'Coal Strike' timetable was introduced for the GWR on 3 March 1912 that scheduled a curtailed and decelerated train service. The 'crack' two-hour expresses between Paddington and Bristol were not affected immediately, but the strike continued, coal supplies dwindled and, from 15 March, only a severely reduced service could be operated. The 1.33 and 7.27 p.m. Faringdon trips were suspended but some branch lines were closed down completely, and on the 22nd, coal stocks had sunk so low that the weekday service was again reduced and that on Sundays suspended, both passenger and goods. However, the GWR did not cut out its milk, perishable or cattle trains so the Faringdon branch continued to play an important part in the life of the local community. A brave effort was made by the GWR to cater for tens of thousands of people who turned up at Paddington and other big stations to go away during the Easter holidays, 3 to 9 April. Additional trains were run, but these were only 'extra' in the context of the 'Coal Strike' service and overcrowding was inevitable. The company was determined that its standards should not fall any more than was absolutely unavoidable and put extra staff on all long-distance trains to assist guards with the stowing of luggage, parcels and people and thus avoid delay at stations. Extra staff were also carried in the restaurant cars. The Faringdon branch train was 'strengthened' by three extra four-wheel coaches, which were sent to Uffington from Swindon on the rear of a stopping passenger train. Easter passed and the week of holidays, but still the miners

During the large-scale military manoeuvres in the Faringdon District in 1909, the hill to the east of the town was used as a viewing point, enabling visiting military experts to see for miles to the north and south. This picture is one of several showing the Crown Prince Wilhelm (1882–1951) of Germany, the son of 'Kaiser Bill', on the hill. His presence at these manoeuvres has always been officially denied. Perhaps he travelled on the Faringdon branch train to add to his pleasure. (Courtesy Jim Brown)

held out for better wages and conditions so that on 12 April permission was given to run any Faringdon branch train 'mixed' if, by so doing, trips with goods trains would be saved. Just when the situation looked gravest, it eased; on the 14th, the main line Sunday passenger service was partially restored, but it was not until the 29th that the branch, in common with the rest of GWR, resumed normal working.

The year 1914 was not a peak year for the prosperity of GWR as a whole, or for the Faringdon branch in particular: the dividend paid by the company that year was slightly less than that paid in 1913. Nor was it a peak year for the train service. To those men working the branch, it would have been much the same as the preceding ten years and certainly no busier than the last seven. A feature of those years leading up to 1914 was the introduction and multiplication of the long-distance, non-stop, vacuum-braked express goods train. There had been just a few freights of this description in broad gauge days, but owing to their grease-lubricated axle bearings, they had not been able to run fast for more than about forty miles without stopping to check the axle bearings. The new express goods trains had oil-lubricated axle bearings on all wagons. Oil flows around the axle bearing much more readily than grease, and the new 'vacuum goods' could be made up to sixty wagons, each one fitted with the vacuum brake, connected by the train pipe to the engine driver's brake controller and permitted to run at a maximum 60 miles an hour for distances of 100 miles non-stop. They could be hauled by Mr Churchward's powerful new 43XX-class 2-6-0 or even his revolutionary express passenger locomotives. These trains moved mainly at night so that, in 1914, the Uffington signalman spent most of his time between 10.45 p.m. and 3.40 a.m. passing a succession of fast 'vacuums' interspersed with 'mails' and 'sleepers'. His work was uncomplicated and almost continuous. According to the working timetable, no train stopped, either to work or to refuge for a faster train to pass; twenty-seven were scheduled to pass and only two of them were not expresses of some sort. All were very important, so unless something was seriously wrong, a place like Uffington would have no business in altering their sequence. Twenty-seven trains in five hours made an average of one train passing every eleven minutes. Each tram was signalled by six separate bell codes, which had to be entered by the minute in the train register – an entry every two minutes – so that the man was kept busy all night, working in the soft light of his oil lamps, moving quietly from the bells and instruments to the signal levers to the train register and occasionally to the single-needle telegraph instrument to receive and pass a 'box to box' message, taking his food standing as the long night wore on.

Some fine trains and sequences of trains ran during that five-hour period. On the down line, the 9.05 p.m. Paddington to Penzance 'Travelling Post Office' went through at 10.45 p.m., going steadily at about 55 mph if it was on time. Six minutes earlier, it had exchanged mail bags whilst travelling through Wantage Road station. The 'Post Office' was followed twelve minutes later by 'Paddy's Mail', the 9.15 p.m. Paddington to Neyland, and after a further twelve minutes, the 9.32 p.m. Acton to Cardiff express goods clattered through. There was a lull on the down line for an hour until the 9.55 p.m. Paddington to Fishguard express goods was due on its non-stop run from Reading to Newport. But on the up line, a succession of trains commenced with the passing of the 4.10 p.m. Milford Haven at 11.45 p.m. The service timetable warned signalmen that this train conveyed 'Trawl Fish. Goods trains to be kept clear'. It was the fastest freight to pass Uffington, and a really hard-slogging job for its enginemen – fish in its ice packing was heavy – and it was scheduled to average 45 mph from its start at Swindon to passing Didcot: Uffington would have been a flash in the dark to the driver as he thundered his heavy train through with speed rising towards 60 mph. This was followed by seven express goods, including the 10.20 p.m. Bristol to Paddington, which called at Chippenham but not Swindon. The working timetable makes a specific reference to this train's motive power, an unusual feature. 'When hauled by locomotive 111 *Great Bear* the load to be increased to 70 wagons beyond Chippenham.' It is not too much to expect that when the *Bear* was on the Bristol the information was passed from box to box so that the signalmen could go to their respective windows for a glimpse of the huge engine as she was caught briefly in the light from the box. Other trains had unusual locomotives. Between the Saints, Stars and Bulldogs on Cardiff, Penzance and Fishguard trains, a couple of Great Central Railway Atlantics passed through, hauling respectively the 1.05 a.m. and 1.18 a.m. Leicester to Bristol passenger trains, passing Uffington at 3.37 a.m. and 4.10 a.m. The end of the night shift brought the slow, loose-coupled freights past Uffington, the 80- and 100-wagon rakes from Stoke Gifford and Southall. They were given a standard allowance of one hour between Didcot and Swindon so that they brought up the rear, the shabby tail of a brilliant parade. One of the last jobs for the night man was to 'refuge' the 2.45 a.m. Paddington to Rogerstone coal empties to make way for the 11.10 p.m. Oxley to Bristol express goods, and he booked off after handling sixty trains, not counting any specials that may have run, in his twelve-hour shift.

Faringdon Branch, June–December 1907

Single line worked by Train Staff and Ticket assisted by Block Telegraph.
Staff: triangular, varnished oak. Ticket: square, buff.

Weekdays

	a.m.	a.m.	a.m.	ECS a.m.	a.m.	noon	p.m.	p.m.	p.m.	p.m.	K p.m.
Faringdon	6.45	8.12	9.22	10L00	11.12	12.00	EBV K	1.32	2.20	3.23	4.45
Uffington	6.53	8.20	9.30	10L08	11.20	12.08		1.40	2.28	3.31	4.55
Uffington	7.45	8.45	9.45	10L18	11.45	12.22	12.43	1.56	2.41	3.59	-
Faringdon	7.55	8.52	9.52	10L25	11.52	12.30	12.55	2.03	2.48	4.07	-
	Mxd			Passr							

		Mxd	Mxd	
	p.m.	p.m.	p.m.	p.m.
Faringdon	6.00	6.55	7.45	8.55
Uffington	6.08	7.05	7.55	9.03
Uffington	6.33	7.18	8.13	9.15
Faringdon	6.40	7.25	8.20	9.22

K = Detached from 12 noon Swindon–Old Oak Common coal
H = Cattle to Swindon
L = First Tuesday of each month

Sundays

	a.m.	p.m.
Uffington	6.53 EBV	6.15 EBV
Faringdon	7.00	6.23
Faringdon	7.30 N	6.40 J
Uffington	7.38	6.48

N = Milk train worked by engine and van off 1.05 a.m. Gloucester goods
J = Milk, goods and cattle worked by engine and van off 5.30 p.m. Swindon goods

Mere figures give a poor insight into the work of the day-shift signalman. He dealt with seventy-six trains during his turn of duty from 6 a.m. to 6 p.m.; twenty-eight were branch trains and, of the remainder, ten stopped to shunt at the station either to pick up or put off traffic or to 'refuge'. A train that simply passed through on the up main required eight lever movements and a train on the down line needed six, but a main line train which required to shunt needed all the main line signals to be operated plus as many point and ground signal levers as was needed for its shunting. A branch train required twenty-one lever movements if the engine did no more than run round its train – any shunting would send the total up considerably, owing to the presence of the various facing-point bolts and catch points.

A train from Faringdon required the branch Home signal to be 'off' in order to enter the station at Uffington – two lever movements, to 'pull it off' and to replace it to 'Danger' when the train had passed. The engine driver gave two blasts on the locomotive's whistle when the carriages had been uncoupled, whereupon the signalman closed the catch point in Baulking siding and lowered the shunt signal, two moves. Once clear of the catch, the driver blew his whistle thrice, the signalman replaced the shunt signal, reversed the loop entry points and cleared the ground disc signal, three moves. The route out of the loop at the Faringdon end could not be set up until the entry points were again reversed so, as the engine cleared them, its driver gave four blasts on the whistle and sped rapidly on towards the exit points, where the catch point was still set in the 'throw-off' position. It was said that drivers would tease the signalmen in this way, making them work very fast in order to close the catch point and set the exit points. He had to replace the ground signal to 'Danger' at the Baulking siding catch point, reverse the catch point and the loop entry point before walloping the loop exit point's facing bolt lock lever into the frame, reverse the exit points and, rather breathless no doubt, operate the ground disc applying to them. The tank engine drifted out onto the branch and came to a stand beyond the Home signal; the driver blew four times on the engine's whistle, whereupon the signalman had to put the ground signal to 'Danger', reverse the facing points, re-bolt them and lower the Home signal, four moves. The engine then came quietly onto its train, wheels squealing a little on the curve, until buffers touched with a soft 'clunk'. While the fireman was coupling the engine and the train, the driver may have gone to the box to fetch the Staff to save the signalman a job and to make up for the teasing. When it was time for the train to leave, the signalman had to lower the starting and advance starting signals, replacing them to 'Danger' when the train had gone, another four lever movements, making twenty-one in all. That was the working at its most straightforward. The signalman had also to operate the block telegraph instruments for the frequent main line trains and keep an account of all this instrument work, minute by minute, in the train register.

At Faringdon, the porter/signalman's job was far simpler, having no ground signals or catch points to operate. He gave 'Line Clear' to Uffington on the block bell, entered the time in his register and when he received 'Train entering Section', two beats on the bell, he lowered his Down Home signal. Seven minutes later, the locomotive steamed into sight out of the shallow cutting and came gently to a stand, the rear of the train close to the signal box. The engine was uncoupled and went forward to the stop blocks clear of the loop points, which were reversed at a 'toot' from the engine's whistle. The locomotive was driven back, over the points, along the run-round loop, past its train and onto the branch main line, the facing points were reversed and the engine went forward to rejoin its coaches. The manoeuvre had taken ten lever movements.

The first branch train of the day conveyed a 'Siphon' van loaded with full milk churns next to the engine and arrived at Uffington three minutes before the 6.30 a.m. Swindon passenger, which was 'all stations' to Didcot – with a connection there to Wolverhampton, and Reading, with connections for Newbury and Basingstoke – before running non-stop from Reading to Paddington, 36 miles in 45 minutes. The branch engine uncoupled from its train and ran into Baulking sidings, making room for the engine of the 6.30 Swindon to come onto the branch platform to collect the 'Siphon' and take it back to the main line train. Nine minutes were allowed for the shunt. By the time the Swindon had left, the 12.35 a.m. ex-Gloucester was 'waiting the road' at Knighton Crossing; the Uffington signalman sent 'Train out of Section' to Knighton and accepted the Gloucester, which was hauling Faringdon traffic, including the station truck, next to the engine. The branch passenger train standing alongside the branch platform had to be pushed back a few yards towards Faringdon so as to clear the points, by the milk dock, which allowed a movement from the branch back into the up refuge. The Gloucester goods came to a stand at the Up Main Home signal about ten minutes after the Swindon had left; the guard walked forward, uncoupled behind the 'Faringdons' and then signalled to the driver, who gave a blast on the engine's whistle. The signalman lowered the Home signal and the engine and wagons rolled forward until they were clear of the up refuge trailing points; another 'toot' the points were reversed and the Faringdon wagons were bumped off into the siding. The signalman set the road straight for the main line engine to go back onto its train and then went to the window to indicate to the branch engine driver that it was all right to come forward with his engine and set back through the milk dock siding to the up refuge. As the main line guard was coupling his 2-8-0 to its train, the branch guard was doing the same for the 517. Both engines were side by side. Now coupled to several trucks, the tank had to shunt any non-vacuum-braked vehicles to some spot chosen by the Uffington porters and put the station truck and any other vacuum-braked wagons on the rear of the branch coaches. Having done that, the engine ran round the train, pushed it properly into the branch platform and all was ready for the trip down to the terminus.

While the Swindon 'stopper' had been collecting the 'Siphon' and the 12.35 a.m. Gloucester was shunting on the upside, the 5.30 a.m. Paddington to Penzance 'Mail and Passenger' went through, which was followed fifteen minutes later by the 5.42 a.m. Pington to Porthcawl, and a few minutes after the branch train had left for Faringdon, the 4.45 a.m. Paddington to Fishguard express goods arrived and put off traffic in the down refuge. Having disposed of this train, the signalman would have had five minutes for a cup of tea before he was called by all three block bells – Faringdon 'asking the road' for the 8.12, Challow and Knighton 'asking' for the 6.49 a.m. Reading and the 8.05 a.m. Swindon respectively. One after the other, the three trains were sent 'on line', the up and down main signals and the branch home were lowered, and all three trains squealed to a halt at the station. The Swindon was 'all stations' to Didcot, where it made a connection with the 6.37 a.m. Southampton to Oxford and the 7.30 a.m. Southampton to Woodford Halse (on the Great Central Railway). After Didcot, it stopped only at Reading. There a traveller could have taken a train to Basingstoke and, after a short wait, an express to Plymouth. The Reading was a stopping train to Weston-super-Mare with some excellent connections at Swindon to Plymouth or Cardiff. When these trains had cleared the station, the branch engine went across to the down refuge to collect the wagons left by the Fishguard. These were all vacuum-braked, and when the engine had run round them, they could be placed at the rear of the branch train. The engine then had to run round the train and was set once more for the return trip to the Town.

Still the signalman had no time for his breakfast, and as he put the signals back to 'Danger' behind the disappearing branch train, the block bells from Challow and Knighton Crossing were ringing to 'ask the road' for the 7.30 a.m. Paddington to Plymouth and the 4.30 a.m. Fishguard boat train respectively. The Fishguard had not stopped at Swindon and went racing through Uffington in fine style, which was just as well, for when the Uffington man sent 'Train out of Section' to Knighton Crossing the man there immediately 'asked on' for the 6.50 a.m. Weston-super-Mare to Paddington. This had also passed through Swindon non-stop only six minutes behind the boat train, which was very close working, and one wonders whether the Weston got a clear run under the circumstances. But the train was running under clear signals past Uffington and dashed through the station just as the 7.30 a.m. Paddington passed in the opposite direction. By 8.56 a.m. the morning's rush was over, having been more or less continuous since six o'clock; the signalman threw the starters back behind the two expresses and with a sigh of relief sat down for a bite to eat.

He had ten minutes in which to relax before one beat on the Knighton Crossing bell heralded another procession of trains. The Knighton signalman was calling attention before 'asking the road' for the 9.15 a.m. Swindon, a milk train, non-stop to Paddington that was due to pass Uffington at 9.30 a.m. At 9.27 a.m., the Faringdon and Knighton bells rang out together – two beats, 'Train entering Section' and the up branch passenger arrived five minutes after the milk had rattled through. Unless it was the first Tuesday of the month, the branch train had nearly forty-five minutes to wait before returning to the terminus, so there was plenty of time for any shunting. The up main line connection for the Faringdon arrived at 9.43, the 8.36 a.m. from Chippenham, which was 'all stations' to Didcot with an Oxford connection, 'all stations' to Reading with trains from there to Basingstoke and Trowbridge, but from Reading it ran non-stop to Paddington in forty-five minutes. As the Chippenham drew out of the station, the 8.45 a.m. Paddington to Fishguard 'Irish Boat Train' passed Didcot with only twenty-one minutes allowed to pass Swindon, a very fast train which would have cleared Uffington at 9.59, if it was on time, running at about 75 mph. Following this magnificent 'hard hitter' was the stolid 7.36 a.m. Slough to Swindon 'all stations', which arrived at Uffington at 10.09 a.m. and gave Faringdon passengers the chance to catch the 9.00 a.m. Paddington to Kingswear at Swindon, the 10.58 a.m. Swindon to Hereford express or the 11.05 'all stations' to Stapleton Road via Badminton. The Slough left Uffington at 10.12 a.m., a Bristol to Paddington express that had run non-stop through Swindon galloped by Uffington at 10.16 a.m. and, two minutes later, the down branch passenger slipped quietly away from the station and steamed out of sight round the sharp curve. At 10.22, the 9.45 a.m. Swindon to Paddington 'H&C and ECS' arrived to pick up and/or put off traffic, the timetable allowing five minutes for the work. The initials stood for 'Horse & Carriage and Empty Coaching Stock'. The 'H&C'-type train had been well known on the Great Western for years, conveying the private carriages and horses of the upper classes over long distances. Five years earlier, there had been no 'ECS' in the title, but as the demand for the original service diminished – the sort of people who could afford a carriage were now buying motor cars – the 'H&C' trains began to convey a variety of empty vehicles, parcels vans, passenger coaches fresh from the works, milk siphons, and in 1915, the first part of the title dropped out of use. However, in 1914, Uffington and Faringdon stations had a horsebox and carriage truck each, allocated on a permanent basis, to be hired out to the local aristocracy.

The 8.50 a.m. Didcot 'Fly', the local pick-up goods, arrived at 10.25 while the 'H&C' was working and probably was reversed into the down refuge, because at 10.29 the 9.00 a.m. Paddington was tearing through Wantage Road – leaving a slip coach behind – and required to find Challow's down distant at 'All Right' by 10.31½ at the latest. Uffington could not give 'Line Clear' to Challow while the 'Fly' was occupying any part of the down main; it would have been unthinkable to give a heavy delay to an express passenger on account of a local goods train so, unless the Uffington signalman was very sure, he would have the goods backed into the refuge.

While the 'Fly' was shunting at Uffington, three up expresses passed, an Exeter, a Fishguard and a Swansea – the last two running non-stop through Swindon. Three main line stopping trains called and the branch train made two visits for connections, the second of these waiting to leave for Faringdon when the pick-up goods eventually got away. Not all the time it was scheduled at Uffington was spent in shunting; the latter part of the allowance was spent waiting for a 'path' to Shrivenham. The 11.15 a.m. Oxford to

Swindon express passed at 11.55, followed by a Bristol two-hour express at 12.05 p.m. and the 10.50 a.m. Paddington to Swansea at 12.15 a.m. This cleared Knighton Crossing at 12.18, leaving the road clear for the 'Fly'. The pick-up goods came out of Baulking sidings, over the crossovers to the down main line, with cans of water on the locomotive's buffer beam for the Knighton Crossing signalman, and because of this water stop, the train was scheduled seventeen minutes for the five miles, Uffington to Shrivenham. The goods would not clear Knighton in less than nine minutes, at 12.29, just as the 11.40 a.m. Paddington to Neyland express was passing Didcot at over 60 mph. This train would need Ashbury Crossing's Distant at 'All Right' at 12.46 p.m., so the goods driver needed to be aware. The distance he had to cover was not great, about 2¾ miles, but his train was loose-coupled, probably quite heavy and his engine small. Not only was starting slow, owing to the need to gently take up the slack in each coupling, but stopping was slow, as only the engine and tender – if there was one – had any brakes, though the guard would do his bit by screwing his handbrake down hard. Having come gently to a stand at Shrivenham, the train had to be shunted into the down sidings or else across to the upside *before* the signalman could allow the express to approach from Ashbury; seventeen minutes was just a comfortable margin.

The complete service of stopping passenger trains at Uffington amounted to fourteen a day; all gave connections at Swindon and Didcot and most met other services at Reading. Passengers did not have to wait more than half an hour for a connecting train as a rule, but there was one train from Swindon to Weymouth that left five minutes before the down 'stopper' arrived. Except for the 3.23 p.m. from Faringdon, all branch trams met a main line passenger and sometimes two.

Besides regular traffic on the main line, there were frequent excursions. This was traffic that had been developing since 1878, but until the twentieth century, relatively few people could afford days, or weekends, away from home, so excursion trains did not form a significant part of GWR's business until about 1905. Of all the day trips ever run by the company, the most enterprising were those from London to Killarney via Fishguard and Rosslare. These commenced running in the summer of 1907, and the Great Western and Great Southern & Western Railways handled the trains with such vigour that tourists arrived in Killarney in plenty of time for an afternoon jaunt by pony and trap around the lakes, followed by tea in the magnificent GS&WR hotel in Killarney. From Fishguard on the return trip, sleeping cars were provided and the intrepid travellers got back to Paddington barely within twenty-four hours of commencing their journey, having covered about one thousand miles. The popularity of this day-adventure was so great that GWR arranged trips to other scenic parts of Ireland, and by 1914, the company were allowing the Great Central Railway's trains, hauled by GWR locomotives, to run via the Banbury & Cheltenham direct line, to Fishguard, for Killarney and others for Killaloe, a beauty spot on the Shannon north of Limerick. These trains were not day trips. They were very fast; those from Paddington ran to Fishguard with an engine-changing stop at Cardiff, and were treated with great respect by the enginemen and signalmen.

The most glamorous trains of any passing Uffington during the pre-war 'Golden Age' were the Ocean Mails from Fishguard. Ships of Booth Line and Blue Funnel Line began calling in 1908, and in August 1909, the enormously prestigious Cunard Line transatlantic liners called to set down mails and any passengers that were in a hurry. Cunard's SS *Campania* – which cut through the Atlantic at 21 knots and once held the Blue Riband for the fastest crossing – dropped anchor in Fishguard Bay on 6 January 1914, and at Uffington, the signalman received the following notice. '6-1-14. SS *Campania* Cunard Line is due at Fishguard at midnight. Please look to my instructions regarding Ocean Mail specials dated 1910.' There is something very grand about the conjunction of a mighty ship and a powerful locomotive in the dead of night. A Great Western Railway express had its own high prestige, but when it ran exclusively for Cunard, pride of the

Empire, it became almost sacred to the signalmen who had the responsibility of keeping its road clear. These gallant trains were well remembered to the end of the steam era, but there were other boat trains that did not have the same aura. Those were the Avonmouth specials. One day in 1914, two specials for Avonmouth passed Uffington, the first full of people sailing to South America in the Royal Mail Steamer *Bayano*, and the second packed with friends going to cheer them from the quay.

Excursions to the seaside, or 'half days' to Windsor or London, were run from Swindon, and these would stop at Uffington to connect with the branch regular service. The branch train service was by then so frequent that it was rarely necessary to run a special except to bring the excursionists home at the end of the day. The tourists would return late at night, or in the small hours of the following day, weary parents carrying sleeping children over the cast-iron footbridge to the branch platform where the 'Faringdon Johnny' was waiting. These were the only occasions when the engine was out of its shed after midnight. Some of these excursions took circuitous routes in order to pick up as many people as possible and the several Swindon to Southsea trips that were made in 1914 ran via the Didcot, Newbury & Southampton line, so one cannot help wondering how much time the excursionists spent on the beach. Excursions to Weymouth started as empty coaches from Didcot, missed out Steventon and began picking up passengers from Wantage Road. Race meetings at Salisbury drew Great Western coaches from Didcot and beyond over the Midland & South Western Junction Railway, though the GWR locomotive did not work beyond Swindon Town. These 'race specials' got back to Uffington in time to catch the last train to Faringdon. More frequent were the horsebox specials that ran from Newmarket to Salisbury, Compton (DN&S) to Bath, Marlborough (MSWJR) to Ascot and so on, many of them stopping at Challow and/or Uffington to pick up horseboxes.

The Bank Holidays of 1914 had little effect on Faringdon branch services. They had reached their peak frequency. Easter, Whitsun and August Monday did not even produce an extra coach for the branch set. Throughout January and February 1915, the Faringdon branch had an extra trip each Saturday night to meet the 'Swindon Late Special' which left at 11.15 p.m. and called at all stations to Wantage Road, arriving at Uffington at 11.35 p.m.

Since 1897, the company's prosperity had grown with that of the country as a whole, and during the period, GWR developed much of the atmosphere of a lordly estate. The employees were relatively well paid, freely liveried and respectful, working within a sharply defined class structure under the directorship of aristocrats and great capitalists – such as Ernest Cunard. The buildings and installations of the line were splendidly maintained – from locomotives to waiting rooms, equipment was of the best quality, and without a doubt Uffington station and the Faringdon branch presented an appearance as trim and well cared for as any Ducal riding stables. The branch was used to a greater extent than ever before to the advantage of the poorer people of the neighbourhood, who could now afford an annual trip to the sea or to London, which was a distinct rise in their living standards. Not only the people of Faringdon benefited: excursions were run from London to the Vale of White Horse on Sundays between 1905 and 1914, calling at all stations from Steventon to Shrivenham – with a special connection to Faringdon – so that for a low fare otherwise city-bound people could be and were introduced to the gentle delights of Berkshire at its most rural. Though not a great traffic, the visitors made a welcome addition to the summer trade of the town, another item in the list of the branch line's modest achievements. It has been said many times that 1914 was the end of an era. This was true in the case of the Faringdon branch and of GWR generally. Four years of awful war caused millions of men to alter radically their traditionally respectful attitude towards the governing classes, and when the European war was over, a new, less lethal conflict began in England; railwaymen were often to the fore in this, and the old 'estate' atmosphere was an early casualty in the struggle.

Faringdon Branch, July 1914

Single line worked by Train Staff and Ticket assisted by Block Telegraph.
Staff: triangular, varnished oak. Ticket: square, buff.

Weekdays

	a.m.	a.m.	a.m.	a.m.	a.m.	noon	p.m.	p.m.	p.m.	p.m.	p.m.
Faringdon	6.45	8.12	9.27	10L03	11.08	12.00	EBV	1.28	2.20	3.23	4L45
				ECS			LK				
Uffington	6.53	8.20	9.35	10L11	11.16	12.08		1.36	2.28	3.31	4L55
Uffington	7.45	8.45	9L50	10.18	11.33	12.25	12.45	1.48	2.41	3.59	K
Faringdon	7.55	8.52	9L57	10.25	11.40	12.32	12.50	1.55	2.48	4.09	-

			Mxd	Gds	
	p.m.	p.m.	p.m.	p.m.	p.m.
Faringdon	5.55	6.52	7.27	8.10	8.55
Uffington	6.03	7.00	7.35	8.20	9.03
Uffington	6.29	7.12	7.45	8.35	9.16
				EBV	
Faringdon	6.36	7.19	7.52	8.42	9.23

L = First Tuesday each month.
K = Comes from Swindon as engine and van, or to Swindon with cattle wagons ex-
Faringdon.

(See Appendix 7)

CHAPTER 9

Locomotive Department

The engine shed at Faringdon was solidly built in stone and measured 20 feet x 40 feet over the ground and its limestone walls rose 15 feet to the eaves of a slated roof. The ridge of the roof carried a raised vent over most of its length, at each end of which rose a square ventilator chimney. The interior of the building was illuminated by large glazed windows and by the south facing entrance. The shed was built to house a broad gauge locomotive, so there was plenty of room for the standard gauge machine and for its crew to work. Facilities were simple, an inspection pit, a hydrant by the east wall, a work bench with vice at the north end, while a stone lean-to against the north-east corner served as an office. Just outside the entrance was a water tank holding 3,280 gallons to supply the locomotive via a water column. Water was also piped from this tank to the cattle pens and stables. The water was pumped from a well in the goods yard by means of a small stationary engine operated by steam from the locomotive. The station's water came from the town main. A few paces from the water tank was the coaling stage, a simple platform made of sleepers. From 1 June 1864 until 10 September 1933, when the shed was closed, the branch engine was serviced here by a team of three to five men, five being the full complement, and in the records of the Swindon factory, the engine shed was given the identification 'FAR'. After the shed's closure, which was part of a larger economy drive throughout GWR, the two drivers, two firemen and cleaner at the shed were transferred to Swindon, and a very much reduced train service was operated by engines and men based at that shed.

From the start of the line, motive power, rolling stock and men had been supplied by GWR, and in 1863, Sir Daniel Gooch, locomotive superintendent of the company, estimated the cost of working the branch 'with locomotive power' as follows:

	£	s	d
Cost of engine £2,500 at 7½%	187	10	0
Cost of repairs annually	230	0	0
Cost of oil and stores	115	0	0
Enginemen's and firemen's wages	210	0	0
Coal	200	0	0
	942	10	0

The coal for Faringdon was supplied to the company by a mine company that contracted to sell at a fixed price over a specified period of time – from one to five years – and in return GWR agreed to take a certain amount, which, during the 1860s and 1870s, was about 700 tons annually. The first contract for the branch shed ran

Faringdon engine shed. A lean-to office at the far end. The branch driver acted as foreman and kept up the small amount of record keeping and answering letters as well as his driving duties. He earned a welcome overtime for this. (Joe Moss/Roger Carpenter Collection)

from 1864 until 1869 and was with the Earl of Dudley's Staffordshire pit for coal at 5s 6d a ton, which was cheap even for those times. The contract was not renewed and thereafter only Welsh steam coal was supplied to the shed. Some famous mines appear in the records; Penrhiwfer, which took the next contract from 1869 until 1873 for 700 tons a year at 6s 4d a ton, then Plas Kynaston, Fothergills of Aberdare, New British of Ruabon, Glyncorrwg at 7s 0d a ton and expensive Dowlais at 7s 6d a ton. This was the most costly fuel supplied to Faringdon, or any other shed for that matter until 1880. Sir Daniel's figure of £200 for coal was £35 below reality in 1864, a 16 per cent error.

His estimate for wages made no allowance for overtime payments but simply allowed each man £1 a week, which was an underestimate of the order of 25 per cent. Two months after the opening of the line, the weekly average wage in the locomotive department was £1 5s 3d, and during December, they earned £1 6s 8d per week. The men's wages remained about this level until 1869 when they began to fluctuate considerably. One week, they might be as low as 17s 0d and the next they were 45s 0d coming back to the average of 26s 0d, or 27s 0d the week after. This was still the pattern in 1873 when the record ceases. These were very high wages for the time; a skilled fitter in the railway factory at Swindon only earned £1 a week, and at first glance, it seems absurd that such wages could be earned at a one-engine shed. But this was a curiosity of the locomotive department 110 years ago – the smallest sheds got the highest wages. In the area bounded by Weymouth, Bristol, Gloucester and Faringdon, the best-paid locomotive men were those at Box and Brimscombe bank engine sheds (according to Joseph Armstrong, GWR Locomotive Superintendent 1864–77). At those two places, the average weekly wage during 1864–74 was 33s 0d a week with peaks as high as 53s, and the peaks were more common than the troughs. These men could only have earned such wages by working dreadfully long hours, perhaps as many as eighteen per day, when a large number of 'specials' had been run, all of them requiring to be assisted in the rear on the Box and Sapperton incline. Footplate staff at Weymouth, Chippenham and Salisbury earned about the same money as the men at Faringdon, while those working from Swindon and Gloucester appeared to earn a regular £1 a week on average. The 1864–74 wages at Faringdon were not bettered until after 1918, when galloping inflation had increased the number of shillings in a man's pocket while their purchasing power had declined. (See Appendix 9.)

Wages Paid at Faringdon Shed, 1864 and 1865
(From Joseph Armstrong's notebook)

	Weekly average per man. 4 men at shed
1 August – 30 October 1864	£1 5s 3d
1 April – 30 October 1865	£1 5s 7d
1 November – 1 December 1865	£1 6s 0d
1 December – 31 December 1865	£1 6s 8d

(See also Appendix 9)

Locomotive records for Faringdon shed cover the period 1902–33 with that for 1920 missing. During those thirty years, it is known that forty-nine different engines were allocated to the shed; with one exception, they were all tank engines. There were thirty-seven 0-4-2s; seven 0-6-0 saddle tanks; two 0-6-0 pannier tanks, a Metro-class 2-4-0, one of the rare 633 class of 0-6-0 side tanks of which only a dozen were built, and one of the common-place (310 were built) 388 class of 0-6-0 tender engines, the outside framed 'Standard Goods' of Joseph Armstrong. The 633 and the 388 were powerful machines that were wasted on the Faringdon line. The former remained only one month before going to Frome, where its small wheels and high tractive effort would be better employed with heavy mineral trains over steep Somerset gradients. But the Armstrong tender engine worked the Faringdon line for a full six months. This was doubly unusual, as the line had no turntable and GWR had given an undertaking in 1864 to work the line only with tank engines. Doubtless the company would have blamed the acute shortage of locomotives had the Board of Trade taken them to task over the matter. Pannier tanks did not become tenants of Faringdon shed until October 1922 when No. 1934 arrived for a month-long tour of duty, and No. 1964 occupied the shed from March to June 1932. Both these engines were of the 1901 series of the 850 class of saddle tank but had been fitted out as panniers when given Belpaire fireboxes. The square 'shoulders' of this type of firebox did not allow a curved saddle tank to be placed over them. The oldest saddle tank of the half dozen that were stabled at Faringdon was No. 736 with 4-foot 6-inch driving wheels and one of the few branch engines to have been built at Swindon, coming out new in January 1873. She had remained in the Swindon area until 1898, when she went to Newport and later Aberdare, returning to Swindon for a general repair in 1902. Then she worked at Faringdon during 1903 and 1904 before moving away to Oxford and the branch lines of that area.

The solitary 2-4-0 Metro tank was No. 1446, which occupied Faringdon shed during October 1916, while 517-class No. 541 went to factory. No. 1446 had been built at Swindon in 1881 and with the rest of the class had been generally employed on the Reading–Paddington suburban passenger services and on the GWR/Metropolitan trains between Henley, Windsor and Aldgate in the City. They gained a reputation for speed and were quite capable of hauling nine eight-wheeled coaches non-stop from Reading to Paddington in 43 minutes, a feat which required top speeds of 65 mph. Their replacements on the main line suburban trains were the massive 4-4-2 County tanks, which, although they towered above the little Metros, were no better at hauling trains. The men at Faringdon were doubtless very pleased to have a Metro tank for a while.

The mainstay of the branch services were the smallest – the most excellent 517-class 0-4-2 side tanks. They were designed by George Armstrong and built at

517-class 0-4-2 tank No. 1158 waits with its connecting service to Faringdon. The main line stopping train is on the right-hand edge of the view. Taken in 1930 by Dr Jack Hollick. (Author's Collection)

Wolverhampton over a period of several years commencing in 1869. The early engines of the class, Nos 517–576, came out as saddle tanks with 16-inch x 24-inch cylinders driving 50-foot-diameter wheels but were later rebuilt at Swindon with side tanks, 17-inch x 24-inch cylinders and 5-foot 2-inch driving wheels to conform to the standard of the remainder of the class, 157 locomotives all told. They gained a good reputation for economy in coal and oil as well as having a fine turn of speed with light loads. They were used all over GWR from Weymouth to Wrexham on branch lines where a light axle load was essential, and on the main lines too. To trace the life histories of all the 517 engines that worked the Faringdon branch would be a lengthy business, complicated by many changes, repairs and renewals before their final journey to 'The Field' at Swindon for scrapping. Complicated though the locomotives' movements were, there does appear to have been some kind of pattern to them. Until 1915, the engines tended to keep to a circuit – ex-works from a heavy repair to Faringdon or Malmesbury for a few weeks 'running-in' and then back to the factory for a week or two before going out, either to one of the local branch sheds or to some distant place like Croes Newydd or Brixham. Those posted away would not usually return to the Swindon area until a heavy repair was due and would fill in their waiting time on one of the nearby branch lines. So Faringdon footplatemen got the best and the worst of the classes. Swindon factory 'shopping control' kept a very close watch on all its locomotives, and it was due largely to the care they had exercised that, when the First World War broke out, the locomotives were able to last so long without factory attention.

Faringdon Branch Working Timetable, July 1912

Single line worked by Train Staff and Ticket assisted by Block Telegraph
Weekdays

	B	B	B	D	B	B	G	B	B	B	E
	a.m.	a.m.	a.m.	a.m.	a.m.	noon	p.m.	p.m.	p.m.	p.m.	p.m.
Faringdon	6.45	8.12	9.27	10L03	11.08	12.00		1.33	2.20	3.23	4L45
				ECS			EBV				
Uffington	6.53	8.20	9.35	10L11	11.16	12.08	X	1.41	2.28	3.31	4L55
Uffington	7.45	8.45	9L50	10.18	11.33	12.25	12L43	1.53	2.41	3.59	V
	Mxd			Mxd							
Faringdon	7.55	8.52	9L57	10.25	11.40	12.32	12L50	2.00	2.48	4.09	

	B	B	B	K	B
	p.m.	p.m.	p.m.	p.m.	p.m.
Faringdon	5.55	6.52	7.27	8.10	8.55
Uffington	6.03	7.00	7.35	8.20	9.03
Uffington	6.29	7.12	7.45	8.35	9.15
				EBV	
Faringdon	6.36	7.19	7.52	8.42	9.22

Sundays

	G	G	
	a.m.	p.m.	
Uffington	6.53	5.23	6.53 Uffington worked by loco and men ex-6.05 a.m. Swindon.
	EBV	EBV	
Faringdon	7.00	5.32	5.32 Uffington worked by loco and men ex-4.00 p.m. Swindon.
	D	E	
Faringdon	7.30	5.50	B, D, G, E, K are locomotive headcodes/ train classifications
Uffington	7.38	5.57	
	Milk	Milk, goods and cattle	X, V from or to Swindon

The careful planning was disrupted by war munition work, which Swindon factory undertook, and by a shortage of materials for anything but the war effort. Swindon factory was the only establishment outside the Royal Arsenals with workers sufficiently skilled to be able to manufacture the barrels for heavy guns. Other railway works made gun carriages but Swindon craftsmen turned out 5.5-inch-diameter rifled barrels for long-range artillery. The work of making guns and limbers took up space that would otherwise have been devoted to locomotive repairs with the result repairs had to be rationed and prioritised. Main line engines were given priority of the reduced accommodation and the engines of minor branch lines had to be, for the most part, neglected. If ever there was a time when it could be said that the branch had a regular engine it was now, and No. 541 of the 517 class worked the line almost continuously from 1916 to 1919. That she kept going for so long is a tribute to the Faringdon men who drove and fired her, to Swindon's earlier repairs and to the general robustness of the steam engine. However, by 1919, she was badly in need of a rest, along with hundreds of other small engines, so it is not surprising that after the war an increasing variety of locomotives came to work the branch as these small engines were put through the works and repaired or scrapped according to how well they had stood up to the years of 'make do and mend'. Between 1921 and 1933, there was an ever-increasing 'turnover' of locomotives at Faringdon shed, and one gets the impression from the record books that it was something of a scramble to find an engine for the job.

No. 541 was built in January 1869 and went from Wolverhampton to Chester. She returned to the factory for a new boiler and general repair when she had run 301,000 miles in May 1905 and came out in October 1905. She came to the Swindon factory in April 1908, having run 318,000 miles, and did not emerge until February 1909 when she was sent to Faringdon to replace No. 1471. Apart from the usual 'check-up' period No. 541 worked the branch for a year before returning to Swindon factory during March 1910 but was soon back at Faringdon. She must have been a well-put-together engine in the first place, for the intervals between repairs are noticeably lengthy. Her next 'heavy' overhaul – after covering 500,000 miles – was one of the most rapid ever, because of the war – in works from 23 February until 22 June 1916. She went back to Faringdon again and five months later was involved in a miserable incident near the terminus. The permanent-way gang, under their ganger's instructions, were pushing a trolley loaded with tools along the track in the direction of Faringdon. The ganger ought to have asked permission from the signalman before fouling the line with the trolley but, relying on his knowledge of the train service, had not done so. He pronounced the fatal statement – 'There's no train for half an hour.' However, No. 541 was running a special from Uffington. He had not even put out a hand signalman with red flag before and behind, and so it was that, just as they reached the part of the line with the shortest forward sighting – a sharp bend, in a cutting, where they were quite invisible to an approaching driver – No. 541 burst into view; the curving cutting banks had cut off the sound of the approaching train. The ganger shouted to his men to jump clear while he tried to run forward, pushing the trolley in a forlorn attempt to give the train more room to pull up, but the engine ran him down and he was killed. At the subsequent inquiry, it was held that his death was his own fault, and one wonders how his widow fared, as she would have received no compensation under those circumstances. Save for one month in each of the years 1917 and 1918, No. 541 worked the branch continuously, but there were several interruptions during 1919, and in February 1920, she went into factory for a very well-deserved 'heavy' repair having covered 528,875 miles, the last 79,000 in three and a half years on the Faringdon line.

Another regular engine on the Faringdon branch was No. 219. She was a 517 of 1876 vintage and had a brilliant career, working at many different locations, giving no trouble and requiring only the usual repairs and those infrequently. Her first four years were spent at Gloucester after which she was re-allocated to Swindon, where she worked until 1890, very probably seeing service on the Faringdon branch during that time. From Swindon, she went to Westbourne Park (Paddington) shed for three years and then re-allocations came frequently. In 1893, she went back to Swindon from there to Llanelly in 1895, Bristol in 1901, Southall in 1903, where she remained until January 1906 when the need for a 'heavy' repair forced her back to Swindon. Even now, she showed her worth and only four months were taken up with repairs against the more usual six. Remarkably, there was no work for her when she came out of shops in April, and she was put in the stock shed. Here she languished for a month until posted to Faringdon as a replacement for No. 540, which was going back to its regular shed, Chippenham. No. 219 worked the Faringdon branch for the next three years, except for occasional and short visits to the factory, and in 1909, when one might have expected her to need some serious factory attention, she headed east to Southall. For six years, she worked in the district, on the Brentford line and on main line suburban work before going to Abingdon in 1915. Still keeping out of Swindon factory, she went from Abingdon to Neath, then even further west, to Carmarthen, and eventually north, to Oswestry. When she did come back to Wiltshire in 1928, it was not for repairs but to be scrapped, and she went to the breaker's yard, opposite Rushey Platt signal box, having covered over 1,100,000 miles, and was one of the last survivors of the 517 class.

Another very successful 517 class to visit Faringdon was No. 829. She began work in South Wales during 1875 and moved on to the West of England, working at Bristol, Taunton, Exeter and Newton Abbot sheds before coming to Swindon in April 1911 for a general repair, having run 778,000 miles. Her overhaul took the usual six months, and she was sent to Malmesbury for a 'running-in' period of six weeks before returning to the factory for final adjustments. She emerged pristine from the works and went to Faringdon. One can imagine how pleased the locomotive crews felt to receive a perfect engine, smooth riding – her bearing surfaces close fitting, her weight evenly distributed over her wheels after the adjustments made to the springs in the factory and free steaming, from a new boiler. When she left Faringdon, on 25 January 1912, she was looking better than when she arrived, for ten weeks of oiling and polishing had smoothed and glazed her raw, new paint and metalwork. Her replacement 517 No. 1443 was driven 'light' to Uffington by a Swindon crew who took over No. 829 when she arrived with a branch train and drove her to Marlborough to replace 517 No. 218, which was required at Swindon factory before going to Brixham. No. 829 never returned to Faringdon but continued to make good mileage elsewhere. Between the 'heavy' repair of 1911 and an 'intermediate' of 1914, she ran 51,500 miles and her total when scrapped was over 1,100,000.

The Faringdon men must have groaned when they saw their new mount, No. 1443, and her suspiciously worn paint. The climb of Barrowbush Hill soon confirmed their fears – No. 1443 had been dumped on them pending a general repair. She left for the factory on 13 February, her place being taken by No. 1436, which worked the line until February 1913, when No. 1443, fresh from works, returned – 1436 going to Shrewsbury but returning to Faringdon for one month during the final year of the operation of the shed.

These constant changes were as nothing to the situation that developed after the war, when in each successive year the tendency was for more and more engines to share the working of the branch. At least five were allocated to Faringdon in 1922, six in 1923, seven in 1924 and in the final 'year' no less than twenty-five engines were sent to the shed. Most of them were 517s due for scrapping, working out their time on local branch lines. All but one of them had seen service on the Faringdon branch in more prosperous days and now made the shed's swansong their own.

Faringdon shed, from its opening, had a complement of two enginemen, two firemen and a cleaner. The drivers received differing wages according to their seniority, the same applied to the firemen; the cleaner, when one was employed, received 5s a week. The firemen at the shed were simply passing through on their promotional way but for many of the drivers at the shed, the Faringdon branch was akin to a convalescent home. One of the first men to be employed at the shed was Edward King who worked there as a fireman from March 1869 until March 1871 when he moved to Swindon for promotion. Suddenly his health became poor, and in March 1872, he was back at Faringdon in the role of 'branch reliefman', apparently standing in for the regular men for whatever reason. This suited him because he held the post until August 1886 when he became 'permanent branch driver' at 5s a day. Sad to relate, he died in December 1887, aged fifty.

George Smith* made some sort of record when he came to Faringdon in April 1882 shortly before his sixty-seventh birthday. He had been on sick leave from Cheltenham shed for a year, and one would have expected the company to retire him on his pension, considering his age and the length of his illness. George worked away quite happily on the branch for three years, until, just before his seventieth birthday, he had the misfortune to lose control of his train as it was approaching Faringdon so that it crashed into the stop blocks. Still his resignation was not requested, and another seven months went by before he retired voluntarily with superannuation. His replacement was Arthur Jones*, who also crashed into the buffer stops at Faringdon. That was in 1890; he was

---

* Fictitious name.

forty-six, and the company fined him £1 and suspended him for five days, so he lost the best part of two weeks' wages for his absent-mindedness. Luckily, no one was hurt. He worked on blamelessly for six years when he began to collect a series of 2s fines for derailing his engine, running axle bearings hot or simply delaying the train for a few minutes. This continued in a desultory manner for three years until he failed his eyesight test, whereupon the company found him a job as pump attendant at Yeovil in 1899.

Occasionally a man would ask to be sent to the branch. A top link engineman from Paddington requested such a move and worked the branch from December 1890 until March 1897, when he returned to express train work at Paddington. Another man had cut short what appeared to be a good career to work on the branch. He had started at Didcot as a cleaner in November 1869 when he was twenty. Redundancy had forced him to move to Fairford and then Witney engine sheds as a cleaner before he eventually found a third class fireman's job back at Didcot in October 1875. Seven years later, he moved to Plymouth for his first class firing job, which occupied him for three years until the next rung of the ladder, engine turner, became vacant for him. An engine turner was qualified to move locomotives within the confines of the engine shed and the shed yard. For this, he moved to Tondu and became a third class engineman there. He rose to second class driver. He moved to Severn Tunnel Junction in 1896 and was promoted into the first class grade with a move to Pembroke Dock in June 1901. Barely a month later, while he was running his express into Cardiff, he overran a signal at Danger, and collided with a horsebox. Six days suspension followed during which time he was unable to shrug off the incident like most men did, and he applied to be put back to second class work or to go to a branch, preferably the Faringdon branch, as it was close to his home. The company was able to oblige him in this, and Churchward, to whom all such applications were made at that time, sent him to Faringdon but only on 5s 6d a day when the usual rate was at least 6s. But such a point did not worry our man, who worked as blamelessly on the branch and retired on his pension in January 1910.

William Beasant arrived at Faringdon shed in January 1910 after a grand tour around GWR. He was a local man, having started at Swindon as a cleaner aged twenty in August 1876, became a third class fireman there in 1878, and in the next five years promotions and redundancy took him to Chippenham, Trowbridge, Devizes, Salisbury and Gloucester, where he was a fireman second class in April 1883. Up to that time, he had had what locomotive men call 'a rough shunt', and still he had to wait another three years for his promotion to first class job, moving to Evesham to get it. From Evesham he moved to Worcester in May 1887 and went back to Swindon as an engine turner in March 1889. Luck never seemed to be in Bill Beasant's favour: he spent two years at Swindon before reaching third class engineman at Cardiff, and between 1891 and 1906, he was posted back and forth across South Wales like a human tennis ball. He saw service from Llantrisant shed, Tondu, Cardiff and Severn Tunnel Junction where he reached the second class grade. It may be that the rigours of his career had adversely affected his health. He had been sent to fourteen sheds in thirty years, often without any promotion, and now, at 'The Tunnel' in December 1909, he severely strained his back while trying to operate a locomotive's steam cock lever, which was very stiff. He was fifty, and the injury would be with him for the rest of his life. Churchward decided that he must be put back to shunting work. Bill with an injured, and without a doubt untreated, back, was put back to driving work, which required more heavy lever reversing actions than any other. He was away from work for three weeks, heard the news on his return, and immediately put in an application for the forthcoming vacancy on the Faringdon branch. Churchward was pleased to concede the request, and so Beasant came to Faringdon. Sometimes the engines on the line were 'rough-uns' waiting to go to factory, and Bill suffered then from his back complaint as he braced himself against their lurching and rolling, but he was of the bulldog breed and kept going through thick and thin until he retired with a pension, aged sixty-three, in July 1919.

According to official reports made in 1912 – by the senior engineman at Faringdon and now enshrined in the public archive – the branch engine was kept in steam continuously from early on Monday morning until 9.30 or 10 p.m. the following Saturday. There was no cleaner at the shed during Ted Glanville's time, 1909 to 1919, and no Sunday work. The drivers worked two shifts – 5.45 a.m. to 4.10 p.m. and 12.10 p.m. to 10.10 p.m. The senior man, Bill Beasant, is said to have been permanently on early turn, leaving the 'young hand' driver, Arthur Taylor, to do the late turn and have his social life ruined. The firemen were supposed to work two shifts alternatively, 2.10 a.m. to 12.10 p.m. and 4.10 p.m. to 2.10 a.m. The period when no fireman was on duty was covered by Arthur Taylor, who therefore fired to Bill Beasant. This arrangement makes it all the more likely that the two drivers kept to their own turns, as Bill, with his bad back, is very unlikely to have done any firing.

The 4.10 p.m. fireman, Ted Glanville, say, relieved Arthur Taylor, who then crossed the footplate to relieve Bill Beasant, who went home. Arthur and Ted worked the rest of the service, and after the last train had arrived at Faringdon, they left the coaches in the platform and ran via the run-round loop to the small pump house. Having topped up the locomotive water-supply tank, they took their engine onto the shed road, cleaned the fire, cleared the smoke box and ashpan, filled the boiler, banked the fire with small coal and dust, and then dropped the engine into the shed. Arthur would ensure that the engine's handbrake was screwed hard on, that the steam cocks on the cylinders were open, that the regulator was shut and the valves left in mid-gear. Having quite immobilised his engine, he could go home and leave his fireman to mind the boiler water level and clean the engine. Theoretically, Ted would clean one side of the engine and leave the other side for the 2.10 a.m. man but what normally happened was that Ted cleaned all the engine and stayed in the shed till 5 a.m. so that his mate could have a decent night in bed – you may therefore be sure that the firemen alternated their shifts.

Steam for the stationary pumping engine in its timber shed was taken from the locomotive's whistle connection. Having first removed the whistle, the whistle operating lever was then held open with a piece of wood to save a man the trouble of standing there for half an hour, but while this seems only natural, it was not good practice, as it left the pump unattended, and on at least one occasion, it sped up to such an extent that its little end broke and its piston, breaking through the cylinder head, disappeared into the night through the side of the shed.

All routine maintenance work on the locomotive was done at night in the shed. At Faringdon, the water contained a high concentration of solids in suspension – while the water at Uffington was very free of impurities. When water is evaporated, these solids are deposited on the tubes as scale and at the bottom of the boiler as mud. Owing to the poor quality of water at Faringdon, it was necessary for the branch engine to have its boiler washed out once a week and a boiler-smith, Jimmy Long, came up from Swindon to do this assisted by the Faringdon night-shift fireman. But cold water jets were used to dislodge the boiler dirt and therefore the boiler should have been cooled down before the wash-out commenced, but this was impossible if the job was to be completed and steam again raised for the day's service, and some considerable strain must have been placed on the hot metal as it was doused with cold water. Hot water wash-out had been introduced at large sheds around 1905, and after 1918, the branch engine was taken to Swindon for boiler cleaning. Swindon men came up with a replacement engine and took the branch engine away. As the boiler did not have to be cooled before hot-water wash-out started, the operation did not take very long, and the branch engine could be back at Faringdon within twenty-four hours.

Firing a 517 on the branch posed no problems. On the up journey, very little steam was needed, as the line was mostly downhill – though if a couple of 'Siphons' loaded with full, 17-gallon milk churns were on the train the difference was felt and heard, as the driver was obliged to 'drop the lever' a notch. Once at the summit of the line, he could shut off and free-wheel the 1¾ miles to Uffington, the only problem being to control speed on the relatively up-grade so as not to overrun the platform. The return trip required the engine to snort a little, and at night, a good display could be seen from the chimney, especially if the 'Siphons' were on the train. Owing to the short length of the line, firing had to be done lightly, with the tip of the shovel, so as not to have a big fire when standing at stations and waste steam through the safety valve. 517-class fireboxes were square and were fired, one shovel in each corner, to produce a saucer-shaped fire that, on the Faringdon line, was always thin except for the little extra put on to get the train up Barrowbush Hill. Skill ensured that this had been burnt away before Faringdon was reached so as to avoid 'blowing off' in the station. Moreover, the driver was paid a bonus for economy in the use of coal and oil and a decent man would share this with his fireman so that both men worked together.

With all the small variations of firing according to what the engine would be doing on its arrival at Uffington or Faringdon, the job must have been a pleasant and an interesting one, with what was virtually one's own engine on one's private branch line. Ted Glanville spent ten happy years there. In all that time, he and Arthur only drove once on the main line-apart from shunting around the station. On this occasion, the day's service had finished when a large party of people from a Conservative Party rally arrived at Faringdon and asked to be taken to Didcot. The branch engine and coaches were turned out and worked right through – non-stop. Arthur Taylor, let loose on the main line for the first time as a driver, gave his 517 her head and they had a terrific gallop to Didcot. With overtime in mind, the return trip, empty stock, was made sedately.

Ted Glanville began his career at Didcot as an engine cleaner in 1905 and became a third class fireman at Faringdon on 21 January 1907. Here he took lodgings in a house with Arthur Taylor – 'a religious sort of chap' – freshly promoted to third class driver from first class fireman at Banbury. The house they both lodged in was owned by a man who was, in his spare time, a Methodist lay preacher. He also took the photographs donated to this book by Mrs Singleton. However, the lodgings were not satisfactory to Arthur – food was barely sufficient, the regime indoors oppressive and the rent high. 'Buying cheap and selling dear' was the sarcastic remark I heard from more than one ancient railwayman concerning what they called 'Holy Joes'. Ted paid 12s for a room out of his 18s 6d weekly wage. Arthur was equally dissatisfied, and after making several complaints, he found a driving job back in Banbury, whereupon Ted was told, very formally, that he was expected to follow his driver's example and leave, which he did.

Eventually, Ted was promoted to second class fireman and went to Slough. One of his jobs there used to take him through Uffington. The working was to take the 'First Workman's', 4.30 a.m. Slough, to Paddington, all stations, thence to Ranelagh Bridge yard for half an hour before working the first down 'stopper' to Swindon. Their engine was a Slough County Tank of the 4-4-2 wheel arrangement or else a 36XX tank – a 2-4-2. Ted used to run his tanks low so that he could get a good fill of the soft, clean Uffington water. At Swindon, the engine was taken on shed for coal and then worked back all stations to Paddington, though Ted and his mate were relieved at Slough.

Ted also recalled that the slightly complicated arrangements with the Train Staff and Ticket at weekends (see Chapter 5) were very occasionally bungled so that a porter from one end of the line would have to walk or cycle to the other carrying the Staff to a waiting train. Sometimes the driver could not be bothered to wait for the Staff and went without it.

Below is a table of mileages worked by the branch line's footplate crews during October and December 1912.

Miles run and round trips completed

Week ending 3 December 1912. Locomotive 1443

Beasant		Taylor	
Passenger trips 46	Miles 322	Passenger trips 26	Miles 182
Goods trips 3	Miles 21	Goods trips 5	Miles 35

Week ending 5 October 1912. Locomotive 1436

Passenger trips 48	Miles 336	Passenger trips 25	Miles 175
Goods trips 6	Miles 42	Goods trips 5	Miles 35

Beasant also worked the first Tuesday of the month special and one other extra passenger trip during the week 5 October 1912 and also a special goods trip every day during that week.

During 1912, the branch engines, Nos 829, 1435 and 1443, burned 308 tons 18 cwt of coal. The official record of locomotive costs (see Appendix 8) puts the figure at 341 tons 15 cwt, but this does not match the total derived from the coal sheets kept at Faringdon by the men who loaded the engines' bunkers with coal from hundredweight-capacity wicker baskets (see Appendix 10). It is interesting to note that while coal consumption had been halved between 1865 and 1912, the price of the fuel had doubled. The locomotives used their coal economically; the totals given in Appendix 10 include coal used in lighting up each week, bringing the fire round each day, shunting and pumping. For example, in the month ending 5 October 1912, 27 tons of coal were burnt, which can be made into a convenient weekly total of 6 tons 15 cwt. Now, in the week ending 5 October 1912, No. 1443 ran 588 miles on 6 tons of coal, roughly 22.8 lb per mile. It will be seen from the table that most fuel was burned during the coldest months and that totals gradually reduced to a minimum in mid-summer. The very low figure for April reflects the reduced train service and special economy in fuel observed by the men during the miners' strike.

The normal weekly consumption of cylinder oil and engine oil by the branch engines during 1912 was 6 pints of the former and 14 pints of the latter. Cylinder oil was a heavy, green/brown oil, stiff as treacle when cold, which was made from crushed seeds for use in the valve chests and cylinders and would not emulsify under the action of steam and hot water as a mineral oil would have done. Engine oil was much lighter, similar in consistency to gear oil used in motor cars, and this was used to lubricate just about everything except the insides of the cylinders and valve chests. When No. 1436 came to Faringdon in 1912, she was fresh from factory and the drivers used two pints more than usual of each kind of oil for a week to assist the machinery to 'run in'. At the end of the week, they were satisfied the engine was running freely and with cool bearings, so with their oil bonus in mind, they reverted to the usual ration. Sometimes the drivers tried to run the engine with less than the usual amount of oil in the hope of a larger bonus. Some weeks they managed with two pints less, but they were obviously uneasy about such economies, and the following week they would use more than usual to make up for their earlier frugality. As the drivers got a bonus for economical working in coal and oil, it seems to have been essential that both men got along happily together to run their engine as carefully as they could. (Cost of working the line – Appendix 8.)

No bonus was attached to 'Blue Billy'. This was the light cleaning oil for locomotive grooming. Twenty-four gallons a year were sent up to Faringdon shed along with five cwt of cotton waste for its application, for polishing brass, cleaning machinery and hands. There were several practical reasons for keeping an engine clean. Cracks in spokes or frames would be impossible to see on a grimy surface and leaks of steam could be difficult to trace; grit around an oil port was obviously a bad thing. Furthermore, enginemen and firemen in those days had to buy their own overalls and did not want them smothered in dirt when they went under the engine each morning to oil the machinery. But, of course, GWR was also concerned about the cleanliness of its locomotives for purely aesthetic reasons, and to ensure that copper, brass and steel was kept in pristine condition, the shed was supplied with 24 pounds of powdered Bath stone for the metal bright-work and 24 pounds of 'jelly petrol' – Vaseline – annually. The fine grit of the Bath stone scoured all metal surfaces producing smoke box door rings, buffers, handrails that looked as if they were made of silver; brass and copper shone like the sun. The jelly petrol was wiped over all this metal to prevent it oxidising, and a really keen cleaner also used it to make 'speed marks' across flat surfaces of paintwork. A rectangular block of cotton waste was drawn carefully across the side tanks that had previously been smeared with the grease and then the block was drawn carefully down the tanks so that the result was a chequer-board pattern. There were other patterns too. The interesting thing about this practice is that it follows directly from stable practice when a freshly groomed thoroughbred horse was 'finished' with contrary brush strokes across its gleaming quarters.

The rolling stock allocated to the branch in 1912 was similar to that reported at Faringdon in 1877. The branch passenger train consisted of three four-wheeled carriages, a third class, No. 327 of Lot 875, a first/second composite, No. 7831 of Lot 733, and the brake van, No. 3110 of Lot 898. There were also vacuum-braked 'Siphons' for milk traffic, a vacuum-braked carriage truck and horsebox. Allocated freight vehicle consisted of one non-vacuum-braked 20-ton brake van, the curiously named 'Toad'. The branch guard therefore had two vans to maintain, both being, so to speak, his private property. The goods brake was branded 'Faringdon R.U.' – the letters standing for 'Regular User' – and the guard's name was painted in small letters down in one corner for all to see. This was part of company policy and the resident guard had strict instructions that, except when he was sick or on leave, he was to padlock the door of the van and take the key home when he finished duty. The guard often returned the compliment by keeping his van in perfect condition, laying linoleum on the floor, draping curtains at the windows and even hanging pictures on the walls.

The freight brake van was used on the evening goods to Uffington, on the one 'mixed' train of the day when it was attached behind the loose-coupled wagon(s) at the rear of the passenger coaches, and for any special goods train that had to be run. The maximum load for the 517 on the branch was 202 tons in the down direction and 302 tons in the up direction, the steep gradient being shorter in the latter case. A Metro was fifty tons better but, as has been noted, this class of engine was hardly ever used on the line. The load limit to Faringdon somewhat restricted the use of the 'mixed' train, as the trailing load of freight wagons may well have brought the total weight of the train over the maximum allowed. If this happened, then some of the traffic would have been left behind and a special trip made to collect them later – as we have seen, Driver Beasant made three such trips a week. (See Appendix 11.)

During February 1912, 290 wagons of freight passed over the branch. There were 181 open wagons, and also seventy-eight covered vans, two meat vans, seven cattle wagons and also an occasional furniture van and fruit van. On market day that month, twenty cattle wagons worked into Faringdon. Some 'foreign' companies' wagons appeared at the branch terminus. For instance, on 8 February 1912, of fourteen open wagons standing in the yard, two belonged to the Midland Railway, two were London & South Western stock and one was from the Great Eastern Railway. In the constant flow of traffic, two open wagons left that day, one the following day, six the day after and twelve went out on the 12th. Thus it can be seen that the line was busy with scheduled freight and special trips, so the branch engine and men were kept very busy. There was also the business of pumping water. The latter operation was probably carried out at least once a day. They may have carried out this job between the 12.32 p.m. arrival at Faringdon and the 1.28 p.m. departure (always supposing they did not have to work a special trip in that interval), or failing that, there was another opportunity between the 4.9 p.m. arrival and the 5.55 p.m. departure.

CHAPTER 10

The Splendour Fades

When England declared war on Germany in August 1914, the attitude of most people was that it would all be over in three or four months and if a man wished to earn a little glory he had best enlist quickly. In this blithe spirit, the nation went about its daily life, and the railway companies actually experienced an increase in passenger traffic, particularly at holiday times. A large number of extra trains had to be run for the Christmas period and during Easter and Whitsun 1915. The level of demand for transport by the public was such that the government had to ask the railway companies to make reductions in their passenger schedules so that the movement of essential supplies would not be hindered by a shortage of locomotives, men, rolling stock and track space. GWR may have been just a little reluctant to withdraw from the heavy civilian traffic, for the cuts it made were often those that should have been made anyhow; for instance, the 3.23 p.m. Faringdon was withdrawn, a train with no main line connections, but the remainder of the lavish service on the branch remained untouched.

Food shortages caused by the submarine warfare of 1916 and the appalling number of families that were losing fathers and brothers in the land battles of that year finally sobered England and from September civilian services were drastically reduced, the pages of the working timetable showing the harsh austerities only too clearly when compared with the grand designs of earlier years. In place of the glittering procession of high-speed express trains, there now ran as many freights carrying barbed wire, food and ammunition under the anonymous and leaden title of 'Government Stores'. Locomotives went into drab livery, as if in mourning for the dead, and speed restrictions were imposed, a general 60 mph on main lines while the previous limit of 25 mph over the points from branch to main at Uffington was reduced to 15 mph and the higher limit was never reinstated. The signalman at Uffington, in common with his mates all over the system, had now to learn some new bell codes. These were

	Headcode	Bell code
Ambulance, Naval or Military special	N	2 pause 3 pause 1
Cordite paste special	C	5 " 3 " 3
Government stores	F	4 " 3 " 3
Admiralty coal train	F	3 " 4 " 4

'N' headcode trains took precedence over all others, while the rest took the precedence indicated by their headcode. The British Army in France was supposed to total around 2,500,000 men in 1917, and all their stores had to be moved by rail, from factory to store depots and from the depots to the docks. Heavy casualties in the army needed replacing, so recruits were taken from training camps and regiments were taken to the ports by train, while long lines of dark-green coaches, each marked with a red cross on a white disc, trailed inland from the southern harbours. It was for this terrible new traffic that cuts were made in the civilian services and ultimately in the Faringdon branch schedules, for there were not the main line trains for the branch services to meet.

Some branch lines were closed down in 1917, and their tracks used in military installations, but the Faringdon branch was too important to the town for this to be done and instead suffered a reduction in its service to five 'mixed' trains a day and one goods train up to Uffington, the engine returning with the brake van alone to the terminus. For the first time since 1892, there was no provision for the Great Cattle Fair on the first Tuesday of each month, which gave rise to much confusion and embarrassment at Faringdon station when drovers herded large numbers of cattle into the station yard only to find that there was no transport.

Faringdon Branch, May to December 1917

Single line worked by Train Staff and Ticket assisted with Block Telegraph

Weekdays

	a.m.	a.m.	p.m.	p.m.	Goods p.m.	p.m.
Faringdon	8.05	9.30	1.25	2.15	4.45	5.45
Uffington	8.13	9.38	1.33	2.23	4.55	5.53
					EBV	
Uffington	8.45	10.18	1.52	2.41	5.05	6.29
Faringdon	8.52	10.25	1.59	2.48	5.15	6.36

All trains ran 'mixed' except as shown.
Sunday service as usual, worked by main line trains.

The 1918 service on the branch was the smallest ever, including the year of closure to passenger traffic, and consisted of three 'mixed' trains leaving Faringdon at 9.30 a.m., 1.35 p.m. and 5.50 p.m., each one meeting two main line passenger trains. The 9.30 a.m. up brought the 'Siphon' loaded with full milk churns, and on arrival at the junction, the branch engine shunted it to a point convenient for the 9.15 a.m. Swindon to London milk train to collect. While this was being done, the 9.20 a.m. Swindon to Paddington arrived and an interchange of passengers and parcels took place. This was the best train of the day for Uffington, as it ran 'fast' from Didcot to Paddington, calling only at Reading. In 1918, the term 'fast' had reverted to its 1870 meaning – a non-stop train – for speeds were very moderate. The 9.20 a.m. Swindon was allowed 23 minutes for the 16 miles from Didcot to Reading and 45 minutes from there to Paddington. This train left Uffington at 9.53 a.m. while the branch engine, 541, was taking water from the column that stood between the two locomotives. The tank engine was coupled to its coaches as the down 'stopping' train arrived. This was the 7.37 a.m. from Slough, 'all stations' to Gloucester, and gave travellers a connection at Swindon with the 9.00 a.m. Paddington to Weston-super-Mare. As the down 'stopper' left Uffington, so the 9.15 a.m. Swindon 'Milk' arrived with ten minutes allowed to pick up the Faringdon 'Siphon', so it often happened that the branch passenger and the milk train left Uffington at the same time for their widely different destinations.

On the first Tuesday of each month, the branch engine ran round its train immediately on arrival at Faringdon and, with a brake van only, returned to the junction at 10.30

to bring back the empty cattle wagons left there around dawn by the 1 a.m. Gloucester goods. This was to avoid any repetitions of the embarrassments of the previous year. A special trip was authorised to run to the junction later in the day with loaded cattle wagons and on their arrival the station staff contacted Didcot via the single-needle telegraph instrument to arrange for the 2.25 p.m. or 4.05 p.m. Reading freights to stop and collect the traffic. Having made these arrangements, they then telegraphed Swindon goods yard to advise the yard inspector of the altered formation of the train, the destination of the wagons, and when the animals were last fed and watered.

The midday connections were made by the 1.15 p.m. Didcot to Swindon calling at 1.52 p.m., and the 2.05 p.m. ex-Swindon arriving at 2.30 p.m., both ordinary stopping trains and of no particular interest. The last down passenger train to call, 4.36 p.m. from Reading 'all stations to Swindon', was booked to be 'shunted' at Uffington – 6.10 to 6.28 p.m. – to allow the 5 p.m. Paddington to Fishguard to pass. The latter was one of the few trains still scheduled to average 60 mph and ran non-stop to Newport, so one can imagine that every effort was made to give it a clear run. According to the working timetable, there was time to cross the Reading to the up main and back again before the arrival of the last up stopping train, the 6.05 p.m. from Swindon, due at 6.28, but timings would have been close both for clearing the down main and dashing the Reading back onto the down main after the passage of the 5 p.m. Paddington.

That was a 1907-type scramble, but in general the character of the main line service through Uffington underwent a drastic change during the war, and by 1918, the number of trains scheduled to pass the station in twenty-four hours had dropped from 130 to 100. In that year, only twenty-four express trains were due through Uffington each day, less than half the 1914 total, and heavy goods trains took up track space during 1918 daylight hours, in considerable numbers. 'Dean Goods' 0-6-0 engines were scheduled to haul enormously long rakes of wagons from Stoke Gifford to Three Bridges, and the sturdy 2-6-0s of the 43XX class rumbled through Uffington with eighty loaded coal tubs en route from Aberdare to Old Oak Common; 1918 and 1919 produced some of the most meagre passenger schedules since 1864. The service at Uffington for 1918 is given overleaf.

Coal trains long ago could have been fairly colourful things with wooden wagons painted red or brown or grey or black. Mr Packer had his 10-ton-capacity, wooden coal wagons painted chocolate brown with white lettering shaded with black to give a 3-D effect. (Author's collection)

Work at Uffington station and on the branch was stopped from 26 September until 5 October 1919 owing to a strike over pay. The government still had control over the railways and the Prime Minister and Cabinet wanted to reduce the cost of wages by taking away the 'war bonus', paid because of wartime inflation, and return all railwaymen – *except footplatemen* – to their 1914 rates of pay. In 1919, the cost of living was at least double what it was in 1914. Footplatemen's wages were to be increased in the hope they would not support a strike by the rest of railwaymen. A total of 94 per cent of signalmen, footplate and station staff and 98 per cent of the Signal & Telegraph Department came out in what was the worst stoppage GWR had then known, and the life of the country was threatened, for most of the food and fuel in the land was distributed by rail. The Prime Minister* wrote to each company as follows: 'I wish you to know that the Government are determined to see this strike through and to use all its resources to this end. Will the General Manager advise his Chief Officers accordingly and instruct them to do everything in their power to carry on and to break the strike.' At the start of the trouble, trains had been stabled in sidings all along the line and the government instructed that companies could seize food and coal thereon and hand it into government centres for distribution. Volunteers were called for from among clerical and supervisory grades and also from railway pensioners, but until these men had finished their 'crash' courses in footplate or signalling work, the train service languished. Men who did not strike and who were not afraid of pickets intimidation managed to run ten long-distance passenger trains on GWR, signalled by the time-interval method, on the first day of the strike, and as the anti-strike organisation got into its stride, more and more trains were run until on the last day of the strike 568 long-distance trains for passengers and mail and forty-eight freight trains were operated. The strike ended with the Government agreeing that the minimum wage for any railwayman should be 52 shillings a week – more for higher grades – so long as the cost of living was 110 per cent above that of 1914.

Faringdon Branch, May to December 1918

Single line worked by Train Staff and Ticket assisted by Block Telegraph

	Weekdays				Sundays	
	a.m.	p.m.	p.m.		a.m.	p.m.
Faringdon	9.30	1.35	5.50	Uffington	6.38	6.05
Uffington	9.39	1.44	5.59		P	N
				Faringdon	6.47	6.14
Uffington	10.10	2.41	6.36	Faringdon	7.15	6.30
Faringdon	10A25	2.50	6.45	Uffington	7.24	6.39
					Milk	Milk, goods and cattle.

All trains run 'mixed'.
A = First Tuesday each month engine and van to return to Uffington and pick up cattle trucks. Cattle traffic ex-Faringdon will work to Uffington by special trip and either 2.25 p.m. Old Oak or 4.05 p.m. Reading may be stopped at Uffington to pick up for Swindon and beyond. Such wagons to be placed so as to be picked up in one shunt. Uffington to ascertain from Didcot the running of these trains and advise the latter as to which will be required to call.

---

* David Lloyd George.

P = Worked by engine and men 5.50 a.m. Swindon.
N = Worked by engine and men 5.00 p.m. Swindon.

Main line trains calling at Uffington

Arr./dep.
6.56/7.05 a.m.; 6.30 a.m. Swindon–Paddington all stations Twyford then fast to Paddington.
9.45/53 a.m.; 9.20 a.m. Swindon–Paddington all stations to Didcot then fast to Paddington.
10.03/06 a.m.; 7.37 a.m. Slough–Gloucester all stations. Connect Swindon for Bristol.
1.52/55 p.m.; 1.15 p.m. Didcot–Gloucester all stations. No connections at Swindon.
2.29/33 p.m.; 2.05 p.m. Swindon–Paddington all stations.
5.16/26 p.m.; 1.45 p.m. Clapham Jcn–Swindon milk empties.
6.10/28 p.m.; 4.30 p.m. Reading–Swindon. Refuge at Uffington for 5 p.m. Paddington Fishg'd.
7.51/53 p.m.; 3.50 p.m. Cardiff–Paddington all stations.
9.09/11 p.m.; 8.42 p.m. Didcot–Swindon all stations. No connections at Swindon.

Faringdon Branch, May to July 1920

Single line worked by Train Staff and Ticket assisted by Block Telegraph.

	Weekdays								Sundays	
	a.m.	a.m.	p.m.	p.m.	p.m.	p.m.	p.m.			p.m.
Faringdon	7.50	9.35	1.00	2.10	3.40	6.00	7.30		Uffington	6.05
Uffington	7.59	9.44	1.09	2.19	3.49	6.09	7.39			EBV
									Faringdon	6.14
Uffington	8.45	10.20	1.30	2.41	4.06	6.46	9.00		Faringdon	6.30
Faringdon	8.54	10.29	1.39	2.50	4.15	6.55	9.09			N
									Uffington	6.39

N = EBV ex-5 p.m. Swindon, brings out milk, goods and cattle.

As can be seen from the table above, the branch regained some of its old vigour in May 1920 when a new service was introduced, though the Sunday trains were cut by half. This improvement was part of a general trend throughout GWR to a return to normality, but it was not the normality of 1914. All was not well with the times. Inflation had doubled operating costs during the four years of conflict, and the introduction of the eight-hour day in 1919 further increased the company's wage bill – perhaps by a third. The uniquely dreadful war had only been 'won' by the vast sacrifice of millions of people. There was throughout the Kingdom great psychological shock. Rationing of food produced semi-starvation in millions of people. This applied to half-starved railwaymen as much as anyone else. There was a huge amount of anger at the carnage, disgust at the generals and the government. Men and women were not prepared to be subservient. There was a need in the working people and returned soldiers, sailors and airmen to kick the government – the ruling classes. A large majority of the nation was reeling, shocked. Demands for nationalisation and socialism were made. As the employer of a large number of men, GWR was bound to be affected by the new mood of the nation. A Labour member of parliament said that the money gathered at railway booking offices belonged to the tax-payers and was therefore the property of the government, a curiously illogical thought but one that found wide approval among working men and many railwaymen.

Naturally, GWR directors felt very uneasy about the spirit of the times in general and particularly about what they considered to be its manifestations within the company. In January 1920, the general manager at Paddington wrote to his divisional superintendent at Bristol: 'Laxity is occurring whereby men book on late and take more than an hour for dinner. They must be properly supervised and stopped.' The attitude of many railwaymen startled the management. They had – naively – expected pre-war standards of behaviour to return, but that was impossible after all that had happened. Such slacking on the part of the men was due to the new feeling in the country and also to mental exhaustion after the tensions and terrors of the Great War. It is significant that during 1919–21 there was an unusually high incidence of goods trains breaking away, either in starting or during running, and also of passing stop signals at 'Danger'. While such accidents are bound to happen from time to time, an epidemic of them must point to a more general carelessness on the part of train guards and drivers. The malaise even affected Uffington and Faringdon; on 1 March, branch engine 541 was driven past a signal showing 'Danger' at Faringdon and became derailed, while at Uffington the signalmen had to deal with two freight trains that broke couplings and thus divided the train whilst in motion.

The incidents were similar. An up loose-coupled freight train had left the loop at Knighton Crossing, the driver, having got his train moving fairly well, accelerated his engine too fiercely, and the resultant 'snatch' had snapped a weak coupling. Had the driver or fireman looked back at the train as they were supposed to do, they would have seen the brake van and a few wagons following slowly behind, the gap between the two parts widening. Unaware, they drove through Uffington with a cheery wave to the signalman. The latter gentleman had sent 'Train entering Section' to Challow – two beats on the bell – and was waiting to send the 'Train out of Section' – two pause one beats – to Knighton Crossing, but no tail lamp-carrying brake van passed his window; the last vehicle was a 'coal tub'. Obviously the train had become divided. A quick look out of the window, bending slightly to see beneath the platform canopy, revealed an empty stretch of track to the west, so there was no danger of the rear part running on into Challow's section, and having made this quick decision, he sent seven beats – 'Stop and Examine Train' – to Challow, replaced his signals to 'Danger', put some fog signals on the line for the benefit of the guard in the breakaway part of the train, and sent 'Train passed without Tail Lamp' – four pause five beats – to Knighton Crossing. Having carried out these prescribed precautions, he looked out of his window again just as the errant wagons came into sight, three quarters of a mile away on the high, curving, embankment. They were running steadily down the 1 in 660 gradient and in five minutes a smiling guard brought them safely to a stand at the platform with a final wrench of his hand brake. He stepped nonchalantly from his van, bowed low to the signalman, who was leaning from the box window, and called out, 'Got the kettle on, mate?'

During 1920 and 1921, as passenger traffic increased, the locomotives shortage grew acute, owing to the numbers under repair, and freight traffic suffered. Goods trains were standing in the big marshalling yards without locomotives to haul them, and this reacted against trains out on the line, for they had to be 'stabled' in loops, refuges and sidings until there was room for them in the yards. At 11 a.m. on 5 February 1920, there were trains to a total of 1,000 wagons standing in sidings at various wayside stations from Uffington to Bridgwater awaiting acceptance from Swindon and Bristol goods yards. This aggravated the motive power shortage, as engines were delayed for hours at these wayside stations and could not maintain their scheduled workings with other trains. A minor effect of these delays was the additional work placed upon the signalman at Uffington. Engines of long-delayed trains standing at Challow, Knighton or Shrivenham that became short of water had to run 'light' to Uffington to fill their tenders from one of the water columns. They then had to be crossed to the opposite line to return to their train. But often they had not sufficient time to go back immediately – an express may be due – so the signalman had to 'park' the engine somewhere until there was a time margin to return it to its train. At Uffington, siding space was at a premium owing to traffic waiting to go to or from Faringdon, a few wagons of coal being unloaded by Toomer's men, and the need for the branch engine to shunt, so that the presence of a 'stabled' train and occasionally an extra 'light' engine made the operation of Uffington signal box an interesting problem. To this very difficult situation must be added the sudden, intense and luckily short-lived demands for transport at the great public holidays, Easter, Whitsun, August Bank and Christmas, when huge crowds queued at the big city stations to fill as many trains as the company could run.

All these operating problems coinciding with very high operating costs made the immediate postwar period a difficult one for GWR, and a microscopic scrutiny was kept on all expenditure – no work costing over £100 could be done without the express approval of the board of directors. To save the cost of a man's night-shift wage, a switching-out device would be installed at a signal box, or a porter who was not fully employed at one post would be moved to another, busier, station. In February 1921, the microscope was focused on Uffington and Faringdon stations. The Bristol divisional superintendent's report to Paddington on the traffic department staff at Faringdon shows their hours of duty:

Station Master	9 a.m. to 1 p.m. & 2 p.m. to 6 p.m.
Clerk 1	9 a.m. to 1 p.m. & 2 p.m. to 6 p.m.
Clerk 2	7.30 a.m. to 11.30 a.m. & 12.30 p.m. to 4.30 p.m.
Guard	7.20 a.m. to 3.20 p.m.
Porter/Guard	12.30 p.m. to 1 p.m. & 2 p.m. to 9.30 p.m.
Checker	8 a.m. to 1 p.m.
Parcels Porter	10.30 a.m. to 2.30 p.m. & 3.15 p.m. to 5 p.m.
Goods Porter 1	7.20 a.m. to 11.30 a.m. & 12.30 p.m. to 4.20 p.m.
Goods Porter 2	12.30 p.m. to 3.30 p.m. & 4.20 p.m. to 9.30 p.m.
Supernumerary Porter	9 a.m. to 1 p.m. & 2 p.m. to 5 p.m.
Carman	9 a.m. to 1 p.m. & 2 p.m. to 5 p.m.

(Guard and Porter/Guard change weekly; Goods Porter 1 and 2 change weekly.)

Nine round trips comprised the branch service in 1921, the first leaving Faringdon at 7.50 a.m. and the last arriving there at 9.09 p.m., and their running time was still the wartime nine minutes. The record shows that a guard and porter opened the station at 7.20 a.m. and the booking clerk arrived at 7.30 a.m. The record fails to mention the porter/signalman who presumably opened the signal box at 7.20 a.m. to work the layout so that the guard could get the engine onto its train. This early guard worked five round trips to the late-turn guard's four, the record offering no explanation for the half hour that the latter was allowed to book, 12.30 p.m. to 1 p.m. The signal box would have been re-manned at 2 p.m., the fresh man working through to 9.30 p.m. Though there was a considerable amount of staff on the station during the day, after six o'clock, it was virtually deserted with only one porter left on duty to 'book' passengers and parcels and answer enquiries. This organisation was reported to Paddington: 'No staff reduction is possible and everything is arranged as economically as possible.'

The post of station master at Uffington was considered to be Class 4 earning £220 per annum. The occupant of the post had the company house for which he paid rates and £30 per annum rent, received twelve days paid holiday per year and was allowed to work overtime to make up for having a day off on other occasions. Under him he had two leading porters, working early and late turns, two porters, a district lampman and three signalmen. The leading porters were responsible to the station master for all outside work and took over the running of the station when the master was away. With a porter to help, they did the loading, sheeting, roping and shunting of wagons, attended to all trains that called, selling and collecting tickets. There was milk in churns to be recorded, wagons in and out of the yard to be booked into the relevant ledger and all the other details that made up the orderly running of a station. They were probably not overworked but gave their time to the company as well as they could by maintaining one of the prettiest station gardens for miles, for which they often won prizes. The district lampman was based at Uffington and to him fell the responsibility of cleaning, trimming and filling every signal lamp from Steventon to Marston Crossing inclusive. A huge amount of lamps to attend to and a lot of miles to walk in doing so. The report did not mention the signalman at Uffington, but these were in Class 3 and there were three of them working round the clock in eight-hour shifts, seven days a week. Their pay was decided by the amount of work they performed in the box during twenty-four hours. For each lever movement, bell signal or delivery of the Train Staff to the engine driver and for all the other duties they had to perform, marks were awarded, the total for twenty-four hours being divided by three to find the classification of the box. Signalmen in 1921–23 were quite well paid, as can be seen from the following table.

Special Class	375 marks minimum	75s
Class 1	300–374 marks	70s
Class 2	225–299 marks	65s
Class 3	150–224 marks	60s
Class 4	75–149 marks	55s
Class 5	30–74 marks	50s
Class 6	1–73 marks	48s

Uffington just got into Class 3 with 169, thanks to the work of the branch trains, while 2½ miles to the east, Challow just missed it with 139 marks. The divisional superintendent, having done a lot of hard pleading on behalf of the Uffington staff, gave the same verdict on the station that he had given for Faringdon.

The year 1922 was when extraordinary expenses were incurred on the branch as wartime neglect was at long last made good. Tracks were re-laid, a culvert just south of Faringdon was replaced for £300, the goods shed roof was repaired for £177 and £250 was spent on renovating the station buildings at the terminus. All seemed ready for a return to 1913 conditions. Receipts in 1923 were very good, the best in sheer quantity that the branch had ever known – or ever would know. A total of 26,000 tons of freight was despatched from Faringdon, 5,000 tons more than in 1913, and though fewer cattle wagons left Faringdon, comparing 1923 with 1913, the 1923 total of 378 was still good. Passenger receipts fell in 1923, 14,000 people buying tickets at Faringdon, 5,000 less than ten years earlier, but the total revenue was £27,500, £10,000 more than in 1913. Even taking into account the fall in the value of the pound, this was an advance on the pre-war performance. The fall in passenger travel from Faringdon from 1923 coincides with the introduction of the first road motor services. The 'City of Oxford Motor Services' began two schedules to Faringdon from Oxford in that year via Wantage and via Buckland, and 'Bristol Tramways' ran buses out from Swindon via Coxwell and from Burford via Thrupp. The Great War had taught tens of thousands of men to drive and to maintain motor vehicles, and many men returned from the war to buy an ex-WD lorry with their accumulated pay and plied as road hauliers; farmers bought lorries and these became cheap and numerous through the new methods of mass production, so it is not surprising that consignments of cattle tended to fall away. Four or six cows presented no problems even to the lorries of those days. In 1931, Thomas Clark of Faringdon began his 'Eagle' coach service regularly from his garages in Marlborough Street to Swindon, and by 1935, he was plying several coaches 'for hire over long or short distances'.

Faringdon Branch, June to September 1923

Single line worked by Train Staff and Ticket assisted by Block Telegraph.

Weekdays

	a.m.	a.m.	a.m.	a.m.	a.m.	p.m.	p.m.	p.m.	p.m.	p.m.	p.m.
Faringdon	6.55	7.55	9.35	11.20	11.55	12.55	2.15	3.35	6.15	7.30	8.35
			Mxd		noon				Mxd		
Uffington	7.02	8.02	9.44	11.27	12.02	1.02	2.22	3.44	6.24	7.37	8.42
Uffington	7.15	8.22	10.18	11.35	12.15	1.12	2.35	3.55	6.45	7.50	8.55
	Mxd	Mxd									
Faringdon	7.24	8.31	10.27	11.42	12.22	1.19	2.44	4.03	6.52	7.57	9.02

Sundays

	p.m.
Uffington	6.05
EBV	
Faringdon	6.14
Faringdon	6.30
Uffington	6.39

Milk, goods and cattle.

Worked by main line freight.

The branch schedules introduced in June 1923 were the ultimate development of the 1920 service and continued unchanged, on weekdays, until July 1933, the best postwar service on the branch. On Sundays from July 1928 until September 1931, a milk train worked up to Uffington from Faringdon, leaving the terminus at 9.00 a.m., the only scheduled Sunday work ever given to the branch engine. The 1923 service is given above.

A small point of interest is that, with the 1923 schedules, some of the trips reverted to pre-war standards of speed with a seven-minute journey time. Plenty of concessionary tickets were issued from Uffington and Faringdon stations, a typical instruction to booking offices being, 'Oxford University *v.* Yorkshire cricket match at Oxford. Cheap tickets from all stations within a radius of sixty miles.' Cheap fares were granted for flower shows and even garden parties and fêtes in some cases. Extra trains ran more frequently on the branch than ever before to connect with the many excursions that were calling at Uffington. During August and September 1926, the year of the great strike, excursion traffic was very heavy and the Faringdon branch engine made several extra trips.

In spite of brave efforts to attract excursion and regular trade, passenger traffic on the branch, never the line's strong point, was leaking steadily away into the seemingly bottomless lake of private motoring and the motor coach. Faringdon's goods tonnages were maintained more successfully, but the figures were shaky and under threat from the petrol engine, so in March 1926, the company set up an inquiry into the branch to see whether its running costs could be reduced or even if they could be removed altogether by the closure of the line. H. L. Wilkinson, assistant superintendent of the line, was given the job and among his terms of reference were these questions, 'How far would the abolition of locomotive power reduce costs?' and a startling one, 'Is there a case for lifting the rails and laying a road for the company's motor buses?'

His report stated,

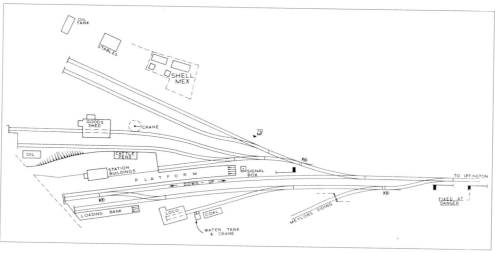

Layout at Faringdon, 1925.

The working of the Faringdon branch, with passengers having to change, gives an advantage in time and convenience to road transport, and private cars are easier. The remoteness of the junction is also a disadvantage which was not the case when the line was built and time and convenience were not of paramount importance. The general and perishable traffic needing quick transit is subject to road competition and is conveyed by mixed train if the traffic is regular. Time is lost attaching such traffic and siding accommodation is often insufficient for wagons to be stabled pending collection by the branch or main line train. This lack is in some part due to heavy goods, such as coal or grain occupying sidings as it waits to be unloaded or to be collected by the branch engine in a special trip.

A steam locomotive on the branch costs 1/6¾d, an auto train 1/5d and a rail motor car 1/4d per mile while a road motor bus could operate for 1/0¾d, but only a steam locomotive can haul freight.

He then went out of his way to criticise rail motor cars.

Rail motor cars are unsuited to branch work owing to the steep gradients encountered and their inability to haul freight. They were first used by the Eastern Counties Railway in 1849 and the fact that there are now only ninety-one at work in the country – of which this Company owns fifty-three – demonstrates their unsuitability for general railway work.

Returning to the Faringdon branch, he continued,

The system of signalling using Train Staff & Ticket assisted by block telegraph is cheap and effective and saves the cost of a token instrument. Whilst I feel that branch sheds should be closed wherever possible I do not think this should be done at Faringdon as the miles of 'light' running to and from Swindon would be wasteful. To save the cost of the electricity at present bought from the 'Eagle' electric light company of Faringdon, might it not be possible for the branch engine to supply steam to a turbine driven dynamo while supplying steam to the well pump and thus charge batteries which could be used to illuminate the station offices at Faringdon. [C. B. Collett, Chief Mechanical Engineer, rejected this idea.] Very little can be done to improve the situation at Faringdon but we will keep an eye on the situation.

The report showed that goods traffic over the line consisted of the same items in 1925 as in 1875, milk, cattle, hay, roadstone, coal, round timber, boards, but with one addition – tinplate boxes. £78 of overtime payments for Sunday work was avoided when the line had to be re-laid by closing it for two days as had been done in 1878, a road motor bus running in place of the trains.

Revenue at Faringdon was less in 1926 than in 1925, partly due to the General Strike, no doubt, for in 1927, takings rose to a peak equalling those of 1923, but thereafter a decline set in, soon to be accelerated by the worst trade depression England had known. It decreased from £23,800 in 1927 to £21,000 by 1929 to a mere £11,000 in 1933. Receipts had increased to nearly £21,000 at the end of 1938, but this was due mainly to fare rises, for traffic carried on the line was decreasing all the time. At Uffington, the situation was worse. There, the decline was so rapid that not even fare increases could influence the trend, and in 1938, the station earned only £1,772, just £500 more than the wage bill.

But the great company did not give up the branch. In July 1928, they reinstated the Sunday morning milk train, now worked by the branch engine, leaving Faringdon at 9 a.m., so that the branch now had a service almost as lavish as that of the 'Golden Age'. The company also introduced a road lorry service, based at Faringdon, to collect and deliver parcels among the outlying villages of the Faringdon district. This was the first 'Country Lorry' service to be operated by GWR, and soon the facility was extended to many other rural branch line termini. How sad it was, as the company must have known, that it was all a desperate, rear-guard action – but how brave to fight to the end!

On the main line, fourteen passenger trains per day called at Uffington and another 128 trains of all types passed through, including fifty-three express passenger trains, and thirty fully vacuum-fitted freights, and these totals increased annually until 1938 or 1939. At holiday times, the public demanded instant transport, and into its already crowded schedule, the company managed to squeeze dozens of extra trains.

Faringdon Branch, July 1929

Single line worked by Train Staff and Ticket assisted by block telegraph.

Weekdays

	a.m.	a.m.	a.m.	a.m.	a.m.	p.m.	p.m.	p.m.	p.m.	p.m.	p.m.
Faringdon	6.58	8.00	10.00 Mxd	11.05	11.55 noon	12.55 Mxd	2.15	3.45 Mxd	6.10	7.40	8.35
Uffington	7.05	8.07	10.07	11.12	12.02	1.04	2.22	3.54	6.17	7.47	8.42
Uffington	7.22	8.36	10.30	11.22	12.15	1.18	2.43 Mxd	4.13	7.00	7.55	8.55
Faringdon	7.31	8.45	10.39	11.29	12.22	1.25	2.52	4.20	7.07	8.02	9.04

On the first Tuesday of each month, the Faringdon Branch engine and guard will return to Uffington immediately after the 10.39 a.m. arrival to collect cattle wagons. The cattle traffic will be worked to Uffington by the special ex-Faringdon and either 2.35 p.m. ex-Southall or 6.00 p.m. ex-Reading may be stopped at Uffington to pick up cattle for Swindon and beyond. Such wagons must be placed ready to be picked up at one shunt. Uffington to ascertain from Didcot the running of these trains and advise latter point which train will be required to call for the cattle traffic.

Sundays

	a.m.	p.m.	p.m.
Faringdon	9.00		6.30
Milk			
Uffington	9.09		6.39
Uffington	9.45	6.05	Milk and cattle. N
Faringdon	9.54	6.14	
	Milk		
	empties		

N = This trip is worked by engine and men of 5.00 p.m. ex-Swindon.

In 1931, Faringdon was again at the centre of a widespread military exercise and again the branch line carried – literally – armies of soldiers and their equipment. The branch engine shuttling up and down the line all day with special trips as well as carrying out the public service.

The eleven-trip weekday schedule continued in use until September 1933, fully ten years since its introduction, but the 9 a.m. ex-Faringdon on Sundays was dropped in June 1931, and just one year later, the Sunday evening trip was abolished, leaving the line without a Sunday service for a while, the first time since 1875. After the closure of the engine shed on 10 September 1933, a light engine came up to Faringdon each day from Swindon to begin the day's service, now reduced to ten round trips, a surprising piece of operation which could not continue for long. On 19 September 1934, the train service was cut to four trips a day with the first train starting from Uffington, and the sudden reduction in the service must have been keenly felt.

An engine and brake van left Swindon daily at 6.30 a.m. (6.20 M.O.) arriving at Uffington about 6.50 a.m. to work the morning trains shown above and working through to Didcot with the 9.28 a.m. ex-Faringdon. The 12.35 p.m. Didcot–Swindon

Scots Guardsmen march at ease, off the train from Faringdon station to their tented camp at Gough's Ground, Wicklesham railway bridge. The picture was taken one Sunday morning in April 1931, by Miss Nancy Bowler with a Kodak 'Brownie' box camera. (Jim Brown Collection)

No. 2007 was an 850-class saddle tank dating from 1892. In Doctor Ian's photo, it is starting to push its empty train back into Baulking siding in February 1931. (Dr Ian Allen)

FARINGDON BRANCH.

Single Line, worked by Train Staff, and only one engine in steam at a time (or two or more coupled).

DOWN TRAINS.

WEEK DAYS. | SUND'YS

Mile Post Distance.	STATIONS.		Station No.	Ruling Gradient 1 in.	Time Allowance for Ordinary Freight Trains. See page 2.			Mixed	Mixed	Pass.	Pass.		Milk E'ties. RR
					Point to Point times.	Allow for stop.	Allow for start.						
	No. of Train.				Mins.	Mins.	Mins.	a.m.	a.m.	p.m.	p.m.		p.m.
M. C.	Uffington	dep.	136	—	10	1	1	7 20	8 30	4 58	6 58	..	5 20
3 41	Faringdon	arr.	168	86 R.			—	7 32	8 42	5 9	7 5	...	5 32

UP TRAINS.

WEEK DAYS. | SUND'YS

STATIONS.		Ruling Gradient 1 in.	Time Allowance for Ordinary Freight Trains. See page 2.			Mixed	Mixed	Mixed	Pass.		Milk RR
			Point to point times.	Allow for stop.	Allow for start.						
No. of Train.			Mins.	Mins.	Mins.	a.m.	a.m.	p.m.	p.m.		p.m.
Faringdon	dep.	—	—	—	1	8 0	9 28	5 50	7 40	..	5 50
Uffington	arr.	86 F.	9	1	—	8 11	9 39	6 1	7 50	....	6 2

Timetable, 1934.

'stopper' was formed with the 'branch' engine and coaches, and they were brought back to the branch as the 4.30 p.m. Swindon to Faringdon. The two evening trips completed, the tank engine left for Swindon with any freight traffic from Faringdon. All this was doubtless cheaper than maintaining an engine shed at Faringdon but did not provide much of a service, although the main line stopping service was actually increased so that those who bothered to get to Uffington, or Challow, still had plenty of trains.

During the Second World War, 1939–45, the branch regained its milk traffic and millions of gallons were carried on the line by 1944. Tanker wagons appeared on the branch to accommodate the heavy loadings and provision was made for a banking engine to be stationed at Uffington to assist overloaded trains on Barrowbush Hill; whether a 'banker' was ever used is not known. The 1936 timetable for the branch continued throughout the war period with only a slight alteration – the 9.28 a.m. from Faringdon no longer ran through to Didcot but ran 'empty stock' to Swindon. The main line thus lost two stopping services, but on the branch an extra 'Sundays Only' milk train ran. Throughout the Great Western system, passenger services were reduced to release fuel, engines and stock for the war effort, but in spite of these austerities, the working timetables of 1941 still carried the traditional exhortation to drivers, asking them to keep a sharp lookout for packs of hounds hunting on the line and to avoid running over them.

Faringdon Branch, October 1944

Single line worked by Train Staff and only one engine in steam at a time (or two or more coupled).

	Weekdays				Sundays	
	a.m.	a.m.	p.m.	p.m.	a.m.	p.m.
Uffington	7.20	8.30	4.58	6.48	8.10	4RRO
	Mxd		Mxd		Milk mt.	Milk mt.
Faringdon	7.32	8.42	5.09	6.55	8.21	4RR11
Faringdon	8.00	9.57	5.50	7.40	8.40	5RR5
	Mxd		Mxd		EBV	Milk
Uffington	8.11	10.08	6.01	7.50	8.51	5RR17

8.10 worked by 7.45 Swindon to Faringdon.

Immediately the war was over, milk traffic returned to road transport. In 1946, the branch carried 1¾ million gallons – one third of the 1944 total – and in 1947 only half a million gallons went by rail.

On 19 November 1947, track circuits were installed to the rear of the up main line Home signal and between the Down Home and Starting signals. This electric device, operated by the presence of a vehicle, prevented the signalman from giving 'Line Clear' to Challow or Knighton Crossing when the track circuit was occupied. This was particularly useful on the up line where the platform canopy obscured the signalman's view of the line. When a train stopped to shunt, the tail of the train was left on the main line and, being out of sight, its presence could have slipped from the signalman's mind. The result of his giving 'Line Clear' to Knighton under these circumstances would have been disastrous. For several years prior to its installation, 'Vehicle on Line' switches had performed a similar function. They were fitted to the station building and to the wall of the waiting shed but they had to be operated by the hand of a porter or guard. At this time, the levers operating the Up Main Advanced Starting signal and

Down Main Starting signal were fitted with electrically operated locks, which were released only when the signalman at Challow or Knighton Crossing gave Uffington a 'Line Clear' indication on the block instrument. These 'new-fangled gadgets' were taken as a personal insult by Elwyn Richards, who resented the implication that he could not be trusted to obtain a 'Line Clear' before lowering his Starting signal.

A horrid incident took place at Uffington station in 1947, which might be mentioned here. A man, a regular traveller on the branch, was in the habit of spending an hour or two each Friday night in the bar of the Junction Hotel before taking the 8.35 p.m. train to Faringdon. On this occasion, the train was ready to leave but the regular traveller was missing so a porter went across to the Junction to fetch him. 'Come on, George,' he called from the door of the bar, 'the train is waiting for you.' George put down his pint. 'Thanks, Bill, but I won't be coming tonight.' Next morning, at 7.20 a.m., the driver of the 6.55 a.m. Swindon to Didcot stopping train was just leaving Uffington when he spotted a body between the down refuge siding and the down main. George had killed himself by lying on the ballast with his neck across the rail of the down main line.

A potentially fatal incident took place between Knighton Crossing and Uffington in 1950. No harm was done, so the event takes on the nature of a farce – but it might have been a tragedy. In 1946, slip coaches were reintroduced on the GWR. The danger inherent in using slip coaches was that they broke two regulations. Once they had been detached from the main train, they formed a second train in the section and two trains in one section together is obviously dangerous. Secondly, a train conveying a slip coach carried two tail lamps, one on the rear of the last coach of the mail train – this being in the form of two lamps side by side within a single body, the whole thing painted white – and that on the rear of the slip coach in the form of two lamps one above the other, one having a red ring and the other a white ring around their respective glasses and both lamps within a single body. The great danger here was that a signalman might see the 'main train-slip gone' lamp and think all was well and then give 'Train out of Section' to the rear and allow another train to enter his section. On 17 October 1950, this happened at Uffington.

The 6.50 a.m. Weston-super-Mare to Paddington conveyed a slip coach for Didcot and should therefore show the 'slip attached' tail lamp up to Didcot and the 'main train-slip gone' lamp beyond. On this morning, the Weston passed Uffington showing the 'main train-slip gone' lamp, but the signalman forgot about the slip coach, saw a tail lamp and confidently assumed the train was complete. He gave 'Train out of Section' to Knighton Crossing and accepted the 8 a.m. Swindon–Didcot 'stopper'. The slip coach – full of passengers for Didcot and its connecting services – was still on the up main line between Uffington and Knighton Crossing because the guard had accidentally operated the slipping lever. The best course of action would have been to allow the coach to run on into Uffington, but he braked and stopped as soon as he could. Luckily for everyone, the coach had passed a very surprised platelayer who then heard the distant but rapid approach of another train and ran towards the sound as fast as he could until the train was close, when he put three detonators on the line and waved 'Danger'. The train consisted of an ex-works Castle and two coaches travelling at about 60 mph and with such a short train – making a shortage of brake power – only just managed to stop short of the stationary slip coach and its very red-faced guard. His was not the only red face on the line. The Weston passed Challow without the signalman noticing that the slip coach was missing, and it might have run all the way to Didcot but for the fact that at the next box, Circourt, the signalman was looking out for his brother – the slip guard of the Weston! The Circourt signalman, Bert Snell, sent the 'Train Divided' bell signal – 5 pause 5 – to Wantage Road and the 'Train passed without Tail lamp' signal – 4 pause 5 – to Challow. The stopping train coupled up to the slip coach and pushed it through to Uffington. There is was shunted onto the stopping train properly and taken through to Didcot.

Faringdon Branch, 7 October 1946 until 4 May 1947

Single line worked by Train Staff and only one engine in steam at a time (or two or more coupled).

	Weekdays						Sundays	
	a.m.	a.m.	a.m.	p.m.	p.m.	p.m.	a.m.	p.m.
Uffington	7.20	8.30	11.25	4.58	6.40	8.35	8B10	4D00
	Mxd	Mxd		Mxd				
Faringdon	7.32	8.42	11.35	5.09	6.50	8.45	8B21	4D11
			noon					
Faringdon	8.00	10.25	12.05	5.50	7.55	8.55	8C40	5E05
	Mxd	Mxd	A	Mxd				
Uffington	8.11	10.36	12.15	6.01	8.05	9.05	8C51	5E17

A = Returns to Swindon as empty coaches.
B = 7.45 a.m. Swindon–Faringdon milk empties. RR.
C = Engine and van Faringdon–Swindon.
D = 3.40 p.m. Swindon–Faringdon milk empties. RR.
E = Loaded milk to Uffington. RR. Collected by 4.15 p.m. Exeter–West Ealing milk train.

The 1946/47 schedules were an improvement on those of pre-war, but the branch could not hope to compete for traffic against the village touring motor bus or the private car. Ford 'Popular' and Morris 'Eight' cars were within reach of most people's means by 1950 so that while the six-trip branch service remained until the withdrawal of passenger trains, traffic dwindled away, though goods tonnages at Faringdon remained respectable. To the bitter end, British Railways tried to interest the people in their nationalised branch line, and even in November 1951, cheap trips were advertised each Saturday from Faringdon to Swindon, mainly for football fans, at 2s 1d return from Faringdon and 1s 6d from Uffington. But this good intention was undermined by the lack of a late train home; an evening on the town after the match was preferable to hurrying back to the station for the teatime train home, so people went to the match by bus or, better still, by car, and few bothered with the branch train.

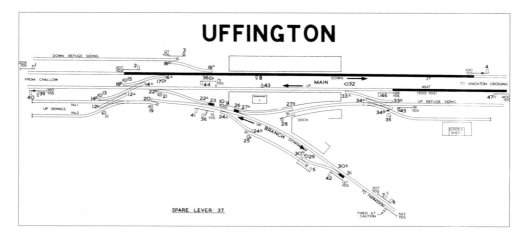

Uffington station layout in 1947, showing signal and point lever numbers. Heavy line indicates a track circuited length.

5700-class 0-6-0 pannier tank No. 4651 arrives at Uffington with the 4.30 p.m. from Swindon for Faringdon in the summer of 1951. (R. H. G. Simpson)

On arrival at the up main platform at Uffington, the 4.30 p.m. Swindon detrained any passengers and then drew forwards clear of the main to branch points and reversed into the branch platform. The engine then had to be uncoupled and 'run round' its coach ready for the 4.58 p.m. departure to Faringdon. Signalman Ken Rowlands looks on from the signal box window and a young John Moody, Assistant Signal & Telegraph Lineman at Uffington in 1951, leans out of a window in the coach. John had served in the Royal Navy during the Second World War and had been a Bofors gunner on HMS *Warspite* when he had had the satisfaction of shooting down 'Stuka' dive-bombers. After the automation of signalling, he became Chief Lineman at the huge signalling complex within the Bristol signalling centre. (R. H. G. Simpson)

On 11 November 1951, a meeting was held at Swindon to discuss the future of the line. The chief civil engineer of the Western Region said, 'Dead wood must be pruned. The Faringdon branch has a six trip a day service with a train of two coaches (contemporary photographs only show one) and costs £2,700 to operate for a return of £300.' No one seems to have objected to the closure of the line. The Faringdon Chamber of Trade and Faringdon Town Council were represented at the meeting and did no more than to ask for an improved motor bus service to Challow station when the branch line was closed.

Faringdon Branch, December 1951

Single line worked by Train Staff and only One Engine in Steam or two or more coupled.

	Weekdays						Sundays	
	a.m.	a.m.	a.m.	p.m.	p.m.	p.m.	a.m.	p.m.
Uffington	7.20	8.30	11.20	4.58	6.40	8.35	8RR10	4RR10
	Mxd	Mxd		Mxd			A	A
Faringdon	7.32	8.42	11.30	5.09	6.50	8.45	8RR21	4RR21
			noon					
Faringdon	8.00	10.25	12.05	5.50	8.05	8.55	8RR40	5RR05
	Mxd	Mxd		Mxd			B	C
Uffington	8.11	10.36	12.15	6.01	8.15	9.05	8RR51	5RR17

Mxd = Mixed train.
RR = Runs if required.
A = Empty milk tanks and vans.
B = Engine and brake van only.
C = Loaded milk train.

The last day of the passenger service on the line was Saturday 29 December 1951, the last train the 8.55 p.m. from Faringdon, and it is likely that pannier tank 4651 hauled it. A large crowd – larger than had ever assembled to buy a ticket and take the train – gathered at Faringdon station to see the train off or to take a last – or first – ride to Uffington. Three station masters were present: J. V. Hale of Faringdon, Arthur Westcott of Uffington and E. W. Major, assistant to the station master at Swindon. Also up from Swindon were Mr and Mrs Coles, who formed a two-piece band on the platform and played 'Auld Lang Syne' while the crowd sang. The throng boarded the train, and Arthur Westcott's young daughter boarded the engine, where she hung on the whistle chain for seven minutes to encourage the musicians in the coach to sing and play louder. Bedlam reigned until the train arrived at Uffington, where another chorus of 'Auld Lang Syne' was sung before the crowd dispersed to their motor cars. Thus came to an end eighty-seven and a half years of public service.

CHAPTER 11

Old Age

Uffington station's decline was not accelerated by the withdrawal of the branch passenger service. At the end of 1952 takings were only £10 less than at the end of 1951, but at Faringdon, forty-one season ticket holders had to look for alternative transport to work or to school. Passenger receipts at Uffington hovered around the £1,000 a year mark from 1952 until 1959 when the record ends, and not even the amazing rise in the number of season ticket holders could improve the situation. These regular travellers were making short journeys on quarterly seasons, civil servants to Reading, workers to government establishments at Steventon, Milton and Harwell, school children and shop assistants to Swindon. Uffington station's goods traffic vanished, and from January 1955, a lorry from Faringdon station called to pick up any parcels. Heavy traffic to and from Faringdon came in via Didcot or Swindon on two local goods trains. One started from Swindon daily at around 7.30 a.m. and called at Shrivenham; the other came down from Didcot, 'all stations' to Uffington, on Mondays, Wednesdays and Fridays only. On the days when both trains met to exchange traffic, Uffington station became a lively place, almost like old times, the sounds of busy shunting and imperative whistles echoing through Baulking cutting, but immediately the trains had gone, the silent, almost gloomy atmosphere of the place closed in once more.

After nationalisation in 1948, the cream and brown coaches of GWR were painted cream and red – or 'rhubarb and custard' as it was very accurately described by railwaymen. The express locomotives remained in Swindon green, though there were some awful experiments with their livery which luckily failed. Between 1950 and 1958, the Western Region management named several express trains, the climax of the scheme coming in 1954 with the reintroduction of the 'Bristolian' running at the pre-war timings. More express passenger trains were running in the period 1954–58 than in 1936, but very few trains in British Railways days were scheduled to run as fast as they had done before the war. They were fast enough, however, and with the gradual introduction of cream and brown coaches from 1954, the signalmen at Uffington might have thought that the 'old days' were back. Certainly they were busier than ever on the main line, wartime excepted. Below is a table showing the named trains on the Didcot–Swindon route.

		Year named
5.55 p.m. Paddington–Swansea 8.45 a.m. Swansea–Paddington	The 'Red Dragon'	1950

11.15 a.m. Paddington–Weston-super-Mare 4.35 p.m. Weston-super-Mare–Paddington	The 'Merchant Venturer'	1951
10.55 a.m. Paddington–Pembroke Dock 7.45 a.m. Pembroke Dock–Paddington	The 'Pembroke Coast Express'	1953
8.45 a.m. Paddington–Bristol 4.30 p.m. Bristol–Paddington	The 'Bristolian'	1954
8.50 a.m. Paddington–Swansea 4.31 p.m. Swansea–Paddington	The 'South Wales Pullman'	1955
3.55 p.m. Paddington–Carmarthen 7.30 a.m. Carmarthen–Paddington	The 'Capitals United'	1956
4.55 p.m. Paddington–Cheltenham 8.00 a.m. Cheltenham–Paddington	The 'Cheltenham Spa Express'	1958

The departure times are those in force in 1958.

All these expresses, with the exception of the 'Bristolian', were creations of British Railways. The 'Bristolian' was introduced by the GWR in 1935 to celebrate the Company's centenary. It was abolished at the outbreak of the Second World War.

After the withdrawal of the passenger service, a variety of small tank engines were used to haul the daily goods from Swindon to Faringdon, including Mr Collett's 14XX class and the 16XX and 37XX pannier tanks. In very cold weather, when water columns were frozen, tender engines of the 22XX class were used. Elwyn Richards, who was a signalman at Uffington from 1943 to 1968, remembered that, in the evenings, unofficial stops were made at the Fernham Road bridge – a short distance from that village – and near Little Coxwell – to allow a passenger(s) to climb down from the carriage and walk home. I always have hoped that these people had bought a ticket to Faringdon, but I fear the worst. Footplate rides to Faringdon became commonplace. Another true story from Elwyn concerns Sid Wilcox, a Swindon driver who worked regularly on the Faringdon trips. One dark winter evening, the branch train was waiting to go down to Faringdon and a group of passengers was standing around the cab of the engine talking to the driver, Sid Wilcox. 'You bin working the "Johnny" a good few years now, Sid,' said one, by way of opening a new subject. 'Aha! and that's a fact,' agreed Sid, leaning over the side of his engine, interested, for by the tone of the man's voice something was 'up'. 'Bet you can't drive up the line blindfold, stop at Fernham bridge and Ringdale Manor and pull up in Faringdon wi'out looking once.' Sid jumped at it. 'Five bob says I can,' there were five men standing near, 'an' one o' you can come up here wi' me to see fair play.' So they blindfolded him with a scarf and off went the train stopping at all the places specified in the wager to the entire satisfaction and wonderment of the laymen. Sid won quite a few shillings after that and sometimes, he said to his fireman as he shared out the winnings, 'Silly buggers, there ain't no difference 'tween driving on a pitch dark night an' bein' blindfolded, 'tis all the same to we.'

   Elwyn told me about a test which was carried out on a WD class 2-8-0 at Uffington in 1951. These locomotives were well known for 'rough riding', a state of affairs brought about by the use of steel rather than lead in the counterbalance weights in the driving wheels. The 2-8-0 was chained down on the Faringdon branch run-round loop and the rails oiled before the regulator was opened wide. Cameras placed around the engine at rail level took photographs, and when the plates were developed, it was found that, momentarily, all the coupled wheels on one side or the other, were clear of the rails.

No. 5016 *Montgomery Castle*, passing Uffington with the 1.15 Paddington–Bristol express on 26 April 1959. Photographed by R. C. Riley from the road bridge as he waited for the Swindon–Faringdon special excursion to arrive. (Transport Treasury)

No. 1019 *County of Merioneth* speeding through Uffington with the 1.18 p.m. Paddington to Weston-super-Mare semi-fast. The train called at Wantage Road and Challow, leaving the latter place at 2.54 p.m. if it was on time. The preceding passenger train was the 1.15 p.m. Paddington–Bristol, Bath first stop. This one was allowed 73 minutes to pass Swindon, 77¼ miles from Paddington, 63.5 mph. From passing Swindon to passing Chippenham, 16¾ miles, the train was allowed 13 minutes, an average of 77.3 mph. (The late Michael Hale)

On at least two occasions, a Castle-class engine was taken onto the branch – as far as the ¾ mile post from Uffington. This happened in the 1950s when the Royal Train, carrying Her Majesty and the Duke of Edinburgh, was stabled overnight on the line. Elwyn was signalman on early turn on both occasions. Before the engine could pass the branch platform and milk dock, the paving stones had to be removed. Those on the milk dock were never replaced. Having squeezed past the platforms and forced its way around the sharp bend beyond, the locomotive rolled down the gradient until the cab was opposite a white post erected specially, thus bringing the rear of the train to a stand on the Faringdon side the branch Up Home signal. Police and soldiers patrolled the track, for the Queen and Duke of Edinburgh were asleep on the train. Elwyn told me that it was 'the duty of the ganger, 'Butty' Martin, Chairman of the Uffington branch of the NUR, to crawl under the train and place a porcelain receptacle emblazoned with the royal arms beneath the discharge pipe of the royal lavatory, and worse, next day, to crawl again under the train and retrieve the now-loaded receptacle, clean it and return it to Buckingham Palace'.

On the first occasion that Elwyn was on early turn with the Royal Train out on the branch, he was taking advantage of a brief lull in signalling activity, at 7 a.m., to eat, undisturbed, his usual boiled egg, bread and tea breakfast. Just as he picked up his spoon, the door opened. 'Oh drat!' said Elwyn to himself, and looked up to see the Duke of Edinburgh coming in. Elwyn was pushing his chair back to stand up but the Duke said, 'Please, get on with your breakfast – I'd just like to come in and sit down and get away from all that down there for a few minutes.' Elwyn said to me, 'He went over and sat in that chair there – by the lavatory – and so I had my back to him. Can you imagine how I felt, eating a boiled egg and 'soldiers' with my back to the Duke of Edinburgh? I offered him a cup of tea but he didn't want one. So I just had to get on. The silence was deadly. I'd just about finished when he got up, thanked me for letting him come in and went out.'

But that was not the end of Elwyn's tale. Two years later, the Royal Train was again stabled on the branch overnight and Elwyn was on duty the next morning. As he sat down to eat his egg at 7 a.m. – being a Churchwarden, Choirmaster and a man of constant habits – the door opened and in walked the Duke of Edinburgh, whose first words were, 'Not still eating that egg!' The Duke sat in the armchair – which was exceedingly filthy in common with most signal box armchairs – and asked about the working of the station and the life of the country around. Elwyn was glad to let his egg grow cold and talk, rather than force food down in an embarrassed silence. After a while, he offered him some tea, but the Duke said his breakfast was probably waiting now, shook hands with his host and left.

A crowd of people had gathered on the down platform to see the Duke leave. The sight and sound of a 'Castle' starting 400 tons of train on a 1 in 140 gradient on a sharp curve would surely have been as magnificent as a Duke. The engine blasted backwards up the hill, through the station and down into Baulking sidings. The crossovers were pulled and as regal an engine as any Duke could have desired came steadily across onto the down main. The small crowd on the platform pressed forward and the inspector on the footplate, sensing disaster, ordered the cylinders' steam cocks opened. Immediately, there appeared a large and very noisy cloud of steam from the front of the engine, which made the most effective broom, sweeping the people back from the edge of the platform, but above the noise was heard a nautical bellow, 'Belay that.' Levers were kicked over snappily in the cab, the shrieking fog abated and the Duke leant out of his window to shake hands with the people as the train drew slowly through the station.

The first diesel locomotive (an AEC diesel rail car had passed over the line some years earlier on a special) to be used on the branch was a 205-hp shunter, which came toiling into Uffington from Swindon with nineteen wagons for Faringdon on 2 January 1962. The weather that winter was so bitterly cold – 15 degrees below freezing

Above and below: Arriving at Uffington. The view from the footplate of No. 3763 0-6-0 pannier tank, 1961. (Author)

Faringdon station looking south from entrance. (Joe Moss/Roger Carpenter Collection)

Faringdon station looking north. (Joe Moss/Roger Carpenter Collection)

was normal for weeks – that all water columns and water troughs from Reading to Swindon were frozen and even those in the engine sheds were kept free from ice only by extreme efforts, but even so, at Swindon shed, there were days when nothing could be done to save them from freezing. A 'King' on the down 'Red Dragon' one evening in January 1962 had stopped specially at Swindon station for water, but the column was frozen solid, and as the men were uncoupling for the engine to go to the shed column for water, the fusible plug in the firebox melted, emptying the contents of the boiler into the fire. They would have found no water on Swindon shed anyhow, the only column in working order that evening was in the works yard.

In these conditions, no tank engine lightweight enough for the branch had the water capacity to make the round trip from Swindon to Uffington, so the foreman at Swindon had used a diesel shunter for the first time. Nineteen wagons would have been a good load for a 37XX tank engine under normal conditions (see Appendix 11), and it is doubtful if one of them could have climbed Barrowbush Hill under the awful conditions of that day, but the driver took the Train Staff and set off for Faringdon. Having a locomotive whose top speed was 20 mph was a distinct disadvantage, for a 'run' could not be made at the incline and halfway up the 1 in 88 the little diesel stalled. On the exposed shoulder of the hill, the guard uncoupled the rear half of the train as the snow hissed across the tracks, and with half a train, the shunter managed to struggle into Faringdon. Next day, a 22XX steam engine was used on the Faringdon. The class was prohibited on the line but the advantage of its 3,500-gallon tender outweighed the ban, and the 'Spinning Jenny', as Elwyn called the 22XXs, continued the working uneventfully until the weather loosened its grip on the water columns at Uffington. The men who had to drive the engine could see no advantage at all in it, for on the return trip from Faringdon to Swindon, they had to go tender first with no protection – other than their canvas storm sheet, which could be rigged from cab roof to tender – from a 10 or 15 degrees below freezing, 30-mph slipstream. Occasionally, the driver, fireman and guard held a conference in the signal box at Uffington on the feasibility of leaving their train at Uffington and going to Didcot 'light engine', which would have been done chimney first, turning the engine on the triangle there and coming back chimney first, picking up their train and going

Faringdon station and engine shed, *c.* 1960. (Joe Moss/Roger Carpenter Collection)

Faringdon goods yard and goods loading/unloading shed, *c.* 1960. (Joe Moss/Roger Carpenter Collection)

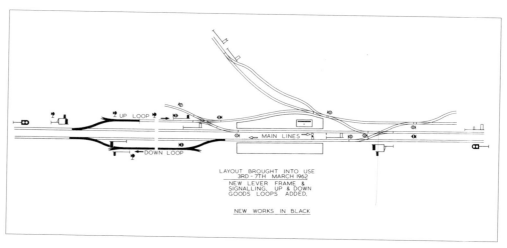

Layout at Uffington, 4 March 1962 to 1 July 1963.

on to Swindon, but they always came to the conclusion that the time taken for the manoeuvre made it impractical.

The practice of using 350-hp diesel shunting locomotives on the Faringdon trips from Swindon grew until, by early 1963, they were commonly on the trains.* They were a great nuisance to the Uffington signalman because of their grindingly low speed of 15–20 mph, which made it almost or actually impossible for him to find a 'path' for the return trip, which would not delay a following train – especially as they had to stop at Knighton Crossing to set down the drinking water cans. For a short period, a new type of shunting diesel capable of running at 40 mph was tried on the trip. They were numbered in the 95XX series and went by the name of 'Teddy Bears', but they very soon were taken off. Sadly, the last train of all to Faringdon was hauled by a 350-hp diesel. The driver handed over the Train Staff to the Uffington signalman for the last time at about midday on 1 July 1963; it was particularly sad because when I mentioned to Alan Jones, the Swindon shed foreman, that I had hoped for a steam engine for the last train to Faringdon, he said, 'Oh, I didn't know, if you'd said I'd have put the 16XX from the Kemble trip on the job.'

On the main line, all types of GWR engines passed through Uffington – the least likely to be seen being the 14XX and 15XX tank engines. The station saw many 'foreign' engines before 1939 in the shape of 4-4-2 'Atlantics' and 4-4-0s from the Great Central and the Great Northern Railways, the latter companies' engines appearing in LNER days. The ex-GNR 4-4-2 were hauling the York, Sheffield and Leicester expresses to Swindon or Bristol. During and after the 1939–45 war, these workings were taken over by the LNER B1-class 4-6-0s. During both great wars, engines from the GER on ambulance trains, LNWR engines on military stores, all kinds of 'foreign' engines might pass through Uffington. Nationalisation brought an increase in the number of LMS locomotives, 0-6-0 4F, 8F 2-8-0, Class 5 4-6-0, and just once I saw an LMS Jubilee. The post-nationalisation locomotive trials at Swindon drew V2 60845 from the ex-LNER, a Royal Scot and a Duchess ex-LMS and, rarest of all, a rebuilt Merchant Navy Pacific from the Southern Region. Outside wartime, it was (almost, I must never say 'never') unknown for ex-Southern Railway engines to work west of Didcot. The Didcot–Uffington pick-up goods, known as the 'Fly', during the period 1950–64, was hauled by the tank engines of 37XX 0-6-0, 56XX (I recall 5643) 0-6-2, 61XX 2-6-2, 53XX tender engines and Manors, I recall 7816. The last 'Fly' working, in November 1964, was with No. 7917, *North Aston Hall*. To see a 'Hall' or lengthy 28XX 2-8-0 – these engines came into Uffington on Sunday engineering trains – squeezed between the milk dock and up main platform at Uffington was almost frightening; one felt sure that it was going to become firmly wedged in the narrow confines. They certainly looked very big machines indeed at that point.

Local main line passenger trains were hauled by locomotives fresh from overhaul in Swindon Works. There were four of these 'running-in' turns on the Swindon–Didcot route. For five days, each train would have a brand-new King or Britannia or other BR standard-class tender engine an ex-GWR County, Hall, Grange, Manor or 47XX locomotive at the head of two coaches. The signalmen along the route looked out for these trains and noted the name of the engines, and the following week, they kept a sharp lookout to see which express 'their' engines were hauling.

During the period 1962–73, various special trains organised by societies of steam engine enthusiasts came through Uffington, occasionally hauled by unusual (in context of the location) engines; an un-rebuilt Merchant Navy in 1962, a Duchess in 1964. Most curiously, the last steam locomotive to be signalled by the old block telegraph system between Didcot and Swindon was No. 4472 *Flying Scotsman* in April 1965. This engine passed by Uffington signal box again in 1966 and spent half an hour in the down goods loop there in 1974. By then, all was automated, abolished and demolished.

---

* Week ending 4 November 1962, D2189 except Friday D2193. Week ending 11 November 1962, D2189 except Wednesday D2143.

The first diesels roared through Uffington from 1958, the earliest being D600-604 of the Warship class. Like many locomotives of this type, they were expensive disappointments and did not remain on the scene long enough to make a good impression upon those who worked along the route. Others followed, 'one-off jobs' like the *Falcon* and *Lion*, the latter elegantly painted in white with brass strips all along its sides. Far more successful were the hard-working Hymeks, which took all the heavy South Wales expresses from the steam engines and always sounded as if they were being 'flogged to death' on these duties. The Hymeks were displaced by the very powerful Western class, but now even these have gone, replaced by the standardised, diesel-electric locomotives of British Railways 31, 47 and 50 classes. But none of these had anything in common with Uffington station or the Faringdon branch. No diesel-hauled train was scheduled to call at Uffington. It was a steam age place, and when it closed, the locomotives that had served it for thirty or even fifty years did not survive another twelve months. Looking in 1975 at the empty site that was Uffington station, it is heart piercing to recall that as late as 1962 or 1963 an ex-works King, No. 6018, had stopped by the red-brick, Brunellian-style buildings, bright in the mid-morning sun, a thin jet of steam hissing from the locomotive's chimney as the brakes were released, and then, with a 'right away' whistle from the guard and an answer from the engine, the train had moved smartly off into Baulking cutting and out of sight through the arch of the bridge, leaving behind the echo of exhaust, a wreath of smoke and sunny stillness.

Despite the large number of trains on the Didcot–Swindon line, the work at Uffington signal box after the withdrawal of passenger services on the branch was very straightforward, simply 'passing' each train – that is, the lowering and raising of the signals. There were no regulating decisions for the signalmen there to make, except when it came time to despatch the 'Fly' to Challow or the Faringdon–Swindon trip Ashbury loop. The situation changed on 4 March 1962 when up and down goods loops were brought into use at Uffington. The down refuge siding was taken out at the same time and the up refuge was converted into an up loop, but it is possible that at this late stage Uffington had the biggest layout in its history, for the branch was still open for freight. Owing to the works for quadrupling in 1901, it was necessary only to build up the embankment on the downside of the main line to accommodate the down loop, for rudimentary earthworks existed on the upside. A new lever frame was provided in the signal box together with new instruments on a new shelf. All this had been ordered from the Western Region signal factory at Reading as far back as 30 May 1958 and had been constructed by 12 October 1961. The frame consisted of thirty-seven levers, numbers 1–47, with ten spaces, and all levers were interlocked by a standard Western Region five-bar vertical tappet machine. The work of installation did not begin until January 1962 and continued quietly for two months until it was necessary to remove the old frame. Then the signalmen were obliged to operate the box while two pneumatic drills broke up the concrete floor of the locking room and two men with oxyacetylene torches burnt through the heavy girders bedded in the floor and walls. The signalmen were forced to spend the entire eight hours of their shift watching to see the bell hammers move, for no bell sound could be heard above the noise. Although this chaos was obviously a danger to safe working, the signalmen were not evacuated to calmer quarters until the floor of the operating room was removed. Having removed the signalmen, the Signal & Telegraph Department disconnected all points and signals from the levers in order to dismantle the old frame.

A temporary block post was installed in a hut at the east end of the up platform. Block instruments, bells and telephones were provided but all signals were at 'Danger' and unworkable except for the Down Starting and Up Advanced Starter, both of which were operated by primitive levers that were pivoted in a quadrant which was spiked into the ground and looked as if it were a survival from broad gauge days. Of course, there was no electrical locking on such levers, so the signalmen had the responsibility of getting 'Line Clear' before 'pulling off'. He also had two hand signalmen working under his instructions and to whom he bawled permission to allow a train to pass a disconnected signal, or to move – with a hefty boot – a set of points. The system worked fairly well during the day but at night it was very difficult, especially when emergency bell signals were received. The signalman could not see his assistants and shouting instructions to the sky in the hope that someone, somewhere might hear and obey was not good for his nerves. The author spent a week on night shift under these circumstances! An interesting demonstration took place when the work was almost complete. A new, down main Home signal with a bracket to carry the goods loop signal had been erected next to the old, straight post Down Home, and the latter signal was quite dwarfed by the bracket signal. But the old signal was still in use and was now lowered for a train to pass. I had just mentioned to the district inspector that the driver of the approaching train was going to get a shock when he came round the corner, to see the large, new signal showing 'Danger', before he realised that the smaller signal was at 'All Right'. The inspector, Phil Millsom, had just replied that the new signal had 'out of use' crosses on each arm when, round the corner and out from under the arch of Baulking bridge, came a Castle running at 55/60 mph at the head of a Paddington to Bristol express. It was about 300 yards from the bridge to the signal and the train was down to walking pace as the engine passed the signal, the district inspector and myself. The driver looked down to us on the track and grinned very sheepishly as he tugged the regulator open even wider in an effort to keep the train moving against the brakes – which were only just beginning to release under the full blast of action of the four-cone ejector. As the train dragged slowly past, I saw the passengers lifting suitcases back onto the racks, truly a remarkable sight and sound.

The Uffington signalmen were surprised to find, on returning to the signal box when the works were complete, that the lever frame was ranged along what had always been considered as the 'back' wall of the building, so that a man had his back to the main line when operating bells or levers. This was standard practice on the old Midland Railway but was very unusual on the old Great Western or its successor, Western Region. The thought behind the layout was that the windows onto the tracks were not obstructed by the instrument shelf or by levers, but the signalmen felt that they could not observe trains so well under the new system. It tended to make a man look over his shoulder at each train whilst replacing the signal levers, while under the normal layout he could operate bells and levers and observe a passing train as he did so. Colour light Distant signals were provided as part of the new work, and power-operated points were installed 'at the west end of the new loops which were about 1,000 yards from the box and therefore beyond the range of manual lever operation. These points were considered to be an innovation by the signalmen in so far as they worked off mains electricity and did not require hand-generated current – though a 'hurdy-gurdy machine', as the Westinghouse hand generator was called, was provided in case of mains failure. Under normal circumstances, all that was necessary to operate the points was to move the correct lever to the halfway position, wait until the repeater instrument showed they had moved to the desired position and then complete the movement of the lever. All levers operating points or signals by electricity had short handles to differentiate them from those that needed a massive pull for their operation. Almost the entire layout was protected by track circuits, which through electric relays operated dead locks or timed release locks on various points and signals, and each track circuit was clearly indicated on a large, new diagram. The old, brass-cased track circuit repeaters were taken away and the position of a train during its passage through Uffington station area was marked by a progression of red lights across the diagram.

Mains electric power was brought into the box to work these devices and the signalmen naturally assumed that they would be able to dispense with the Tilley lamps, thinking the box was going to be illuminated by electricity. They were astonished when told that no plans had been made for electric lighting. However, Western Region quickly put matters right and very kindly included the men in their improvement plans and for good measure gave them a fine, long-burning stove as well.

Though no one working Uffington box at the time realised this, the new loops were part of the scheme for Multiple Aspect Signalling – an unheard-of phrase amongst country signalmen then, but one with which they were to become all-too-familiar four years later. In 1962, traffic on the railway was less than it had been in 1958, and the signalmen were therefore puzzled over the installation of the loops when those at Challow and Ashbury had sufficed in the busier past. But under the future scheme of things, Uffington would be the most central place between Didcot and Swindon and therefore the best place to locate goods loops. Uffington did a lot of 'trade' with its loops, taking work from Challow in the matter of regulation. In fact, a drastic change was effected in goods train working between Didcot and Swindon in 1962 owing to the new loops, the decline in the number of trains and the introduction of diesel locomotives to ordinary goods trains. Hitherto, diesels had not been much employed on such work but with the new D10XX-class locomotives becoming available to augment the Hymek and Warship fleets, even loose-coupled goods trains could have diesel power. Where this was done, a remarkable change came over the running, particularly in the matter of acceleration from rest or from a 'check', and, of course, top speeds tended to be higher. A goods train, diesel hauled, would be allowed to run from Steventon to Uffington before 'going in for the fast', whereas, steam hauled, it would have been side-tracked at Wantage Road to trundle down the relief line to Challow and be turned out from there when there was time. To signalmen used to finding 'paths' for goods trains hauled by 28XX-class 2-8-0s or 43XX-class 2-6-0s, the performance of diesel engines, the Hymeks and particularly the D1000 class was quite astonishing.

The plan of Uffington station in March 1962 looked quite impressive with the branch and loops, but this was to be short-lived. The branch was closed to freight traffic on 1 July 1963, the trailing connection with the main line was lifted in October, and during 1964, the entire line was dismantled. Much of the trackbed was sold to bordering farms, the biggest bridge, that over the Fernham–Shellingford road, was dismantled about 1970, but the tubular steel post of the up branch Distant signal was still standing in the summer of 1974. During the winters of 1962 and 1963, there were days when many of the villages of the White Horse Vale were isolated by heavy falls of snow. Several local inhabitants, businessmen who had never used the station, struggled through the lanes and demanded that the signalmen – me among them – stop the very next express to London for them – and stopped the next train was – but the station's new-found patronage melted with the snow. In the last three or four years of its existence, the station brooded under an air of dank decay and odd things happened. For instance, most of its regular passengers – there were about twenty a day – travelled to Swindon and got into the habit of issuing themselves with tickets, taking them from the racks, date-stamping them and putting the money in the till. Accounts were kept by the sole person in charge, a porter, but in such haywire writing as to defy comprehension. The railway accountant simply took the supervising station master's word that all was in order and let the matter rest.

From June 1964, travellers from Uffington had the following trains at their service:

7.50 a.m.	Didcot–Swindon	2B76	8.24/25 a.m.
1.58 p.m.	Didcot–Swindon	2B76	2.27/28 p.m.
6.01 p.m.	Didcot–Swindon	2B76	6.33/34 p.m.
6.45 a.m.	Swindon–Didcot	2A76	7.05/06 a.m.
4.15 p.m.	Swindon–Paddington	2A76	4.29 p.m.
5.51 p.m.	Swindon–Didcot	2A76	6.12/13 p.m.

The 1.58 p.m. Didcot and its return working, the 4.15 p.m. Swindon, were scheduled to be worked by diesel multiple units, but to the best of my knowledge, all six stopping trains were hauled by steam engines until the end of the service. In the last few months, 61XX-class 2-6-2 tank engines from Didcot shed were the usual locomotives, with 6159, 6145 and 6136 the most regular performers. Their load was rarely more than three coaches in 1964, though on occasions empty coaching stock had to be transferred from Didcot to Swindon on the 7.50 a.m. Didcot, when the powerful tanks managed to keep approximately to the two-coach schedule while hauling fourteen coaches. On 28 November 1964, No. 6145 worked the afternoon service with the usual load of two coaches. I travelled on the footplate on all three trips and recorded some very rapid acceleration between stations and top speeds of 77 mph between Shrivenham and Uffington.

Uffington station, with the rest of the wayside stations between Didcot and Swindon, was closed forever after the last stopping train – hauled by No. 6136 – on 7 December 1964. It was closed in spite of its porter's protest that the platform rose garden would suffer if he could no longer prune it; he had won several prizes over the years for 'The Best Kept Station'. During 1965, when the buildings were being destroyed, his roses were buried under piles of clay and rubble. Daffodils and narcissus, which had been planted by the same porter on the downside cutting bank, survived to brighten the spring of 1966 before they were crushed in full bloom by bulldozer-driven clay.

The last passenger to use the station did so early in 1966 – by mistake! He was travelling from Paddington to Swindon and had been told that his destination was 'next stop after Didcot'. This would have been true under normal circumstances, but single-line working was in force between Uffington and Ashbury and the train was brought to a stand at Uffington to pick up the pilotman for the temporary single line. When the train drew away, a very bewildered man, a suitcase in each hand, was left standing on the banks of rubble that had once been platforms! 'Is this Swindon?' he asked. I regret to say that no one present could control their laughter, but to make up for what might have been bad manners, the unfortunate man was given some tea and cake and was put onto the next westbound train, which made a special call at Swindon to set him down.

The closure of the station was not the end of Uffington as a place of work on the London–Bristol main line, for the signal box was retained in operation. Indeed, it could be argued that the climax of its career was yet to come. A scheme to automate the signalling from Oxford, Uffington, Theale, through Reading to Twyford, with a control room at Reading, was underway in 1964. Late in that year, work commenced at Uffington on the relay room that was to house the switch-gear necessary to operate points and signals when the manually operated signal box was abolished. The whole scheme was realised, in stages, the last being the abolition of Wantage Road and Challow signal boxes. This took place on 30 May 1965, and from 3.25 p.m., Uffington signal box worked directly with the control room ('Panel') at Reading.

The layout at Uffington, by 30 May 1965, consisted of the up and down main lines and goods loops, the old 'trailing' crossover and a new 'facing' crossover, the latter having been installed several weeks earlier and brought into use on 30 May. Uffington's semaphore signals were now replaced by three-aspect colour lights while some four-aspect lights were installed between Uffington and Shrivenham on both roads. The block indicator to Challow was replaced by a 'train describer' (which had come second-hand from the demolished 'Reading East Main' signal box). By means of this instrument, the control room operator in Reading Panel and the signalman at Uffington could advise each other of the trains that were approaching by dialling and transmitting the correct number to 'describe' a train. Thus the 3.50 p.m. Cheltenham express was identified as '1A76'. The bell to Challow was retained but rerouted to Reading for use when emergency bell signals had to be sent – 'Stop & Examine' or 'Obstruction Danger' for instance – or for use when the describer failed, which it did frequently and for hours at a stretch. During such times, the trains could be 'described' by bell codes rung out in the traditional manner.

Block telegraph working to Knighton Crossing continued until 12 November 1966 when all signal boxes from the latter place to Highworth Junction (exclusive) were taken out of use. This was the first stage in a scheme to introduce another 'Panel' control room at Swindon. At Knighton and Ashbury level crossings, automatic barriers replaced the manually operated gates, while a facing crossover was added to the existing trailing crossover at Ashbury, and a siding, the remains of the old up goods loop, was also brought into use. Similar crossovers had been installed at Challow in 1965, and all these items together with sixteen miles of track and signals became the responsibility of the signalman at Uffington.

The box was now at the height of its powers. Most of its equipment was new and suffered considerably from what was excused as 'teething troubles'. Massive failure in electrical equipment, rare in the simple equipment previously employed in signalling, became commonplace, and the history of the next two years would fill a book. Without any official rules to guide them for many months, the three signalmen at Uffington coped with all manner of emergencies never envisaged before; indeed, much of the routine improvised by the signalmen on these occasions was enshrined

On the night of 7 January 1966, an axle bearing on a wagon loaded with pig iron in the 9.02 p.m. Acton to Cardiff express goods became overheated. The lubricating oil was ablaze, and with no signalmen to see and stop the train, it had run for many miles until the bearing disintegrated. The wheels of the wagon fell off and still the train was dragged along at speed, smashing sleepers and throwing whole rails. Some rails were found in fields well away from the railway track. If the driver of the train had had a steam engine, he would have felt the greatly increased 'drag' of the train and stopped, but the train was diesel hauled and the power of the engine was such that the driver noticed nothing amiss. When the train came into view of the signalman at Uffington – the author of this book – he saw the streams of fiery sparks in the darkness and immediately realised that the train was derailed. He took the necessary action and the train was brought to a stand by the driver a mile west of the signal box. (Author's collection)

in later official instructions sent to the box from headquarters! The great problem of train operating after the abolition of signal boxes was that of freight trains that ran for many miles without any lineside supervision. Diesel locomotives were hauling relatively old-fashioned wagons at high speeds and for long periods with the result that axle bearings on the wagons overheated and finally broke down. Three crashes took place at Uffington from this cause during 1965 and 1966, the worst being on 7 January 1966 at 12.21 a.m. when the 9.2 p.m. ex-Acton vacuum freight became derailed, bringing fourteen wagons off the road and destroying one mile of track. There were some other 'near miss' situations between Uffington and Reading until, sometime in 1966, hot axle box detectors were installed on the lineside at Wantage Road with 'read-out' instruments in the box at Uffington.

This instrument applied only to down trains – those approaching Uffington. If an overheated bearing triggered the alarm, the signalman could put his signals to 'Danger' on up and down lines until the crippled train had arrived intact at the box, when it could be put into the down goods loop and any up train that had been detained could go on its way. This was an improvement on the previous arrangement – or lack of arrangement – but the defective wagon still had to be trusted to stay in one piece for six miles after passing Wantage, and any up train that had passed Uffington before the alarm sounded had to take its chance in passing, at full speed, a crippled train. The signalmen at Uffington were forced to allow a situation to exist that went against all their training and instinct and which would have brought them a 'Severe Reprimand' in 1964 – a repetition would have resulted in removal from signal box work. The signalmen found the new railway a very strange place.

The signal box was finally taken out of use on 3 March 1968. The layout was not altered but simply came under the control of the new 'Panel' at Swindon. Men still came to Uffington to operate the emergency crossovers on Sundays when engineering work was in progress, and this situation continued for seven more years. But on 23 November 1975, the crossovers were taken out of use, and from that time, manual operation of the railway at Uffington ceased.

Epilogue

Charitable grass is gradually covering the lineside scars that mark the site of Uffington station. Travellers in the sleek, steel trains would have to be sharp to catch a glimpse of what is left of the remote, old place; the brick bridge, the tree-lined cutting, an old house and a black, steel bridge, the scene is passed as quickly as these words are read. For a few more seconds, the modern loops fly parallel to the tinted windows and the train is again in open country. One hundred years of history, the men, their livelihoods and occasionally their tragedies are left behind unguessed at, receding at 125 miles per hour. Should you, reader, indulge yourself in the pleasures of a day out among the villages of the White Horse, pass close to the old station and salute a century of honest industry.

One hundred years of progress: the site of Uffington station in 1966.

APPENDIX 1

Faringdon Branch: Main Line Connections, July 1864

Train Title: Up line	Uffington dep.	Didcot arr.	Reading arr.	Paddington
8.55 a.m. Swindon. All stns. Reading, semi-fast Paddn.	9.16 a.m. (9 a.m. Faringdon)	9.50 a.m. *10.30 W'h'ton*	10.50 a.m. *11.50 a.m. B'stoke* *12.05 p.m. T'bridge*	12.25 p.m.
10.20 a.m. Bristol fast to Paddington	12.10 p.m. (11.50 a.m. Faringdon)	12.37 p.m. *12.45 Oxford*	1.07 p.m. *No Connections*	2.25 p.m.
11.30 a.m. Bristol all stations to Paddington	2.14 p.m. (1.55 p.m. Faringdon)	2.50 p.m. *3.35 p.m. B'ham*	3.30 p.m. *4.35 p.m. Devizes* 5.55 p.m. B'stoke	5.40 p.m.
4.20 p.m. Bristol ('Plymouth Cheap')	6.35 p.m. (6.15 p.m. Faringdon)	7.05 p.m. *7.23 p.m. W'h'ton*	7.55 p.m. *No Connections*	9.20 p.m.

Down Line	Uffington dep.	Swindon arr.	Chippenham arr.	Bristol
6 a.m. Paddington ('Plymouth Cheap')	8.33 a.m. (8.10 a.m. Faringdon)	9 a.m. *9.25 a.m. C'diff*	9.40 a.m. *No Connections*	11 a.m.
7.15 a.m. Paddington ('Bristol Cheap')	11.12 a.m. (11.15 a.m. Uffington)	11.40 a.m. 11.50 a.m. *No Connections*	12.28 p.m. *No Connections*	1.45 p.m.
10 a.m. Paddington all stns Bristol	12.35 p.m. (11.50 a.m. Faringdon)	1.05 p.m. *1.35 p.m. C'diff*	1.55 p.m. *2 p.m. Weymouth*	2.50 p.m.
2.45 p.m. Paddington all stns Bristol	5.22 p.m. (5 p.m. Faringdon)	5.50 p.m. *No Connections*	6.28 p.m. *7.20 p.m. Weymouth*	7.30 p.m.

5.10 p.m. Paddington	7.56 p.m.	8.20 p.m.
all stns Swindon	(8 p.m. Uffington)	Terminates
		8.30 p.m. Gloucester

W'h'ton = Wolverhampton
B'stoke = Basingstoke
T'bridge = Trowbridge
C'diff = Cardiff

Connecting service shown below arrival time at stations: departure time and destination.

APPENDIX 2

Faringdon Branch: Main Line Connections, June 1887

Train Title: Up line	Uffington dep.	Didcot arr.	Reading arr.	Paddington
7.05 a.m. Swindon all stns to Reading, fast to Paddington	7.49 a.m. (7.17 a.m. Faringdon)	8.20 a.m. 8.25 *a.m. W'h'ton Express*	9.25 a.m. 9.50 *a.m. B'stoke* 10 *a.m. T'bridge*	10.15 a.m.
9.15 a.m. Swindon all stns to Paddington	9.45 a.m. (9.25 a.m. Faringdon)	10.20 a.m. 10.30 *W'h'ton* 10.30 *a.m. W'chester*	11.05 a.m. 11.55 *a.m. B'stoke*	12.35 p.m.
10 a.m. Bristol all stns to Reading, fast to Paddington Broad Gauge	12.17 p.m. (12 noon Faringdon)	12.50 p.m. 1 *p.m. Oxford* 1 *p.m. W'chester*	1.25 p.m. (Slips at Slough) 1.45 *p.m. B'stoke* 2.10 *p.m. T'bridge*	2.30 p.m.
1.45 p.m. Swindon all stns to Paddington	2.12 p.m. (1.10 p.m. Faringdon)	2.45 p.m. 3.50 *p.m. Oxford* 5.30 *p.m. W'chester*	3.33 p.m. 4.42 *p.m. B'stoke* 4.52 *p.m. T'bridge*	4.55 p.m.
'Plymouth' all stns to Paddington Broad Gauge	6.12 p.m. (5.45 p.m. Faringdon)	6.55 p.m. 7.20 *p.m. Oxford*	8.05 p.m. 9.55 *p.m. B'stoke*	9.40 p.m.

Down line	Uffington dep.	Swindon arr.		
8.40 a.m. Reading all stns to Swindon	10.10 a.m. (9.25 a.m. Faringdon)	10.35 a.m. 10.55 *a.m. Plymouth* 11.05 *a.m. Bristol*	*Broad Gauge Express* *All stations*	
11.30 a.m. Reading all stns to Swindon	1.28 p.m. (1.10 p.m. Faringdon)	1.55 p.m. 2.05 *p.m. (SO) Bristol* 2.20 *p.m. Swansea* 2.25 *p.m. Weymouth*		

2.30 p.m. Paddington all stns to Bristol	6.11 p.m. (5.45 p.m. Faringdon)	6.40 p.m. *7.08 p.m. Bristol* *7.35 p.m. Weymouth* *7 p.m. Exeter*	*Broad Gauge Express*
5.30 p.m. Paddington all stations to Swindon	9.01 p.m. (8.45 p.m. Faringdon)	9.30 p.m. *11.02 p.m. Plymouth*	*'Western Mail & Passenger'.* *Broad Gauge*

APPENDIX 3

Men's Service Records

Walter John Thomas. Born 1885.

			Wages per week
Joined service	June 1902	Cart Boy, Paddington	10s
	April 1905	Porter, Royal Oak	17s
	March 1906	Signal/Porter, Marlow	18s
	May 1907	Groundman, Paddington (see note below)	21s
	May 1908	Signalman, Greenford	22s
	July 1908	Signalman, Shrivenham	22s
	Feb. 1914	Signalman, Uffington	28s

Retired in 1951

Outside the Arrival signal box at Paddington, there was a four-lever ground frame, each lever bolting or releasing one of the signals giving access to a platform. This ground frame was operated by the groundman. When a train entered a platform and the signal was placed to Danger behind it by the signalman, the groundman's duty was to operate the lever bolting that signal to Danger until the signalman came to the window and asked for the lock to be removed. This was pre-electric track circuit safety device.

Alfred Joyce. Born 23 April 1880

Joined service	July 1899	Signal/Porter, Highclere		18s
	July 1900	Signalman, Lavington		19s
	Nov. 1903	Signalman, Wantage Road		21s
	Sept. 1905	Signalman, Yarnton		23s
	Nov. 1905	Signalman, Bedwyn		22s
	Sept. 1910	Signalman, Uffington		24s
			In 1915	31s

Retired in 1945

APPENDIX 4

Milk and Passenger Traffic at Uffington

Week ending 21 July 1894

	Passengers		Full churns and empties	
	up	down	full	MTs
16 July	23	9	55	54
17 July	7	7	57	55
18 July	7	5	55	57
19 July	5	17	59	55
20 July	10	17	57	59
21 July	16	25	56	57
	68	80	339	337

No. of passenger trains calling daily		No. of goods trains calling daily		No. of passenger trains passing daily		No of goods trains passing daily	
up	down	up	down	up	down	up	down
5	5	5	4	22	21	29	30

APPENDIX 5

Statement of Shunting at Uffington interfering with Level Crossing

6 a.m. 21 July 1894 until 6 p.m. 23 July 1894

Author's remarks

21 July	6.15 a.m. – 6.30 a.m.	15 mins	1.40 a.m. Paddington–Aberdare due 6.25/30 a.m.
	6.50 a.m. – 6.53 a.m.	3 mins	Branch engine shunting
	7.30 a.m. – 8.00 a.m.	30 mins	Branch engine shunting
	9.40 a.m. – 9.45 a.m.	5 mins	9.15 a.m. Swindon–Paddington due 9.39/43 a.m.
	10.16 a.m. – 10.20 a.m.	4 mins	7.50 a.m. Slough–Swindon due 10.09/12 a.m.
	10.26 a.m. – 10.50 a.m.	24 mins	
	11.06 a.m. – 11.09 a.m.	3 mins	8.30 a.m. Didcot–Bristol goods due 10.50/11.05 a.m.
	11.21 a.m. – 11.24 a.m.	3 mins	3 a.m. Wolverhampton goods due 11. 15/29 a.m.
	5.16 p.m. – 5.23 p.m.	7 mins	2.10 p.m. Paddington–Swindon Horse & Carriage train due 5.07/15 p.m.
	5.36 p.m. – 5.40 p.m.	4 mins	
	5.43 p.m. – 5.46 p.m.	3 mins	
		————	
		101 mins	

21 July	6.20 p.m. – 6.34 p.m.	14 mins	4.15 p.m. Bath–Reading passenger to 'refuge' for 11.05 a.m. Penzance. 6.19/32 p.m.
	7.53 p.m. – 7.56 p.m.	3 mins	
	10.45 p.m. – 11.08 p.m.	23 mins	3 a.m. Paddington goods due 10.33/11.05 p.m.

22 July	1.14 a.m. – 1.17 a.m.	3 mins	
	5.19 a.m. – 5.28 a.m.	9 mins	9.55 p.m. Gloucester goods due 5.20/40 a.m.
	5.55 a.m. – 5.58 a.m.	3 mins	
		————	
		55 mins	

22 July	6.04 a.m. – 6.08 a.m.	4 mins	
	7.05 a.m. – 7.08 a.m.	3 mins	
	7.24 a.m. – 7.27 a.m.	3 mins	6.55 a.m. Swindon–Paddiongton due 7.21/26 a.m.
	8.48 a.m. – 8.51 a.m.	3 mins	

	9.10 a.m. – 9.13 a.m.	3 mins	
	12.45 p.m. – 12.48 p.m.	3 mins	
	4.37 p.m. – 4.41 p.m.	4 mins	8.50 a.m. Bristol–Didcot goods due 4.00/4.35 p.m.
		———	
		23 mins	

22 July	6.45 p.m. – 6.48 p.m.	3 mins
	7.52 p.m. – 8.00 p.m.	8 mins
	8.16 p.m. – 8.20 p.m.	4 mins
23 July	5.50 a.m. – 5.54 a.m.	4 mins
		———
		19 mins

23 July	7.23 a.m. – 7.26 a.m.	3 mins	
	7.30 a.m. – 7.40 a.m.	10 mins	
	8.20 a.m. – 8.25 a.m.	5 mins	
	8.35 a.m. – 8.38 a.m.	3 mins	
	9.40 a.m. – 9.50 a.m.	10 mins	
	10.26 a.m. – 10.34 a.m.	8 mins	
	10.52 a.m. – 11.00 a.m.	8 mins	8.30 a.m. Didcot–Bristol goods due 10.50/11.05 a.m.
	11.14 a.m. – 11.17 a.m.	3 mins	
	12.06 p.m. – 12.10 p.m.	4 mins	
	3.50 p.m. – 3.53 p.m.	3 mins	
	5.05 p.m. – 5.10 p.m.	5 mins	
		———	
		62 mins	

APPENDIX 6

Traffic Receipts and Statistics, Faringdon, 1903–59

	Staff	Pay	£ Total Revenue	Tickets Sold	Seasons	Coal Tons	Goods in	Tons out	Loaded Cattle Wagons	Milk gallons
1903	7	517	15,678	15,678	NK	NK		19,000	259	NK
1913	9	415	17,667	19,023	NK	NK		21,000	491	NK
1923	11	1,783	27,537	14,051	5	NK		26,000	343	NK
1924	11	1,786	23,083	14,397	NK	NK		22,000	378	NK
1925	11	1,798	25,692	14,353	NK	NK		21,000	370	NK
1926	11	1,686	23,874	11,214	NK	NK		21,000	351	NK
1927	11	1,702	27,347	12,325	NK	NK		23,000	309	NK
1928	10	1,764	23,516	10,919	NK	NK		20,000	334	NK
1929	10	1,717	21,704	9,281	14	NK		20,000	297	NK
1930	11	1,760	21,690	8,168	18	NK		23,000	207	NK
1931	11	1,671	17,950	10,480	NK	NK		19,000	125	NK
1932	10	1,609	11,611	6,390	NK	NK		17,000	78	NK
1933	8	1,457	11,036	4,569	NK	NK		18,000	55	NK
1935	8	1,260	11,225	1,699	NK	NK	19,000		43	NK
1936	8	1,244	15,684	1,594	4	NK	20,000		31	NK
1937	8	1,215	20,769	1,445	Nil	NK	16,000		65	NK
1938	8	1,273	19,829	1,566	2	NK	16,000		27	NK
1941	8	1,610	7,840	3,733	4	NK	11,000		13	34,970
1942	8	1,629	8,700		NK	NK	13,000		8	See below
1943	8	1,920	13,163	NK	NK	NK	15,000		28	See below
1944	8	2,159	20,248	3,844	6	NK	19,000		17	3,780,109
1945	8	2,018	19,188	NK	NK	NK	14,000		13	3,565,621
1946	8	2,056	11,848	4,572	33	NK	12,000		16	1,857,932
1947	8	3,736	5,069	3,723	19	NK	15,000		11	514,455
1948	20	5,713	2,969	NK	NK	NK	20,000		26	60,595
1949	20	5,811	4,400	3,209	49	NK	18,000		12	89,307
1950	NK	NK	2,237	NK	27	NK	21,000		10	5,133
1951	NK	NK	2,874	NK	41	NK	19,000		21	Nil
1952	NK	NK	776	—	—	NK	17,000		4	Nil
1953	NK	NK	984			4,626	14,000		6	Nil
1954	NK	NK	759			4,364	12,000		Nil	Nil
1955	NK	NK	602			3,475	11,000		3	Nil
1956	NK	NK	539			3,571	12,000		1	Nil

1957	NK	NK	599	3,950	12,000	1	Nil
1958	NK	NK	543	3,000	10,000	2	Nil
1959	NK	NK	610	1,911	7,000	Nil	Nil

NK = Figures not known

Tonnages for goods are the combined in/out total from 1935. Prior to that the figure represents the outward tonnage only.

Figures for revenue after 1941 are for passenger and parcels traffic only.

Milk in 1941 was conveyed in 3,497 churns and 558 tank wagons. Income was £7,150.
Milk in 1942 was conveyed in 821 churns and 526 tank wagons. Income was £7,082.
Milk in 1943 was conveyed in 2,411 churns and 867 tank wagons. Income was £11,208.
Milk in 1944 was conveyed in 236 churns and 1,366 tank wagons. Income was £17,000 plus.
Milk in 1945 was conveyed in 1,312 tank wagons. Income was £9,334.
Milk in 1946 was conveyed in 738 tank wagons. Income was £9,334.
Milk in 1947 was conveyed in 662 churns and 231 tank wagons. Income was £2,955.
Milk in 1948 was conveyed in 6,262 churns and 1 tank wagon. Income was £650.

Traffic Receipts and Statistics, Uffington, 1903–59

	Staff	Pay	£ Total Income	Tickets Sold	Seasons	Goods Out	Tons In	Loaded Cattle Wagons	Milk Gallons
1903	6	412	4,929	12,000	NK	3,900		Nil	NK
1913	8	662	4,490	10,000	NK	4,400		Nil	NK
1923	8	1,507	6,354	9,000	NK	5,000		1	NK
1924	8	1,406	6,301	10,000	NK	4,800		15	NK
1925	8	1,428	5,831	9,000	NK	4,300		6	NK
1926	8	1,351	7,494	8,000	NK	7,900		9	NK
1927	8	1,428	7,308	9,000	NK	8,000		10	NK
1928	8	1,406	6,088	9,000	NK	5,900		Nil	NK
1929	8	1,381	5,046	8,000	NK	3,700		5	NK
1930	8	1,331	6,256	7,000	NK	7,300		4	NK
1931	8	1,328	4,493	7,000	NK	2,200		7	NK
1932	7	1,108	2,877	7,000	NK	2,200		8	NK
1933	7	1,146	2,176	6,000	NK	1,900		5	NK
1935	7	1,579	1,579	5,000	4		1,691	2	NK
1936	7	1,134	2,426	4,700	10		3,882	8	NK
1937	7	1,148	1,937	4,700	9		2,613	2	NK
1938	7	1,209	1,772	4,500	10		2,199	2	NK
1941	7	1,551	1,670	9,128	24	450	2,200	3	90
1942	7	1,768	1,616	9,934	2	493	2,623	Nil	NK
1943	7	2,027	2,000	11,400	7	790	2,709	Nil	NK
1944	7	2,112	2,931	10,884	19	1,009	3,427	2	NK
1945	7	2,077	1,879	10,063	19	1,031	2,983	Nil	NK
1946	7	2,191	1,689	8,783	23	692	2,717	2	NK
1947	7	2,144	1,581	8,615	47	569	2,033	2	3,789
1948	7	2,523	1,659	7,859	40	527	1,911	Nil	10,131
1949	7	2,664	1,550	7,756	52	514	1,904	Nil	13,071
1950	7	NK	1,250	6,746	51	300	1,985	Nil	9,324
1951	7	NK	1,240	6,588	99	426	1,753	Nil	1,050
1952	7	NK	1,230	4,123	92	201	1,829	Nil	19,151
1953	NK	NK	1,163	3,889	173	233	1,676	Nil	11,012
1954	NK	NK	949	3,839	224	94	1,320	Nil	6,000
1955	NK	NK	887	3,889	275	Freight now concentrated at Faringdon			
1956	NK	NK	997	3,412	386				

1957	NK	NK	1,120	4,477	380
1958	NK	NK	1,035	4,057	394
1959	NK	NK	1,138	3,569	479

Goods tonnages 1935–38 are combined in/out figures.

Revenue from milk: 1948 £92; 1949 £98; 1950 £83; 1951 £14; 1952 £250.

NK = Figures not known.

Faringdon Branch:
Main Line Connections, 1914

Train title: Up line	Uffington dep.	Didcot arr./dep.	Reading arr./dep.
6.30 a.m. Swindon all stations Reading, fast to Paddington	7.05 a.m. (6.45 a.m. Faringdon)	7.46/55 8.10 *Wolverhampton*	8.40/47 8.49 *Basingstoke* 8.53 *Newbury*
8.05 a.m. Swindon fast Paddington from Didcot	8.30 a.m. (8.12 a.m. Faringdon)	9.05/17 9.34 *Oxford* 10.03 *Woodford Halse*	9.35/38 9.58 *Basingstoke* 10.22 *Plymouth*
8.36 a.m. Chippenham all stations Reading, fast to Paddington	9.43/48 a.m. (9.27 a.m. Faringdon)	10.24/33 10.33 *Oxford*	11.09/17 11.22 *Trowbridge* 11.55 *Basingstoke*
11.52 a.m. Swindon all stations Slough, fast to Paddington	12.18 p.m. (12 noon Faringdon)	12.51/56 1.10 *p.m. Oxford*	1.38/46 *No connections*
2.10 p.m. Swindon all stations Maidenhead, fast to Paddington	2.38 p.m. (2.20 p.m. Faringdon)	3.15/27 3.35 *p.m. Oxford*	4.07/15 *No connections* Arr. Paddington 5.15 p.m.
5.55 p.m. Swindon all stations to Reading	6.24 p.m. (5.55 p.m. Faringdon)	7.00/06 7.25 *p.m. 'Motor' to Oxford*	7.45 Terminates
7.15 p.m. Swindon all stations to Reading	7.38 p.m. (7.27 p.m. Faringdon)	8.05/38 *8.15 Oxford* *8.40 Banbury* *Also connects with the* *2.50 p.m. York–* *Southampton* *via Compton (DN&S line).*	9.22 Terminates *10.15 p.m. Basingstoke* *10.35 p.m. Paddington fast* *11.40 p.m.* *All stns Paddington*

Faringdon Branch:
Main Line Connections, 1914

Train title: Down line	Uffington dep.	Swindon arr./dep.
6.49 a.m. Reading all stations to Weston-super-Mare	8.28 a.m. (8.12 a.m. Faringdon)	8.53/9.20 a.m. *7.30 a.m. Paddington–Plymouth express 9.13* *9.16 a.m. Swindon–Cardiff express*
7.36 a.m. Slough all stations to Swindon	10.12 a.m. (10.18 Uffington)	10.35 a.m. Terminates *9 a.m. Paddington–Kingswear express 10.54* *10.58 Swindon–Hereford express* *11.05 Swindon–Stapleton Road via Badminton all stations*
10 a.m. Reading–Swindon all stations	11.23 a.m. (11.08 a.m. Faringdon)	11.45/12.20 (to Taunton) all stations *10.50 a.m. Paddington –Neyland 12.37 p.m. express* *1 p.m. Swindon–Chippenham 'Motor' all stations*
1.07 p.m. Didcot all stations Swindon	1.44 p.m. (1.28 p.m. Faringdon)	2.07 p.m. (Misses express to Weymouth by 12 minutes) *1.10 p.m. Paddington–Cardiff express 3.01 p.m.* *3.07 p.m. Swindon–Exeter express* *3.12 p.m. Swindon–Cheltenham all stations* *3.15 p.m. Swindon–Bath all stations*
1.20 p.m. Paddington all stations to Swindon	3.45 p.m. (3.23 p.m. Faringdon)	4.08 p.m. Terminates *2.28 p.m. Paddington–Bristol express 4.20 p.m* *3.15 p.m. Paddington–Cheltenham express 4.47 p.m.* *5.10 p.m. Swindon 'Cheddar Valley Passenger' all stations*
3.50 p.m. Paddington all stations to Swindon	6.23 p.m. (5.55 p.m. Faringdon)	6.48 p.m. Terminates *5.15 p.m. Paddington–Bristol express 7.11 p.m.* *6.10 p.m. Paddington–Swansea express 7.43 p.m.*
5.05 p.m. Paddington all stations to Cardiff	7.10 p.m. (6.52 p.m. Faringdon)	7.30/49 p.m. *8.05 p.m. Swindon–Portishead all stations*
8.33 p.m. Didcot all stations to Swindon	9.11 p.m. (8.55 p.m. Faringdon)	9.33 p.m. Terminates 8.00 p.m. Paddington–Bristol 10 p.m.

APPENDIX 8

Cost of Locomotive Power and Rolling Stock on Faringdon Branch, 1912

	£	s	d	% per train mile
Locomotive Expenses				
Salaries	25	6	1	.21d
Running Expenses				
Wages to Enginemen & Firemen	372	0	10	3.09d
Contribution to E'men & F'men's fund	2	8	2	.02d
Wages to cleaner	13	0	0	.11d
Water	22	18	0	.19d
Oil, tallow, sundry stores	17	3	0	.14d
Coal at 13s 6d ton, 341¾ tons	230	0	0	1.19d
Total running expenses	658	3	9	5.41d
Renewal & repair of locomotive	343	9	3	2.85d
Retiring allowance & gratuities	6	0	6	.05d
Total locomotive expenses	1,007	13	6	8.31d
Interest on stock				
1⅓ engines = £2,133 at 4 per cent	85	6	8	
Carriage expenses				
Repair & renewal	270	5	0	2.52d
(estimated in proportion to value of stock used)				
Interest on stock = £1,618 at 4 per cent	64	14	5	.60d
Wagon expenses				
Repair & renewal	61	8	11	4.63d
Interest on stock (original cost)	93	8	0	7.04d

APPENDIX 9

Average Wages of Footplate Crews, Faringdon Shed, 1867–72

Week ending	Faringdon	Box	Brimscombe	Cirencester
8.2.67	24s 5d			
22.2.67	24s 5d			
4.8.67	24s 6d	30s	32s 11d	28s 9d
5.9.67	39s 1d	32s 7d		22s 9d
19.9.67	25s 2d	32s 7d		22s 9d
25.1.68	24s 1d			
8.2.68	24s 8d			
22.2.68	24s 11d			
5.9.68	45s 2d	33s 6d		29s 7d
19.9.68	24s 4d	33s 6d		29s 7d

1 April – 31 July 1869: average 24s 6d per week
June 1864 – February 1872: there were five men at the shed
February – 11 May: three men at the shed
11 May – 31 December: four men at the shed and then five men again

		Faringdon		
January & February	1870	24s		
Week ending	5.3.70	21s 5d		
	19.3.70	17s 10d		
	2.4.70	18s 1d		
	16.4.70	18s 1d		
During May		25s		
June & August		24s		
Week ending	3.8.70	45s 2d	Previous year Faringdon	
Week ending	3.9.71	29s 2d	25s 2d	
	16.9.71	27s 9d	25s 2d	
	30.9.71	27s 9d	25s 2d	
	14.10.71	28s 3d	24s 7d	
	28.10.71	21s 9d	24s 5d	
	11.11.71	25s	25s 2d	
	25.11.71	22s 9d	25s 2d	
	9.12.71	28s 6d	25s 2d	
	23.17.71	28s 6d	25s 2d	

Week ending	3.2.72	20s 6d	23s 9d
	17.2.72	19s 10d	23s 9d
	2.3.72	21s 8d	19s 5d
	16.3.72	27s 7d	20s 7d
	30.3.72	27s 9d	22s 9d
	13.4.72	30s 4d	25s 2d
	27.4.72	21s 8d	25s 2d
	11.5.72	21s 8d	25s
	25.5.72	18s	25s
	8.6.72	22s 4d	25s
	22.3.72	28s 3d	28s

APPENDIX 10

Coal Placed on Locomotives, Faringdon, 1912

1–27 January 30 tons	Up to 24.2.12 28 tons 13 cwt	Up to 23.3.12 25 tons 3 cwt	Up to 26.4.12 12 tons 8 cwt
Up to 18.5.12 24 tons 10 cwt	From 13.7.12. to 10.8.12 25 tons	Up to 7.9.12 25 tons 10 cwt	Up to 5.10.12 27 tons 1 cwt
Up to 2.11.12 30 tons 12 cwt	Up to 30.11.12 30 tons 17 cwt		

Locomotives at Faringdon during this time were No. 829 until 25 January 1912, No. 1443 from 26 January 1912 to 13 February 1912 and No. 1436 from 13 February 1912 until 28 February 1913.

Maximum loads for branch locomotives, 1902 and 1927

1902
517-class 0-4-2 tank engine

Coal or mineral	15 wagons up	11 wagons down
Goods	22 wagons up	16 wagons down
Mixed train	26 wagons up	19 wagons down
Empties	30 wagons up	22 wagons down

Other locomotives permitted to run over the branch:

Type 23 Single frame, tender goods. 17-inch by 24-inch cyl. TE 15, 102 lb. Weight 31 1/2 tons.
Type 24 Double frame, tender goods. 17-inch by 24-inch cyl. TE 15, 102 lb. Weight 31 1/2 tons.

(Statistics taken from a GWR report to the Board of Trade, 1902)

1927

3521 class
0-6-0T & Standard Goods
0-6-0 Ex-Cambrian Rly Belpaire boiler   } Uffington to Faringdon 286 tons
0-6-0 Ex-M&SW Jc Old boiler   Faringdon to Uffington 364 tons

3232–3251
2-4-0T Metro
4-4-4T Ex-M&SW Jc Rly   } Uffington to Faringdon 242 tons
1328 & 1329 Ex-Cambrian Rly   Faringdon to Uffington 336 tons

0-4-2T 517 class
0-4-4T Ex-M&SW Jc Rly   } Uffington to Faringson 202 tons
2-4-0 Ex-M&SW Jc Rly   Faringdon to Uffington 308 tons

(Taken from the 1927 Working Timetable)

Note: The loadings for 1927 were still in force in 1947.

Main Line Connections, September 1936

Down Line

Train Title	Uffington dep.	Swindon arr./dep.	Chippenham dep.
6.52 a.m. Reading–Bristol all stations	8.13 a.m.	8.35/9.20 a.m. *9.03 a.m. Plymouth fast* *9.12 a.m. Gloucester slow* *9.55 a.m. Malmesbury*	9.50 a.m. *10.05 a.m. T'bridge*
8.11 a.m. Slough–Gloucester all stations	10.20 a.m.	10.40/11.12 a.m. *10.58 a.m. Weston-super-Mare fast* *11.15 a.m. Westbury slow* *11.20 a.m. Bristol slow*	11.27 a.m. *11.38 a.m. T'bridge*
9.20 a.m. Slough–Swindon all stations	11.16 a.m.	11.36 a.m. *12.16 p.m. Kemble*	*Nil*
12.33 p.m. Didcot–Swindon all stations	1.05 p.m.	1.30 p.m. *1.45 p.m. Bristol slow (via Badminton)* *1.58 Cirencester (via Kemble)* *2.05 p.m. Weymouth slow*	2.25 p.m.
2.38 p.m. Reading–Swindon all stations	3.57 p.m.	4.18 p.m. *4.51 p.m. Cheltenham fast* *5.00 p.m. Bristol slow* *5.15 p.m. Gloucester slow* *5.20 p.m. Bristol slow* *(via Badminton)*	5.30 p.m. *5.50 p.m. T'bridge*
2.30 p.m. Paddington–Swindon all stations	6.30 p.m.	6.50 p.m.	*Nil*
5.15 p.m. Paddigton–Bristol fast (did not call in 1929)	6.54 p.m.	7.08/14 p.m. *7.26 p.m. Fishguard*	7.47 p.m. *8.27 p.m. Westbury*

8.20 p.m. Didcot–Swindon 8.50 p.m.

9.10 p.m.
9.25 p.m. Malmesbury (Th & SO) Nil
9.40 p.m. Bristol slow

8.47 p.m. Oxford–Swindon Calls if requested

10.8 p.m.   11.21 p.m.
11.00 p.m. Westbury (Th & SO)
11.15 p.m. Neyland Passenger & Mail

Up Line

Train Title	Uffington dep.	Didcot	Reading	Paddington
6.55 a.m. Swindon–Paddington all stations Reading fast to Paddington	7.17 a.m.	7.48 a.m. *8.15 a.m. Oxford slow* *8.34 a.m. Wolverhampton fast*	8.42/50 a.m. *9.00 a.m. Portsmouth* *9.31 a.m. T'bridge* *9.39 a.m. Pembroke Dock (non-stop Newport)*	9.30 a.m.
7.48 a.m. Swindon–Didcot all stations	8.15 a.m.	9.00 a.m. *9.20 a.m. Paddington fast* *9.51 a.m. Birmingham fast* *10.18 a.m. Eastleigh*	9.39 a.m. (slip coach) *9.46 a.m. Basingstoke* *10.20 a.m. Hereford*	10.17 a.m.
9.30 a.m. Faringdon–Didcot	9.45 a.m.	10.22 a.m. *10.30 a.m. Paddington all stations to Reading fast Paddington* *10.43 a.m. Oxford slow*	11.08/15 a.m. *11.18 Basingstoke* *11.46 T'bridge*	11.55 a.m.
10.22 a.m. Swindon–Didcot all stations	10.42 a.m.	11.10 a.m. *11.23 a.m. Paddington fast* *11.30 a.m. Leamington slow* *12.35 p.m. Southampton*	11.43/50 *11.46 T'bridge* *12.12 Portsmouth*	12.30 p.m.
12 noon Swindon–Didcot	12.20 p.m.	12.45 p.m. *1 p.m. Oxford slow* *1.05 p.m. Paddington fast*	1.25/31 p.m. *1.30 p.m. Newbury (Th O)* *1.47 p.m. Portsmouth* *2.10 p.m.Basingstoke (SO)* *2.17 p.m. Plymouth fast*	2.10 p.m.
5.45 p.m. Swindon–Didcot	6.04/05 p.m.	6.35 p.m. *6.45 p.m. Reading slow* *6.47 p.m. Southampton* *6.52 p.m. Oxford slow*	7.18 p.m. *7.29 p.m. Paddington fast* *8.38 p.m.m Basingstoke* *8.47 p.m. Hungerford*	8.10 p.m.
2.10 p.m. Swansea–Paddington all stations (7.35 p.m. Swindon)	7.56/57 p.m.	8.24/9.00 p.m. *8.48 p.m. Oxford fast* *(Diesel rail car)* *8.56 p.m. Banbury slow*	9.33/10.25 p.m. *10.45 p.m. Newbury* *10.50 p.m. Basingstoke*	11.58 p.m.

Locomotives Known to Have Been Allocated to Faringdon Shed, 1903–16 and 1921–33

Loco	217	218	219	220	519	521	525	529	539	540	541
Year	1926	1925	1906	1916	1923	1933	1929	1914	1923	1927	1906
	1931	1907	1931	1931		1933	1933	1924	1930	1926	
	1933		1908	1932				1926			
				1933				1927			
								1928			
								1933			

Loco	549	552	558	560	576	638	727	736	829	837	839
Year	1927	1914	1908	1905	1925	1922	1906	1903	1911	1926	1921
	1928	1915				1933		1904	1912	1929	1922
	1933	1932									1933

Loco	844	857	858	944	964	1154	1155	1158	1164	1426	1427
Year	1902	1929	1924	1921	1905	1925	1932	1930	1923	1932	1927
					1933					1933	1924
					1933						1933

Loco	1428	1436	1438	1439	1440	1443	1446	1471	1476	1477
Year	1910	1912	1923	1929	1904	1911	1916	1909	1913	1928
	1911	1913	1924	1933		1913				1930
	1928	1932	1933			1914				1933
	1931	1933								
	1933									

Loco	1934	1964	2007	2014	2044
Year	1922	1932	1931	1928	1931
	1924	1933		1933	1933
		1933			

Locomotives Identified

Nos 217–576; 829–858; 1154–1443; 1471–1477: 517-class 0-4-2 Side Tanks.

Nos 727 and 736: 1076 (Buffalo) -class 0-6-0 Saddle Tanks.

Nos 1934 and 1964: 1901-class 0-6-0 Pannier Tanks. Rebuilt from Saddle Tank.

Nos 2007 and 2014: 850-class (1901 Series) 0-6-0 Saddle Tanks.

No. 2044: 2021-class 0-6-0 Saddle Tank. (Slightly enlarged 850.)

No. 1446: Metro-class 2-4-0 Side Tank.

No. 638: 633-class 0-6-0 Side Tank. (Several of this class fitted with condensing gear but not 638.)

No. 944: 'Armstrong Standard Goods' 0-6-0 Tender Engine.

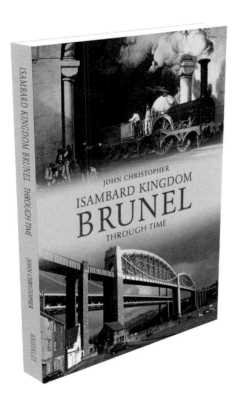

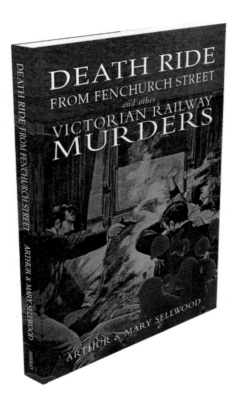